Midland Main Lines to
St Pancras and Cross Country

Sheffield to Bristol 1957–1963

Midland Main Lines to
St Pancras and Cross Country

Sheffield to Bristol 1957–1963

John Palmer

PEN & SWORD
TRANSPORT

First published in Great Britain in 2017 by
Pen & Sword Transport
an imprint of
Pen & Sword Books Ltd
47 Church Street
Barnsley
South Yorkshire
S70 2AS

ISBN 978 1 47388 557 8

A CIP catalogue record for this book is available from the British Library

Typeset in Ehrhardt by
Mac Style Ltd, Bridlington, East Yorkshire
Printed and bound by Replika Press Pvt. Ltd.

Front cover: photograph taken in 1961 at Heeley, Sheffield shows a cross country train hauled by a Royal Scot locomotive. David Marriott

Pen & Sword Books Ltd incorporates the imprints of Pen & Sword Archaeology, Atlas, Aviation, Battleground, Discovery, Family History, History, Maritime, Military, Naval, Politics, Railways, Select, Transport, True Crime, and Fiction, Frontline Books, Leo Cooper, Praetorian Press, Seaforth Publishing and Wharncliffe.

For a complete list of Pen & Sword titles please contact
PEN & SWORD BOOKS LIMITED
47 Church Street, Barnsley, South Yorkshire, S70 2AS, England
E-mail: enquiries@pen-and-sword.co.uk
Website: www.pen-and-sword.co.uk

Contents

Acknowledgements

Researching and writing this book has given me considerable pleasure over a period of three years. Along the way I have been fortunate to find individuals who have given their time to respond to my requests; maybe a confirmation of a perceived fact, recollections of practices from some sixty years ago, photographs taken at particular locations or the depot to which certain locomotives were allocated at a particular date.

In particular I would like to thank the following:

Steve Leyland who painstakingly identified locomotive allocations for motive power depots of particular interest and also for locomotives rarely seen along the routes and therefore of great interest. Chris Holmes who has helped considerably with the production of maps. Don Magson of the British Transport Pensioners' Federation, Tyseley Branch for information relating to workings from Aston depot. Alan Butler and Alan Binder who added detail to information concerning workings at Bromsgrove and Saltley respectively. Pat Heydon who provided information from his father concerning the Cromford and High Peak railway and an incident at Hazel Grove. Geoffrey Morris, Leslie Askin and Alan Grice who provided detail for 'The Human Element.'

The photographers and holders of collections:

David Postle at Kidderminster Railway Museum
Paul Chancellor of Colour-rail
Jeremy Suter (E.R. Morten)
Midland Railway Trust Ltd Photo Archive
Phil Waterfield
David Marriott (with assistance of Rhys Jones)
John Carter
Keith Platt
Bob Jones
National Railway Museum (John F. Henton collection)
Tessa Johnson and Karen Proudler for their patience in accepting and processing the manuscripts as provided and on many occasions later revised.

Maps of the Routes

To assist all readers, but particularly those who do not have a knowledge of railway geography, a selection of maps has been included. In summary the maps are of:

- an overview of the main routes
- the Derby/Nottingham/Burton areas
- the Trent area
- Derby and Trent to Sheffield (via Ambergate and via the Erewash Valley route to Clay Cross)
- the Peak line to Manchester via Peak Forest
- Peaks, Dales and Moorlands routes (including the Cromford and High Peak)
- the Ambergate station area
- the Stockport area
- Burton-upon-Trent to Birmingham and to Leicester
- the Birmingham area
- Birmingham area to Bristol
- the Bristol area
- Nottingham to Leicester and Kettering (via Edwalton and via Trent)
- Leicester to Bedford overview
- the Midland (Railway) extension from Bedford towards St Pancras
- the final approach to St Pancras.

With over 400 route miles and a history of up to 125 years covered in the book some compromises had to be reached. The end result has been to include as much detail as is relevant for the references made in the various chapters. The maps should enable readers to follow the specific routes taken by particular trains of interest; for example the trains diverted away from the Manchester (London Road)–Euston route and the excursions for visitors to the new cathedral at Coventry. In particular areas, for example along the Nottingham–Sheffield route, there were other railways which featured strongly (for example the former Great Central), but because they were not directly featured in more than a passing way in this book the relevant map does not show them. By Act of Parliament (1865) railway companies were obliged to display distances along their routes in miles and quarter miles from an originating point. Nowadays these posts can still be seen to one side of the tracks and are painted yellow with numerals in black. From 1907 the Midland Railway adopted a standard approach and for the Derby to Bristol line milepost 0 can be seen at the west end of Derby station. The Midland (with a network of alternative routes) always indicated the shortest distance to its route destination so, for example, London to Sheffield via Sharnbrook Summit, Kettering, Leicester, Trent, Clay Cross and Dronfield (and not, for example, from Trent to Clay Cross via Derby and Ambergate) and, because 1907 was the date applicable, the slightly shorter route between Derby and Birmingham by use of the chord between Kingsbury and Water Orton post dated it by two years and was, therefore, not taken into account.

OVERVIEW OF THE MAIN ROUTES

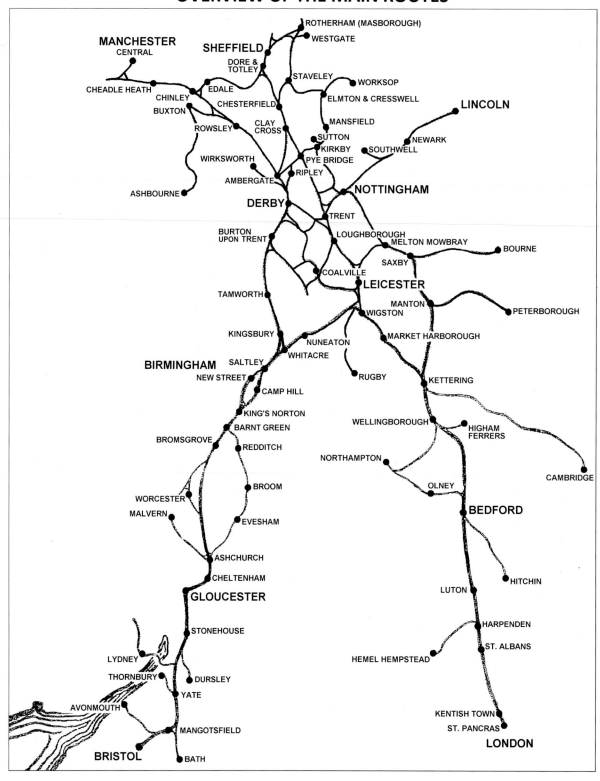

DERBY / NOTTINGHAM / BURTON AREAS

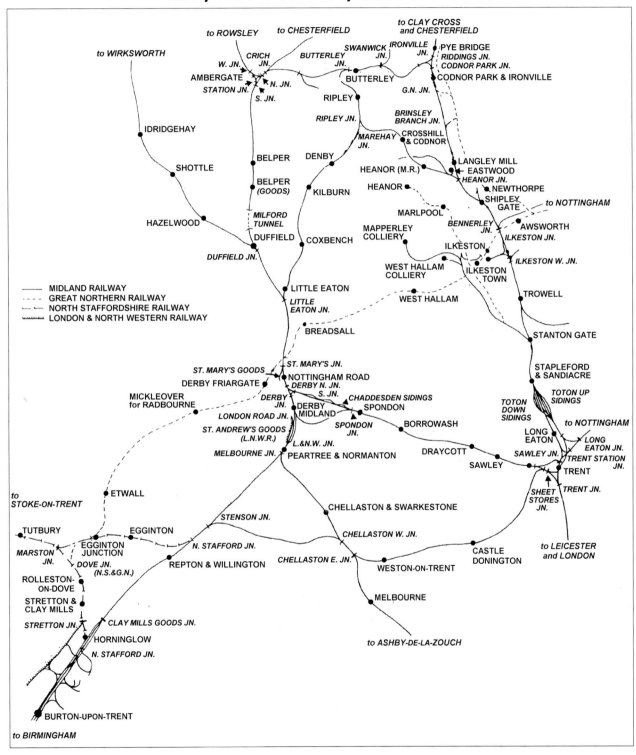

TRENT AREA

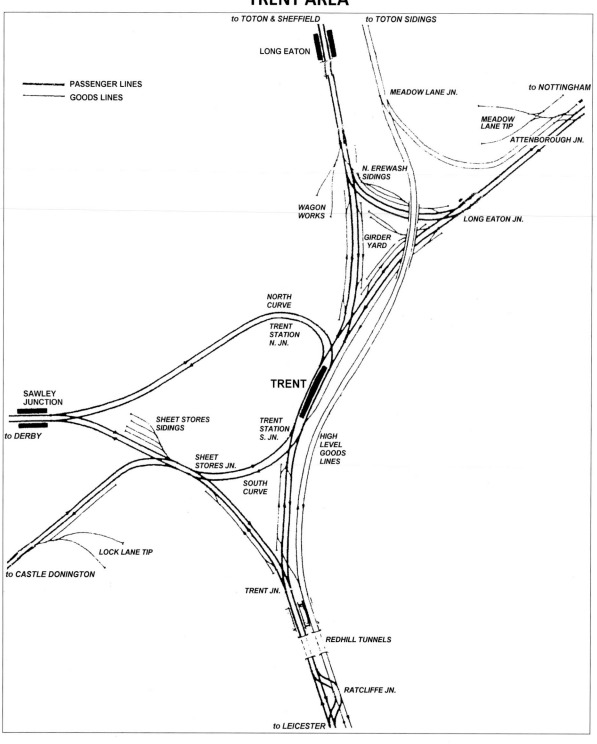

DERBY / TRENT TO SHEFFIELD

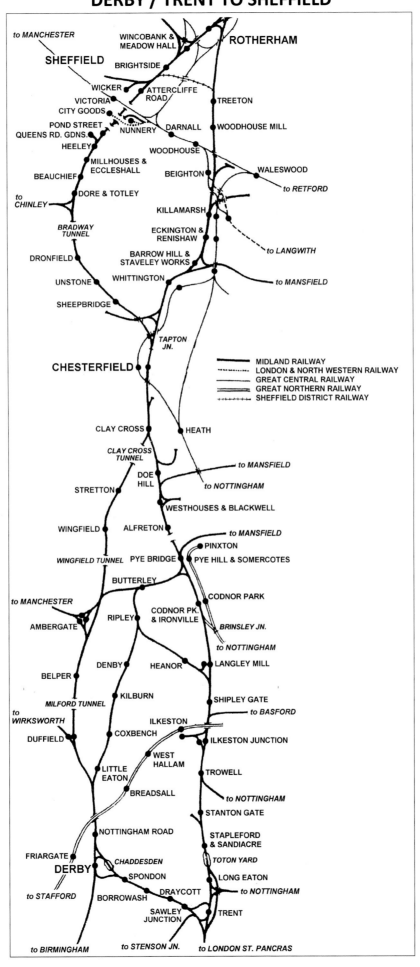

to MANCHESTER

WINCOBANK & MEADOW HALL

ROTHERHAM

SHEFFIELD

BRIGHTSIDE

WICKER

VICTORIA

ATTERCLIFFE ROAD

TREETON

CITY GOODS

POND STREET

DARNALL

WOODHOUSE MILL

QUEENS RD. GDNS.

NUNNERY

HEELEY

WOODHOUSE

MILLHOUSES & ECCLESHALL

WALESWOOD

BEAUCHIEF

BEIGHTON

to RETFORD

DORE & TOTLEY

to CHINLEY

KILLAMARSH

to LANGWITH

BRADWAY TUNNEL

ECKINGTON & RENISHAW

DRONFIELD

BARROW HILL & STAVELEY WORKS

UNSTONE

WHITTINGTON

to MANSFIELD

SHEEPBRIDGE

TAPTON JN.

CHESTERFIELD

MIDLAND RAILWAY
LONDON & NORTH WESTERN RAILWAY
GREAT CENTRAL RAILWAY
GREAT NORTHERN RAILWAY
SHEFFIELD DISTRICT RAILWAY

CLAY CROSS

HEATH

CLAY CROSS TUNNEL

DOE HILL

to MANSFIELD

STRETTON

to NOTTINGHAM

WESTHOUSES & BLACKWELL

WINGFIELD

ALFRETON

to MANSFIELD

PINXTON

WINGFIELD TUNNEL

PYE BRIDGE

PYE HILL & SOMERCOTES

BUTTERLEY

CODNOR PARK

to MANCHESTER

RIPLEY

CODNOR PK. & IRONVILLE

BRINSLEY JN.

AMBERGATE

to NOTTINGHAM

DENBY

HEANOR

LANGLEY MILL

BELPER

KILBURN

SHIPLEY GATE

MILFORD TUNNEL

to BASFORD

to WIRKSWORTH

ILKESTON

DUFFIELD

COXBENCH

ILKESTON JUNCTION

WEST HALLAM

TROWELL

LITTLE EATON

BREADSALL

to NOTTINGHAM

STANTON GATE

NOTTINGHAM ROAD

STAPLEFORD & SANDIACRE

FRIARGATE

CHADDESDEN

TOTON YARD

DERBY

SPONDON

LONG EATON

to STAFFORD

BORROWASH

DRAYCOTT

to NOTTINGHAM

SAWLEY JUNCTION

TRENT

to BIRMINGHAM

to STENSON JN.

to LONDON ST. PANCRAS

PEAK LINE TO MANCHESTER

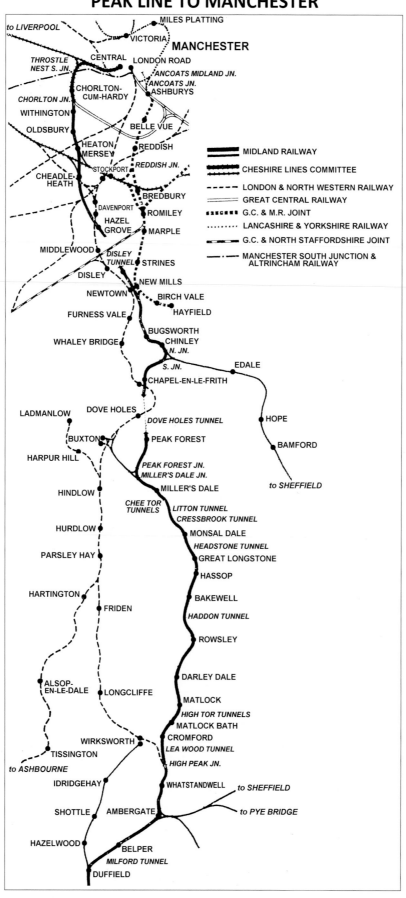

PEAKS, DALES AND MOORLANDS

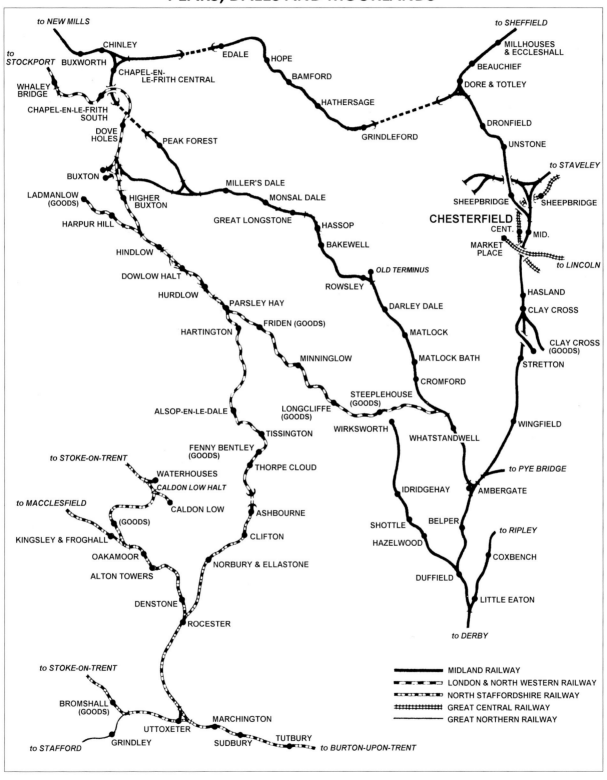

AMBERGATE STATION AREA

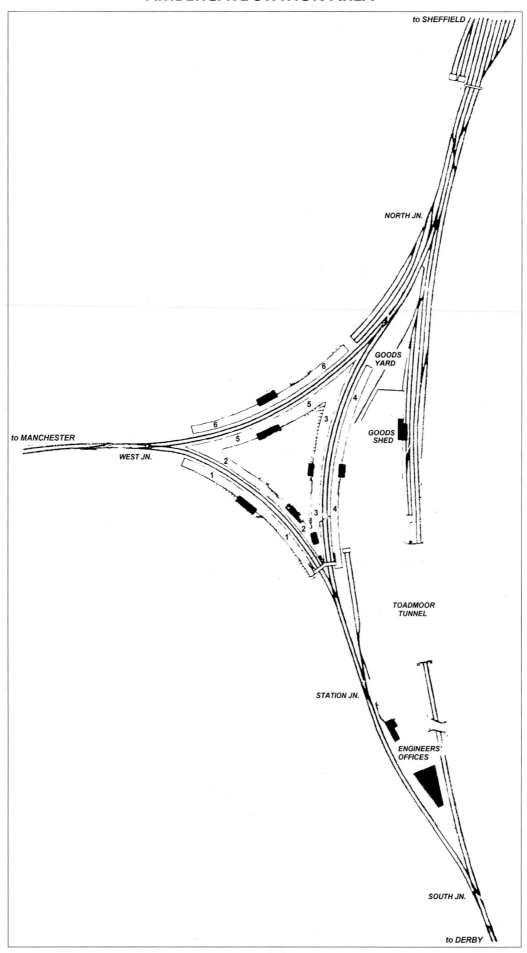

STOCKPORT AREA

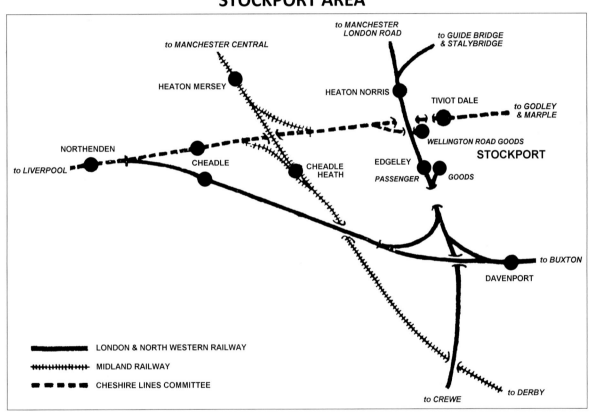

BURTON-UPON-TRENT TO BIRMINGHAM / LEICESTER

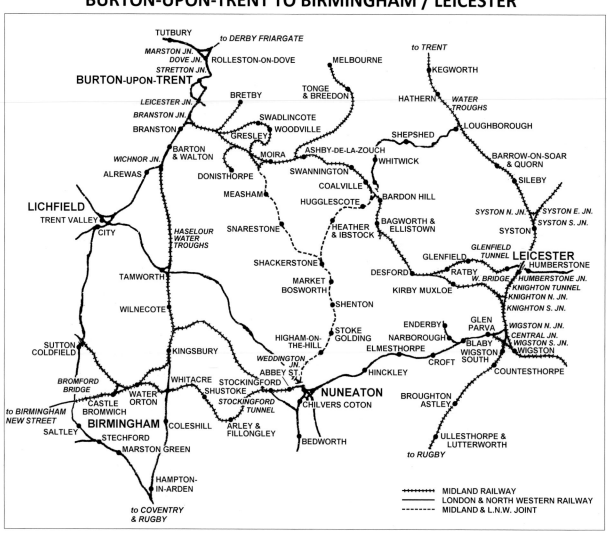

BIRMINGHAM AREA

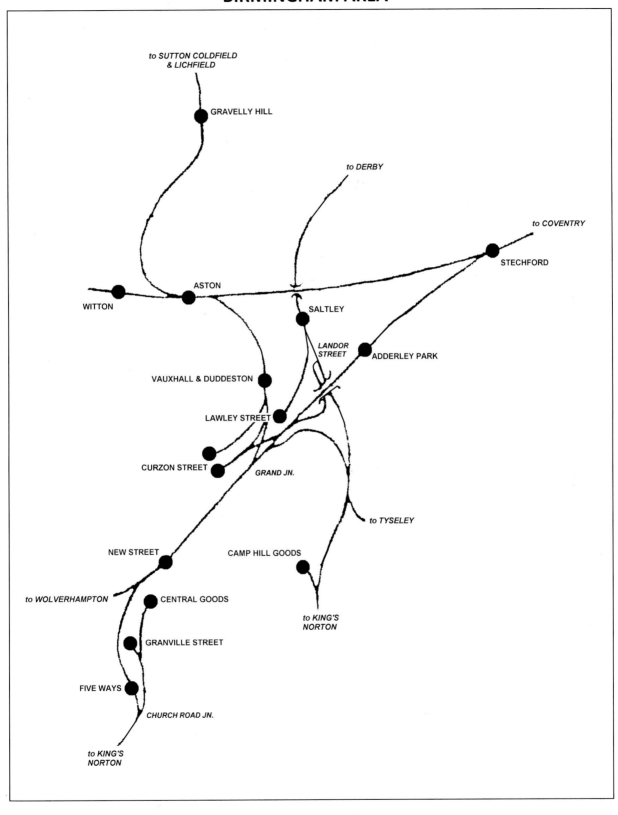

BIRMINGHAM TO BRISTOL

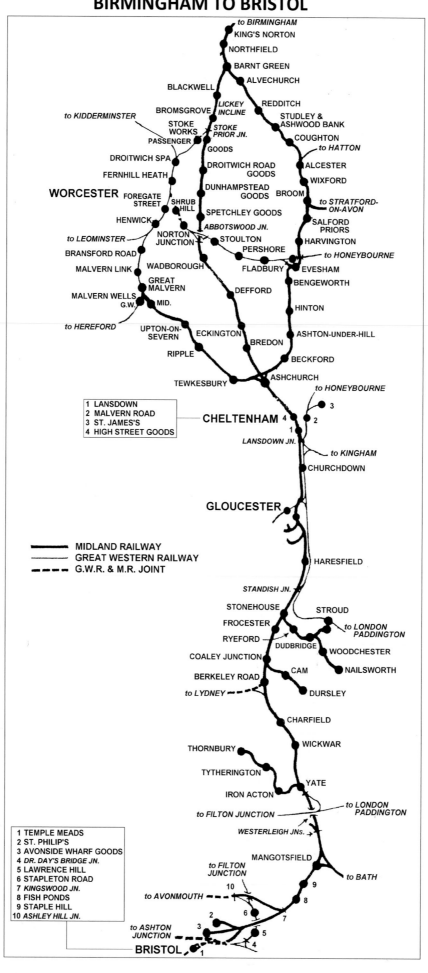

to BIRMINGHAM
KING'S NORTON
NORTHFIELD
BARNT GREEN
ALVECHURCH
BLACKWELL
LICKEY INCLINE
REDDITCH
BROMSGROVE
STUDLEY & ASHWOOD BANK
to KIDDERMINSTER
STOKE WORKS
STOKE PRIOR JN.
COUGHTON
PASSENGER
to HATTON
GOODS
DROITWICH SPA
DROITWICH ROAD GOODS
ALCESTER
FERNHILL HEATH
WIXFORD
DUNHAMPSTEAD GOODS
BROOM
WORCESTER
FOREGATE STREET
to STRATFORD-ON-AVON
SHRUB HILL
SPETCHLEY GOODS
SALFORD PRIORS
HENWICK
ABBOTSWOOD JN.
STOULTON
HARVINGTON
to LEOMINSTER
NORTON JUNCTION
PERSHORE
to HONEYBOURNE
BRANSFORD ROAD
WADBOROUGH
FLADBURY
EVESHAM
MALVERN LINK
GREAT MALVERN
BENGEWORTH
DEFFORD
MALVERN WELLS
G.W. MID.
HINTON
to HEREFORD
UPTON-ON-SEVERN
ECKINGTON
ASHTON-UNDER-HILL
BREDON
RIPPLE
BECKFORD
TEWKESBURY
ASHCHURCH
to HONEYBOURNE

1 LANSDOWN
2 MALVERN ROAD
3 ST. JAMES'S
4 HIGH STREET GOODS

CHELTENHAM 4
3
2
1
LANSDOWN JN.
to KINGHAM
CHURCHDOWN

GLOUCESTER

	MIDLAND RAILWAY
	GREAT WESTERN RAILWAY
	G.W.R. & M.R. JOINT

HARESFIELD

STANDISH JN.
STONEHOUSE
STROUD
FROCESTER
to LONDON PADDINGTON
RYEFORD
DUDBRIDGE
WOODCHESTER
COALEY JUNCTION
CAM
NAILSWORTH
BERKELEY ROAD
to LYDNEY
DURSLEY
CHARFIELD
WICKWAR
THORNBURY
TYTHERINGTON
YATE
IRON ACTON
to LONDON PADDINGTON
to FILTON JUNCTION
WESTERLEIGH JNS.
MANGOTSFIELD
to FILTON JUNCTION
10
to BATH
to AVONMOUTH
9
8
7
6
5
4
3
2
to ASHTON JUNCTION
1

1 TEMPLE MEADS
2 ST. PHILIP'S
3 AVONSIDE WHARF GOODS
4 DR. DAY'S BRIDGE JN.
5 LAWRENCE HILL
6 STAPLETON ROAD
7 KINGSWOOD JN.
8 FISH PONDS
9 STAPLE HILL
10 ASHLEY HILL JN.

BRISTOL

BRISTOL AREA

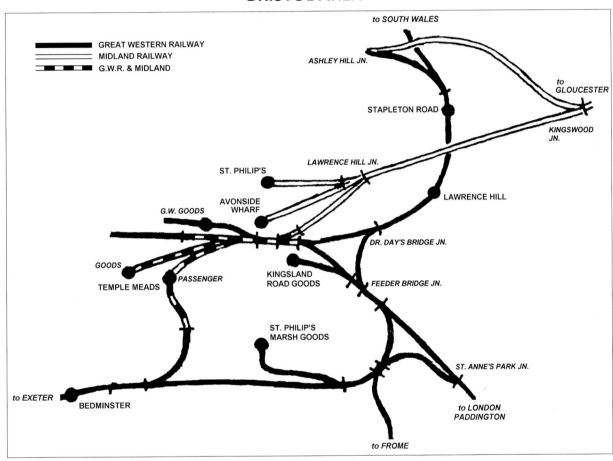

GREAT WESTERN RAILWAY
MIDLAND RAILWAY
G.W.R. & MIDLAND

to SOUTH WALES

ASHLEY HILL JN.

to GLOUCESTER

STAPLETON ROAD

KINGSWOOD JN.

ST. PHILIP'S

LAWRENCE HILL JN.

AVONSIDE WHARF

LAWRENCE HILL

G.W. GOODS

DR. DAY'S BRIDGE JN.

GOODS

KINGSLAND ROAD GOODS

FEEDER BRIDGE JN.

TEMPLE MEADS

PASSENGER

ST. PHILIP'S MARSH GOODS

ST. ANNE'S PARK JN.

to EXETER

BEDMINSTER

to LONDON PADDINGTON

to FROME

NOTTINGHAM TO LEICESTER AND KETTERING

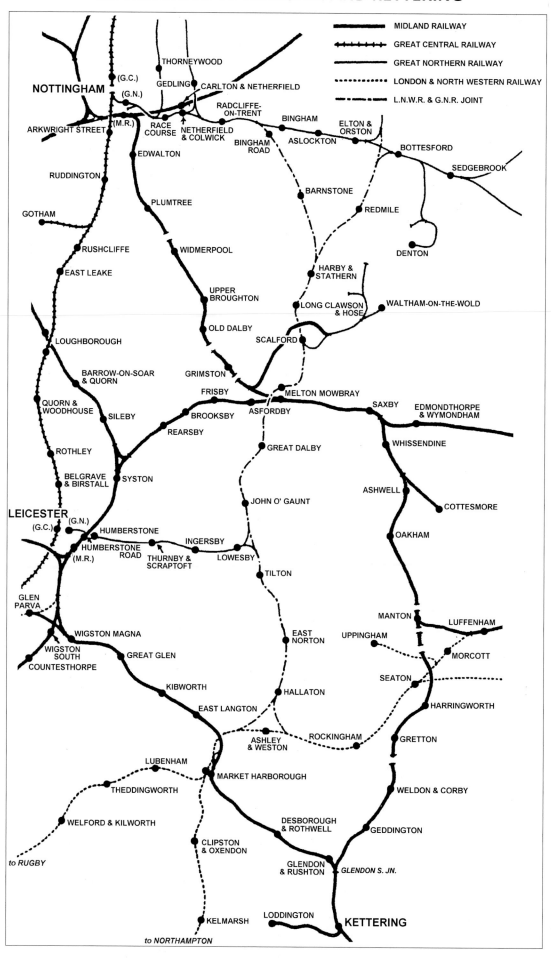

LEICESTER TO BEDFORD OVERVIEW

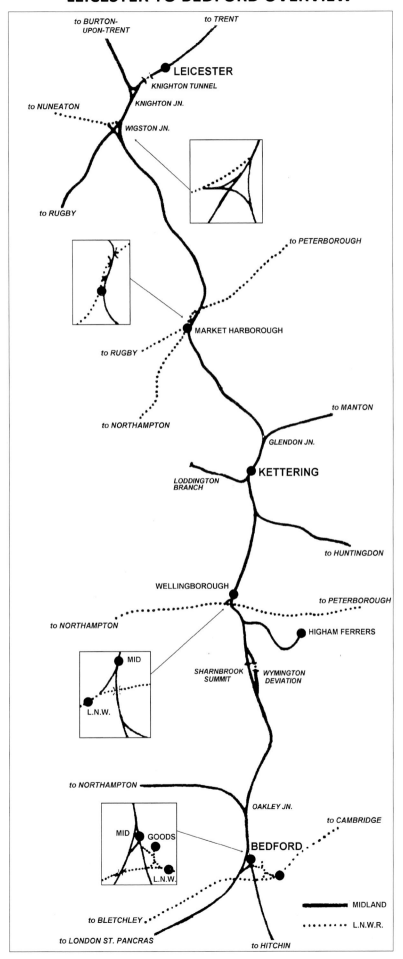

to BURTON-UPON-TRENT

to TRENT

LEICESTER

KNIGHTON TUNNEL

KNIGHTON JN.

to NUNEATON

WIGSTON JN.

to RUGBY

to PETERBOROUGH

MARKET HARBOROUGH

to RUGBY

to NORTHAMPTON

to MANTON

GLENDON JN.

KETTERING

LODDINGTON BRANCH

to HUNTINGDON

WELLINGBOROUGH

to PETERBOROUGH

to NORTHAMPTON

HIGHAM FERRERS

MID

SHARNBROOK SUMMIT

WYMINGTON DEVIATION

L.N.W.

to NORTHAMPTON

OAKLEY JN.

to CAMBRIDGE

MID   GOODS

BEDFORD

L.N.W.

to BLETCHLEY

to LONDON ST. PANCRAS

to HITCHIN

———— MIDLAND

·········· L.N.W.

THE MIDLAND EXTENSION TO ST. PANCRAS

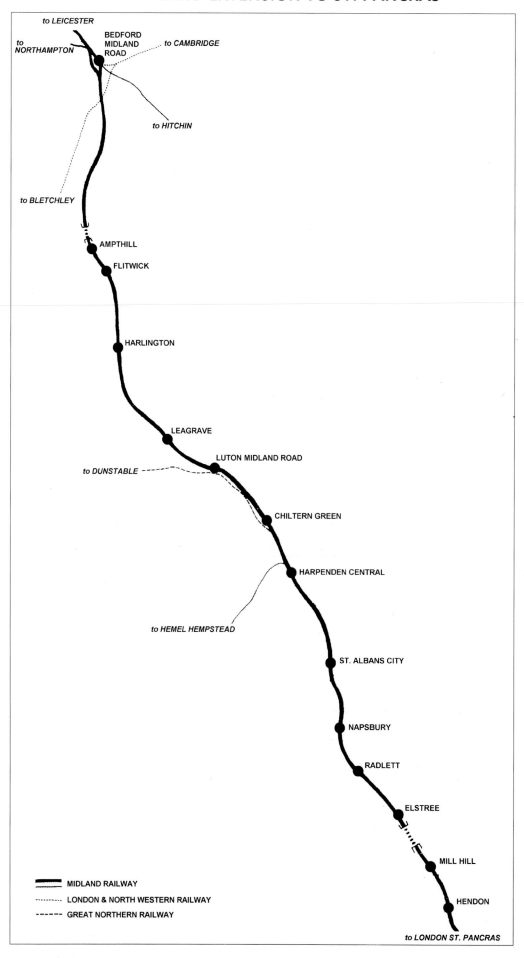

to LEICESTER

to NORTHAMPTON

BEDFORD MIDLAND ROAD

to CAMBRIDGE

to HITCHIN

to BLETCHLEY

AMPTHILL

FLITWICK

HARLINGTON

LEAGRAVE

LUTON MIDLAND ROAD

to DUNSTABLE

CHILTERN GREEN

HARPENDEN CENTRAL

to HEMEL HEMPSTEAD

ST. ALBANS CITY

NAPSBURY

RADLETT

ELSTREE

MILL HILL

HENDON

to LONDON ST. PANCRAS

—— MIDLAND RAILWAY

---------- LONDON & NORTH WESTERN RAILWAY

- - - - GREAT NORTHERN RAILWAY

FINAL APPROACH TO ST. PANCRAS

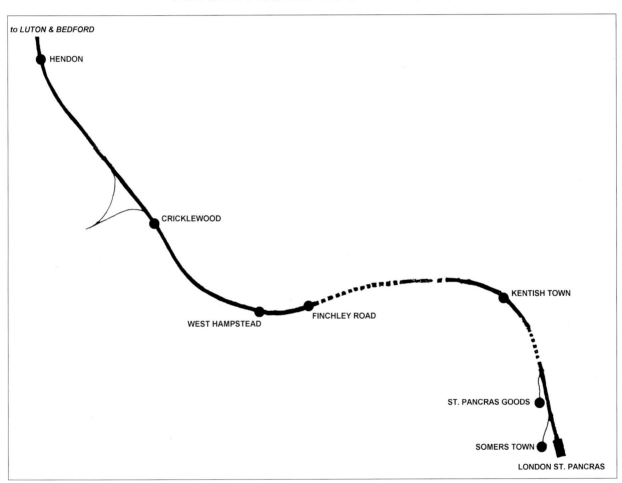

Glossary of Terms

As the readership of this book may extend beyond railway enthusiasts I have included the following glossary as a guide. At the end of the glossary is a conversion table for distances, weight and volume and a few of the distances between railway locations.

Term	Meaning
banker(s)	locomotive(s) used to push trains up an incline
cess	drainage area alongside track
clacks	non-return valves
Conductor (Driver)	Driver who knows the detail of a section of railway who accompanies another Driver who is unfamiliar with that section
continental loading gauge	maximum width/height greater than was usual on British Railways
cross country	within this book the route between Leeds/York and Bristol via Derby and Birmingham
dampers	method of allowing air to be admitted
diagram	several workings by a locomotive/train in a sequence
disposed	fire cleaning of locomotive at end of a turn of duty
distant signal	a signal indicating either caution or a clear section ahead to the next signal
down	direction away from St Pancras or towards Bristol from Derby
fire devil	a portable, self-contained steel basket into which a fire was made. Used in times of extreme cold to prevent running water from freezing
football coupons	weekly listings of football matches on which entrants predicted the results
fusible plug	safety device to indicate danger if water level in boiler dropped
gross (weight)	laden weight
GPO	General Post Office
High Level goods lines	sets of tracks at Trent to allow freedom of movement of freight trains
1 in 100	a gradient equivalent to one unit in every one hundred; one foot in every 100 feet travelled
injector pipes	method used to force water into boilers
Klinger valve	safety device used if engine separated from tender/train
lodging turns	duties where railway personnel were obliged to take a period of rest prior to working back to home depot
loose coupled	linkages between wagons/locomotive without continuous brake
jinties	popular name for some 0-6-0 and some 0-4-0 locomotives
open station	station having no ticket barriers
outshopped	released from a workshop
pannier tank	type of locomotive with water tanks straddling the boiler
path	specific timing within overall timetable
perishables	vegetables/fish with limited 'shelf' life
permanent way	track
pilot engine	locomotive leading another
pilotman	person with local knowledge to guide Driver, e.g. during a local diversion due to engineering work
pinned down	brakes on wagons activated
powertrain	on diesel multiple units, all components leading to movement

Glossary of Terms

Q trains	trains which ran as required
Railway Mania	period in the nineteenth century when applications to build new railways were at their peak
reverser	mechanism by which varying amounts of steam could be admitted to cylinders of locomotive and determine direction of travel
roller bearings	modern axlebox technology
roundhouse	circular building into which locomotives could be placed around a turnable
ruling gradient	limit set by civil engineer regarding steepness of track over a given distance
run in	settling period of running following overhaul
saturated steam	wet steam (not superheated)
semifast	passenger train calling at selected intermediate stations
shedplate	small plate affixed to smokebox of locomotive to indicate home depot
signed for the road	allowed to drive a train over a certain section
Special Limit	maximum tonnage of train allowed within timetable allowance
superheater elements	method of drying wet steam
telephony	electronic communication system
ticket platform	final station before open station where tickets could be checked
top nut	top point visible in water gauge glass
train engine	rear engine of double headed train
tripping	local freight train
turn	duty of crew or locomotive
unbalanced locomotive working	a one-way journey with no timetabled arrangement for the return
up	direction towards St Pancras or from Bristol towards Derby
up to the mark	the point at which the boiler pressure causes the safety valves to allow steam to escape into the atmosphere
vacuum braking	a method of braking by removing air under pressure
washing out	cleaning of interiors of boilers to remove scale and other particulates
way and works	trackside infrastructure
XL Limit	As for Special Limit

Conversions

1 mile	= 1.60934 kilometre
1 yard	= 0.9164 metre
1 foot	= 0.3048 metre
1 inch	= 2.54 centimetres
1 gallon	= 4.54596 litres
1 ton	= 1.016 tonne

Note: Mileposts and quarter mile posts are still in place along the lines of routes of interest to the book.

Mileages between major railway locations

St Pancras to Manchester Central via Derby	190
St Pancras to Sheffield Midland via Derby/Dronfield	165
St Pancras to Nottingham via Trent	127
St Pancras to Nottingham via Edwalton	123
Sheffield Midland to Derby Midland via Dronfield	36
Derby Midland to Bristol Temple Meads via Birmingham New Street/Spetchley/Mangotsfield	132

Preface

This is a book about railways and change. In this case the railways are those from Sheffield (Midland) and Manchester (Central) to London (St Pancras) and also from Sheffield (Midland) to Bristol (Temple Meads). The period of change of particular interest is 1957–1963 inclusive.

The routes saw a great amount of change – organisational, motive power, timetabling – and for those directly involved, a wide range of challenges – statutory, infrastructure, resources, training, adapting from the perceived old to the new – and throughout it all a constant need to provide a service by keeping the trains moving.

This, then, is a book for those with an interest in the detail of railway operations, for those with a passion for locomotives and for social historians.

Researching for the book has resulted in the availability of a large volume of detail about the day-to-day workings of steam locomotives and, in response to an undeniably high level of interest, there is a Chapter specifically on that topic. Reflecting the interest of the time period covered, that Chapter is entitled 'You'll never guess what has been through!' and there were certainly some rare sightings to be enjoyed.

During the time period reviewed lives were being transformed; external influences such as rationing was coming to an end, in a matter of a few years ownership of private cars would double, motorways would be built, cleaner industries would lure away from the grime and unsocial hours of the railway many of the artisan staff, competition from the road haulage industry would intensify and politicians would take more and more interest in placing a control on the shape of the future national railway. Challenges within the railway would include modernisation with massive investment in diesel traction, electrification, improvements to the infrastructure, a need for fewer footplate staff, re-training for many, redundancy for some, opportunities for others, new traffic flows to pursue, others to try to protect, new skills to build and maintain diesel and electric traction. The traditional role of the main workshops would be significantly affected, new marshalling yards would eliminate scores of shunting yards, duplicated routes between major centres would be identified and future direction would be sought.

Improvements would include the progressive extension of the fitment of automatic warning systems into the cabs of steam and diesel/electric locomotives, an extension also of the use of continuous vacuum braking of freight trains and a general recovery from the effects of under investment and over utilisation of assets during and immediately after the Second World War.

But for the time being there was, at the end of 1956, a complex and varied railway scene to be enjoyed, in fact the essential role of the railways had come to the fore as a result of the Suez Canal becoming unavailable for the shipping of oil supplies to Europe and particularly Great Britain. Rationing of petrol had been introduced and the railway management was responding as best it could to the needs of the nation.

The book starts with a review of the origins of the routes of interest and the main characteristics of each. That is followed by a Chapter to set the scene for a review, year by year, of what was a fascinating period of change. Human interest is not overlooked and examples of parts of working lives on the railway have been included.

I feel that I was fortunate to have been born into a railway family. My paternal grandfather had retired as Station Master, Derby Midland, and had been followed into the LMS by one of his sons, my father. My other grandfather had worked at Derby Locomotive Works as a time-served machinist and had been followed there by one son and two sons-in-law.

My father had started his railway career as a locomotive/train recorder at Ambergate South Junction signal box and then progressed through various operating grades including Duffield, with responsibility for the stations along the branch line to Wirksworth, then during wartime firstly as a relief Station Master for anywhere on the Midland Division and later in Derby District Control and at Manchester. Later a move into personnel work took him to Leicester and Nottingham divisions prior to him being made redundant and working out the final few months of a forty-year career at St Mary's yard in Derby. Our family lived near the railway and with my father opting to lodge or travel during the working week rather than disturb our schooling the nearby Breadsall Crossing became my spare-time haunt. A near neighbour was a Locomotive Inspector – by that I mean he was responsible for inspecting footplate crews in carrying out their duties – and during bus journeys he would tell my father about motive power developments. Overhearing that he would be away for a few days learning about Britannias had my antennae switched to full power!

Although the consequences of the acceptance of the proposals in 'The Re-Shaping of British Railways' report were well underway when I was seeking employment, my heart was set on joining the railway. I started at the offices of the Chief Mechanical and Electrical Engineer, London Midland Region and was placed into what was called the Shopping Bureau. There, the daily tasks were to cajole carriage depots to release vehicles due for overhaul, to listen as the Inspectorate at the various carriage and wagon works demanded a flow of vehicles to satisfy the workshop management, to listen as carriage depot managers demanded overhauled vehicles back from works before sending any more vehicles, to liaise with the operators for the movement of stock trains to and from the sidings where the carriages would be sorted and, it seemed, to keep the Section Manager sane. I loved it and spent the lunch hour watching the stock trains/shunts. It was second nature to me. Soon I was asked whether I would report for work early, go to Maintenance Control and extract from the daily log all instances of failures of diesel traction, reported reason for the failure and effect upon services. Then to prepare a summary by locomotive type (Sulzer/E.E./Metrovick/other) and have it typed up so that it was on various desks by 8.30am. How I used to love to add something along the lines of 'Assisted forward to Preston by 70013 with gain of 8 minutes on schedule' or, on one occasion 'D328, third failure of this nature in the last month with this locomotive.' The Section Manager responsible for English Electric type 4s cornered me later and demanded to know how I could know that. He found it difficult to accept that it was purely from interest and second nature for me to remember.

I was then fortunate to be accepted as an internal candidate for one of the Management Training Schemes of the British Railways Board. The Board supported my pursuit of a Degree and enabled me to embark on an enjoyable career of some thirty years. Privatisation of the railways at the end of the 1990s threatened redundancy, but together with some twenty of my colleagues, a private company was formed and further opportunities to work for the new railway organisation and for others were created.

John Palmer
Allestree
Derby, 2016

Chapter One

Origins and Characteristics

Within the boundaries set for this book there is a lengthy list of originating railway companies. Along the routes of interest the high quality of the surveying work and engineering standards can still be admired by travellers of today (Rowsley to Chinley, Leicester to Rugby and Nottingham to Egginton Junction/Burton and Nottingham to Melton Mowbray being the main exceptions) and it is appropriate that the origins and some of the enduring characteristics be acknowledged.

Each originating railway is listed within an individual line of route.

Midland Counties Railway (MCR)
Nottingham to Derby	opened 1839
Trent Junc to Leicester	opened 1840
Leicester to Rugby	opened 1840

Birmingham and Derby Junction Railway (B&DJR)
Derby to Hampton	opened 1839
Whitacre Junc to Birmingham	opened 1842

North Midland Railway (NMR)
Derby to Masborough (Rotherham)	opened 1840

(*Note:* Midland Railway formed in 1844 by amalgamation of MCR, B&DJR and NMR)

Midland Railway (MR) Nottingham and Erewash Valley
	opened 1847
Trent to Pinxton	opened 1847
Nottingham to Kirkby	opened 1848
Kirkby to Mansfield	opened 1849
Pye Bridge to Clay Cross	opened 1875

Birmingham and Gloucester Railway (B&GR) and the Bristol and Gloucester Railway
Birmingham to Gloucester	opened 1840
Bristol to Gloucester	opened 1844 (broad gauge)
	opened 1854 (standard gauge)

Midland Railway South to London
Leicester to Hitchin via Bedford	opened 1857
Bedford to Kentish Town via Luton	opened 1868
St Pancras station	opened 1868

Midland Railway North to Manchester
Ambergate to Rowsley	opened 1849
Rowsley to Miller's Dale	opened 1863
Miller's Dale to New Mills	opened 1867
Trains into Manchester (Central)	opened 1902

Cromford and High Peak Railway (C&HPR)
Cromford to Whaley Bridge   opened 1831

Great Northern Railway (GNR)
Grantham to Nottingham   opened 1852
Colwick to Pinxton via Kimberley and Codnor Park   opened 1876
Kimberley to Egginton Junc (thence to Burton via
North Staffordshire Railway and to Tutbury via London North Western Railway)   opened 1881

The origins, development and, in some cases, the decline of these railways has been well documented before. The summaries included in this section are to assist the reader in an understanding of the operating characteristics and the background to duplications of routes under National rather than private ownership. A set of maps is included elsewhere in the book.

The demand for coal provides a starting point; demand in Leicester to be specific and in the period around 1825. At that time the coal was carried in bulk some 30 miles from the pits of the Erewash Valley in Nottinghamshire using the canal; slow but economical. Although there were coal reserves closer to Leicester the lack of a canal or waggonway or railway meant that the local colliers could not compete. The Stockton and Darlington Railway had demonstrated the relative efficiency of movement of loads by train hauled by steam locomotives. In response to the frustrations of the local colliers a locally based, wealthy Quaker – John Ellis – invited Mr George Stephenson and his son Robert to consider an invitation to survey and construct a railway over the 16 miles between Swannington and Leicester. The invitation was accepted and after overcoming various setbacks over a period of six years the line was opened in 1833.

For every winner there is a loser and the miners of Eastwood in Nottinghamshire were unhappy about the loss of a market outlet. They, in turn, decided to have another railway built, this one being from the Erewash Valley to Leicester. In engineer William Jessop they had an influential supporter and he took the outline proposal to a group of financiers known as the Liverpool Party. The financiers were attracted to the idea of a new railway, though on a far more extensive scale. The destination was to be Rugby, thence with traffic taken on to the huge market of London. The Midland Counties Railway (MCR) was conceived and was to be built in three sections: Nottingham to Derby, Trent to Leicester and Leicester to Rugby. At Rugby the MCR line would join the London and Birmingham Railway (L&BR). No doubt the backers were also aware of the intention of the Birmingham and Derby Junction Railway (B&DJR) to have a line to Hampton-in-Arden,

thus opening a second potential route. The only people who lost out on this were the very ones who started the process; the miners of Eastwood would have to wait (until 1847) before they could send coal to Leicester (and South thereafter) by rail.

The construction of a new railway was subject to the parliamentary process of Bill/Act/Assent with arrangements for minimum subscription of Shares a pre-requisite to commencement. Those requirements having been met and the relevant Act having been passed into law in 1836, construction in line with the survey of Vignoles of the new railway from Nottingham via Beeston, Sawley, Spondon and Chaddesden was underway in 1838. The formal opening of the 16 miles was on 30 May 1839 with the first train from Nottingham being hauled by the delightfully named locomotive *Sunbeam*.

Out of chronological sequence, but logically relevant here are notes about the opening in 1867 of an alternative line from an area between Trent and Derby (Pear Tree to Melbourne 1868, Sheet Stores Junction to Weston-on-Trent 1869 and Weston-on-Trent to Stenson Junction 1873). In 1901, high level goods lines were added at Trent and with the extensive range of junctions then complete, the MR had a facility to re-route trains as demand and incidents may dictate.

Back to the opening of the MCR Nottingham to Derby line in 1839 and it is relevant to note that an extension of the line Eastwards to Lincoln was opened in 1846. At that time a new Nottingham station was opened and remains today largely on that site.

The line from Trent Junction to Leicester was opened in May 1840 and the section of 20 miles from Leicester to Rugby via Broughton Astley was opened in July of that same year.

A route to link with the London & Birmingham Railway (L&BR) and thus gain access to the line to London (at that time there being just that one from the North) had also been in the minds of the promoters of and backers for the Birmingham and Derby Junction Railway (B&DJR). The potential route for this was surveyed by the Stephensons and achieved Hampton-in-Arden via Burton-on-Trent, Tamworth and Whitacre.

The line opened in August 1839 and the Directors of the B&DJR would surely have been upset by the arrival of the MCR at Rugby and with the L&BR in accepting additional traffic onto its line to London. Competition had arrived. The choice of the B&DJR to pursue a line to Hampton rather than Birmingham (reached in 1842 via a line from Whitacre) conveyed adequately where the best market was deemed to exist. (The link between Kingsbury and Water Orton was built in 1909).

In the area twenty or so miles north and east of Derby, industrialisation had been developing since the late eighteenth century and momentum having been established, was attracting interest from further afield:

1771   The first successful water-powered cotton-mill had been built by (Sir) Richard Arkwright at Cromford.

1776   The building of cotton mills extended south along the River Derwent to Belper where Jedediah Strutt started construction.

1779   The Erewash Canal linked Langley Mill to Trent.

1780   The first Derbyshire coke iron furnace was opened.

1783   Mill at Matlock Bath opened.

1790   Butterley Engineering Company founded by Benjamin Outram. By 1796 the Company was producing 1,000 tons of pig iron annually (and by 1820 annual production there and at Codnor Park totalled 4,500).

1794   Promoted by Benjamin Outram and engineered by William Jessop the Cromford Canal opened, linking Cromford with Langley Mill and establishing a route via locks, to the Erewash Canal. This enabled an exchange of traffic; coal to Cromford, limestone and lead to Langley Mill. In digging the tunnel for the canal near Butterley further deposits of iron ore and coal were discovered.

1795   Railway from Denby to Little Eaton built by Benjamin Outram opened, thence by Derby Canal West to the Trent and Mersey Canal at Swarkestone and east to the Erewash Canal at Sandiacre with access to the River Trent.

1799   Coal extracted during the year from shallow pits on Nottinghamshire side of Erewash Valley amounted to 384,000 tons.

1804   North Mill at Belper built by William Strutt.

Here, then were means of production, actual production and trade products in various forms requiring transportation to market places.

The North Midland Railway (NMR) was enacted by parliament in summer 1836 and within a few weeks the route from Derby to Leeds – some 72 miles – was being surveyed by George Stephenson and his son. Their intention was to limit gradients to nothing more taxing than 1 in 330 (that is a rise or fall of 1 foot in every 330) and, in support of this, to follow, whenever possible, the valleys of the rivers Derwent, Amber, Rother, Don, Dearne, Calder and Aire. Whilst that civil-engineering led desire was very largely met, it did mean that the route would not pass directly through the emerging industrial centre of Sheffield and the coal rich areas of Barnsley and Wakefield. Sheffield would, though, be connected at Masborough (Rotherham) by a line which was pre-existing by the time the NMR reached there. Following tunnels (originally seven with a total length of roundly 3,120 yards) which cost the lives of fifteen contractors' employees and with the cost of fees to landowners, compensation to others and the building of a station at Derby (also for the MCR and B&DJR) the outturn total cost was twice that originally budgeted.

However, in June 1840 a fine railway was opened, some of its stylistic stations having been the work of Francis Thompson. To complete the outline of the route of prime interest to this book, a new line was built by the Midland Railway (successor body to the NMR) between 1865–70. This was from Tapton Junction (north of Chesterfield) via Dronfield and Dore to Sheffield with gradients and physical barriers which were such an anathema to the Stephensons. Once that direct route became available and with the emergence of Sheffield as being worthy of a direct Leeds to Birmingham route, the route between Tapton Junction and Rotherham via Killamarsh (which became known as the Old Road) suffered a reduction in passenger, though not freight, traffic. In fact, the section between Cudworth and Toton would, within twenty-five years, become the most congested section of the Midland's growing network. With the opening of the line to Leeds the design, development, production and sales of products (for example rails, wheels, axles, castings, brakegear and steel tyres) specifically for railways burgeoned particularly in South Yorkshire.

We now return to the area of the Erewash Valley, where it will be recalled the aspirations of the coal miners to have a railway link to Leicester had failed to materialise in 1839/40. The necessary backing and statutory process having been successfully secured by the MR a new route was opened in 1847 between Trent and Codnor Park; Nottingham to Kirkby (1848) and followed shortly afterwards by a branch line to Mansfield (1848) joining the Mansfield to Pinxton

In steam days telegraph poles and wires were an ever present fact of life for photography. Here, though, they are out of the way and allow a clear view of 8F 48199 crossing Unstone viaduct (approaching Dronfield from Chesterfield) lifting 450 tons of coal for Gowhole exchange sidings up the 1 in 100 gradient. (*Rail-online*)

tramway at Kirkby-in-Ashfield. Thereafter the owners of collieries quickly developed a network of sidings to which, and from which, the MR could return/collect privately owned wagons of coal, and iron ore/limestone/ steel products could flow to others in the area. It was the era of Railway Mania.

For geographical completeness two other sections of the route are included here; Pye Bridge to Clay Cross (there to join the Derby to Chesterfield line) opened in 1862 and between Radford and Trowell (to provide a new connection between Lincoln/Nottingham and the Erewash Valley route) opened in 1875.

The foregoing two paragraphs rather understate the development of the network of lines along the Erewash and the need for some co-ordination of the railway traffic arising therein. Out of this need emerged shunting yards around Sandiacre-Toton which, during the first half of the twentieth century, were continually developed by first the MR then its successor the London Midland and Scottish Railway to a point when

the yards ranked as the largest in Europe. The need, up to 1948, for privately owned wagons to be segregated and returned/ collected from owners – particularly the collieries and in some cases the customers such as gas works – presented a time-consuming and inefficient challenge. From 1907 the MR introduced a method of co-ordinating control – initially for the Cudworth-Toton section and within a few years matters were much improved. The availability of more powerful locomotives, frequently working in pairs, enabled the tonnage of loaded trains to be increased and from 1927–30 a new Class of locomotive – the 33 Beyer Garratts – were able to take up to 87 loaded 13 ton capacity wagons of coal to the yard at Brent, North London. To stable some of those huge locomotives between duties a longitudinal section of line was used between two of the three roundhouses at the Toton motive power depot. A roundhouse contained a turntable upon which the locomotives (shorter than Beyer Garratts) could be turned and then placed on to any of up to 12/16 short lines radiating from the turntable. The Garratts equipped with rotary coal bunkers could be run in whichever way they faced though in theory the few with conventional, self-trimming bunkers would be turned by use of various junctions.

The Birmingham and Gloucester Railway (B&GR) was conceived in the 1830s as a link between the inland port of Gloucester and the developing West Midlands. The backers of the proposed line engaged Isambard Kingdom Brunel and a Captain Moorson and debate ensued as to the route to be selected. From a traffic generation perspective there was not a lot between the two ends to excite the backers – Worcester showed no interest – and it became a discussion around how best to tackle the physical barrier between the valley of the River Severn and the plateau of the Midlands; the then conventional practice of seeking a gradient ideally no more arduous than 1 in 300 as a practicable proposition being unattainable.

Following advice that there was in America a type of locomotive that would be capable of surmounting a climb over the same 2 miles at a gradient in excess of 1 in 40, the decision was taken to engineer the climb by a dead straight section at 1 in 37¾ between Bromsgrove and Blackwell, the Lickey incline.

The B&GR was opened in stages in 1840; between Bromsgrove and Cheltenham in June, and Gloucester in November and from Bromsgrove via Kings Norton to the (original) terminus near Camp Hill in December. In the following year the railway was extended to make a junction with the L&BR and was able to utilise facilities at the latter railway's Birmingham terminus at Curzon Street. The section between Bromsgrove and Cheltenham included a short branch line from Ashchurch to Tewkesbury. Ashchurch became a three-sided station due to other developments. An Act of Parliament in 1860 authorised the extension of the Tewkesbury branch towards the (GWR) Worcester to Hereford line, meeting it South of Malvern (Malvern Hanley Road). In 1861 the Midland Railway was given approval for a line from Ashchurch to Evesham (opened October 1864), later extended by the Evesham and Redditch Railway to create from 1868 a particularly attractive diversionary route from the Midland Railway between Barnt Green and Ashchurch. (The Barnt Green to Redditch MR line having been in operation since September 1859). The Midland later absorbed both the 'new' lines from Ashchurch; that to Redditch in 1874, that to Malvern in 1876 and between Evesham and Redditch in 1882. The section between Malvern and Upton upon Severn was closed in December 1952 and the dates of other closures and noted later in this book.

As already noted, Worcester was not ready for the new world of railways, but once the attractions became clear to those who chose to make a difficult journey by a roadway to Abbots Wood Junction, the city fathers agreed to a railway being laid, thus completing a link back to Stoke Works, 2 miles South of Bromsgrove.

Gloucester having been reached resulted in passengers who wished to journey to Bristol and beyond having to change to the broad gauge (7 feet, as opposed to the standard 4'8½"), as did all accompanying luggage and general merchandise. The broad gauge had been laid by the Bristol and Gloucester Railway over the 23 miles of the route of an earlier tramroad North from Westerleigh, to Standish Junction, with the route aligned to benefit from the relatively flat vale of the River Severn. Any consequent need for major earthworks was minimal and there was just one tunnel, at Wickwar. The intermediate stations at Yate, Charfield, Berkeley Road and Frocester were Italianate in style and each had a wagon turntable allowing five short storage/unloading bay stubs from the two access lines. The availability of a standard gauge railway to Bristol/Birmingham and beyond as a means of transporting products attracted the flour millers and traders of the Cam Valley. By Act of Parliment (1855) the 2½ mile Dursley & Midland Junction Railway was incorporated and opened to business the following year; the junction station (close to milepost 105), along with the Midland, was known variously as Dursley Junction, Coaley and Coaley (for Dursley). The railway was taken over by the Midland from 1861 and survived until 1962. Whilst there is no longer a branch railway, there is at Cam & Dursley (near milepost 105¼) a new station opened in 1994. From Standish Junction the final 7 miles to Gloucester were used as agreed with the Cheltenham and Great Western Union Railway. From 1872 Yate was the junction for the line to Thornbury (closed to passenger traffic from 1944) though still open to Tytherington for stone traffic. From 1908 a line was added from Yate to join the Badminton line of the GWR (and since 1969 has formed the cross country route to Bristol Parkway/ Temple Meads).

Around this time (1844) the Midland Railway was formed with the aforementioned John Ellis very much involved. Mr Ellis was mindful of the fact that the MR would need a terminus in Bristol and that the Great Western Railway had its eyes on expansion in the Midlands. The Bristol and Gloucester Railway was struggling to make adequate returns for investors and knowing of this Ellis bided his time until it was appropriate to offer outright purchase, an offer that was

The up *Devonian* has changed locomotives at Bristol Temple Meads and Barrow Road's Jubilee 45662 *Kempenfelt* is departing for Bradford and with the Jubilee and its crew working through to Leeds. All very business-like and a regular working for one of the Barrow Road long term allocation of Jubilees … *Eire, Bengal, Shovell, Rooke, Kempenfelt, Trafalgar, Barfleur, Leander* and *Galatea*, of which the final two in the list survived into preservation. (*Kidderminster Railway Museum 002068, Courtesy R. J. Leonard*)

accepted. By this process the Midland Railway acquired a new main line, a terminus at Temple Meads, Bristol and stopped the incursion of the Great Western and its broad gauge. The broad gauge was gradually replaced and by 1854 the standard gauge 'through' trains reached Bristol. The joint use of separate parts of Temple Meads station by the Midland with the Great Western Railway dates from June 1865 and the re-built station as a single unit was completed on 1 January 1878.

To conclude the details for Birmingham to Bristol, reference needs to be made to the history of the establishment of Birmingham New Street station and the MR route through that station. The station jointly used by the B&GR at Curzon Street (from 1841) quickly became very busy and its owner – the London and Birmingham Railway – obtained authority to build nearby at New Street a new station. It was that year – 1846 – that the L&BR, the Grand Junction Railway and the Manchester and Birmingham Railway merged to form

the London and North Western Railway (L&NWR). New Street opened on 1 June 1854 and gradually took over the timetabled passenger services previously dealt with at Curzon Street. The MR continued to use the Camp Hill to Kings Norton route, but decided that it would construct a new, two track section beyond New Street to Church Road (approximately one mile) where it joined an existing line from Granville Street towards Kings Norton. From 1885 the MR ran through services via New Street as well as via Camp Hill and, by 1889, the Midland had its own station adjacent to that of the L&NWR with a central road carriage driveway between the two.

The operating characteristics of the Birmingham to Bristol line include the outstanding interest of the Lickey incline. The choice of route made in the 1830s put in place a 125-year-long need for most trains to stop at the foot of the incline to be assisted up by banking locomotive(s), and until such time as continuous braking was available, for all trains to stop at the top of the incline prior to descending at restricted speed. As traffic and train weights increased the two track incline also became a constriction on operations. The incline also became one of the most fascinating places at which to watch an undoubted spectacle.

Early trials at Bromsgrove with an experimental tank locomotive went disastrously wrong with an explosion of the boiler and the loss of life of the two enginemen. The locomotive selected for use as the first bankers and also for use elsewhere on the Birmingham and Gloucester Railway were of the Norris type, originally built in Philadelphia. However, the engineer of the B&GR was less than impressed with the Norris for use as a banker and in 1845 had built an 0-6-0 wheel arrangement saddle tank locomotive – *Great Britain* – for use exclusively on the incline. The lifetime of *Great Britain* is an unknown, but at some stage it was replaced by locomotives with the same wheel arrangement, though with a tender for coal and water, from the extensive stocks of the Midland Railway Goods type. This design, originally by Kirtley, and with follow-on designs by Johnson (1878–92 and 1895–99) served

the needs of the Railway through to 1920, when their ranks at Bromsgrove were augmented by the arrival of a bespoke design locomotive. The new locomotive was an 0-10-0 tender type, officially un-named, but known to all as 'Big Bertha'. The locomotive was designed for the production of a high tractive effort throughout each climb and over the years until withdrawal in 1956 a mileage of 800,000 (mainly in round trips of 4¼ miles!) accrued. In 1924 the locomotive was used also on trials with heavy coal trains between Toton and Brent, but the results were either not deemed sufficiently successful to encourage further building or possibly they were successful, but the thoughts of the LMS (successor body to the Midland) had turned to the development of Garratt locomotives. Whatever, the 0-10-0 became a mainstay of operations on the Lickey with regular scheduled overhauls at Derby Works, where time out of service was minimised by the fitment of the 'spare' boiler.

Two different types of Garratt were tried on the Lickey: the 2-6-0 + 0-6-2 type and the larger London and North Eastern Railway's sole 2-8-0 + 0-8-2, but neither type lingered and nor did either of two types of eight

All set for its role as a banker on the Lickey incline 92079 (9F) stands outside the Paint Shop at Crewe Works. The locomotive has been fitted with the headlamp previously fitted to 58100 to assist in hours of darkness and in addition has the tender off 92009, the design of which was better suited to the coaling stage facilities at Bromsgrove. (*Colour-rail std 15*)

coupled tank locomotives of the former Great Western Railway when they were tried following the withdrawal of the 0-10-0. For banking duties Bromsgrove shed had allocated to it 0-6-0 side tank locomotives known as Jinties, but when a Regional operating boundary change took effect in 1958 responsibility passed from the London Midland Region to the Western Region. For a time the Western Class 84XX/94XX pannier tank locomotives – some of which had the advantage of superheater elements – worked alongside the Jinties – which like most of the 84XX and 94XX were saturated steam – and the new star of the show; British Railways designed and built Class 9F 2-10-0 92079 (which carried the large headlamp which had previously adorned the 0-10-0).

In the lead up to the time period of interest to this book, trials had been held (in 1955) to ascertain the extent to which power classes 5 and 6 could cope with loads of 222 tons/252 tons respectively. The first test was started from Stoke Works with a 30mph maximum speed through Bromsgrove, followed by a second test which incorporated stops and then re-starting at three different locations on the incline, with a third test from a dead stand at Bromsgrove. The normal arrangements were left undisturbed; possibly because density of varying traffic, timetabling, pathing of trains into Birmingham, consistency of availability of varying classes of power for certain trains and unpredictable weather conditions played a part in the grand consideration.

The use of the locomotive's whistle when passing Stoke Works Signal Box was the method of communication employed by Drivers of Northbound trains, one, two or three indicated his requirement for banking locomotive(s) based upon the weight/number of wagons/steaming of his locomotive. The signalman at Stoke Works would advise his contemporary at Bromsgrove South Signal Box who, in turn would advise the requirement across to the coaling stage

This is on the Lickey incline and I am sorry that I have no way of including the sound to accompany the illustration. The Cardiff–Newcastle passenger train was usually of twelve carriages and following a change of locomotives at Gloucester was normally double-headed as far as Sheffield, before another change took place. Here in June 1958 a Gloucester Compound (41163) is piloting Millhouses' Jubilee 45725 (*Repulse*) banked in the rear by (the equivalent of) three 0-6-0 tank engines; the 2-10-0 banker, if employed being considered the equivalent of two 0-6-0s. (*Kidderminster Railway Museum 150951, Courtesy A. Donaldson*)

The Cardiff-Newcastle train again (6 June 1959) and the train engines (45268/73155) are well out of sight as the photographer concentrates on the bankers; 8400/6/2. All part of a daily spectacle for well-nigh 125 years. The train here is at the start of the climb. (*Kidderminster Railway Museum 093244, Courtesy P. J. Lynch*)

area where the bankers waited. The 0-10-0/2-10-0 was the equivalent of two 0-6-0s. Of the two footplate men, the Fireman had by far the most interesting and demanding tasks. On a Jinty the requirement would be a fire at the back of the firebox built up to the lower level of the firehole, shallower fire at the front, water level well up to the top nut, damper open to keep away the potential for clinkering as the fire set on the firebars and, of course, steam pressure right up to the mark. As soon as the train arrived the banker(s) would be released and having 'buffered up', but not coupled to either the train or themselves, an exchange of coded whistles from and back to the train engine(s) and away, subject of course to the signal being 'off'. The Fireman on a Jinty would then have lifted the flap half way up the firehole door and would fire over the top of it, just four shovelfuls of coal at a time; the blast from the chimney would 'take' the coal and the 'big' back of the fire would start to naturally move forward. The climb would typically take eight to ten minutes for a passenger train, thirteen to fifteen for a freight and approaching the 'distant' (for Blackwell) the Driver would be looking

for an indication from the Signalman. A green flag, or in hours of darkness a green light, would indicate the banker(s) were to return immediately to Bromsgrove; the alternative being to stand in a centre refuge between the 'up' and 'down' tracks awaiting a path (with other bankers) or possibly to provide additional braking force for a descending freight train. Whilst the Driver was looking for that indication the Fireman would be taking the very first opportunity he could to get some more water into the boiler. The firing techniques for an 84XX and for the 2-10-0/0-10-0 varied from that described for a Jinty, but the ever present need to balance fire/water/pressure requirements was a constant. Meantime, the Fireman of the train engine – particularly if there was also a pilot/leading engine going only as far as Birmingham/Derby – may decide, with his Driver's acquiescence, to not disturb his fire too much for the sake of a short duration thrash.

Not every train was required to be banked. For the start of the period of interest to this book (1957) the maximum load unassisted for a passenger train was a mere 90 tons (or up to 16 empty two axle wagons).

One 0-6-0 banker for a power class five up to 250 tons passenger train weight or for power class size 270 tons, then two (or the 2-10-0) if the weight was up to 350–370 tons respectively and for trains of exceptional weight three or the 2-10-0 plus a 0-6-0. For freight trains it was a similar equation of power class/quantity of loaded two axle equivalent wagons providing a basis for the allocation of up to three bankers; power class three 24/36/48, power class four 26/38/48, power class five 27/39/51, power class eight 33/46/59.

With a combination of freight and passenger trains the signalling arrangements on the incline allowed for a second train to safely be started from Bromsgrove before the preceding train had reached the summit.

In the 'down' direction all loose coupled freight trains were required to stop at Blackwell where a proportion of the brakes would be 'pinned down' to allow brakeblocks to be applied to the surface of the wheels. Descent would be at a maximum of 11mph. For passenger trains, it was a case of slowing to 10mph through Bromsgrove station, 27mph down the incline and if stopping in the station at Bromsgrove, 10mph over the crossing point into the platform.

Over a period of time 92079 was replaced by other 9F 2-10-0s and then, when diesels arrived, continuous braking of freight trains became more widespread and the great constriction of well over a century began to lose its aura. The history of the Lickey incline and filmed sequences of the drama of the operation are available elsewhere and are recommended.

Attention is now directed towards the line South from Rugby towards London. Whilst having such a route for its increasing traffic it was courtesy of rights granted by the London and Birmingham Railway (L&BR). The L&BR also enjoyed an increase in traffic and, consequently, occupation of sections of the two track route was at a high level and not ideal for either Railway. Following the amalgamation of companies including the L&BR, to form the London North Western Railway, the allocation of available capacity became more of a concern and to the detriment of the Midland Railway. Unsurprisingly, the Midland sought an alternative route into the capital.

Heading North out of London (Kings Cross station being opened in 1852) were the tracks of the Great Northern Railway (GNR), via Hitchin to Peterborough, Grantham and – right into the territory of the Midland

Whilst banking engines on the Lickey incline would normally run back light engine(s) from Blackwell, they were on occasions required to pilot locomotives on trains descending to Bromsgrove; the reason could be to make available additional brake force. Here 8402 has been attached to 9F 92052. 17 July 1961. (*Kidderminster Railway Museum 008507, Courtesy B. Moone*)

– Nottingham. Whilst wishing to take advantage of the alternative route into London, the Midland did not take at all kindly to the arrival of the GNR at Nottingham (1852) and having taken illegal possession of the locomotive of the latter, locked it away for several weeks. The GNR was to have a greater role in the railways of the East Midlands, but that will follow.

During 1853 the three Railways with a developing interest in services to/from London from/to the North – L&NWR, MR and GNR – proposed to join together, but parliament would have none of such. The Midland was losing out to the L&NWR and began an extension South from near Leicester towards Bedford (some 46 miles) via Market Harborough and Kettering and 16 miles from there across to join the GNR at Hitchin. The line, engineered by contractor Thomas Brassey opened in 1857 and John Ellis was able (just) to witness the first MR through trains into and out of London in February 1858. Out of the L&NWR frying pan and into

the fire. Capacity along the two track route constrained by tunnels resulted in the GNR traffic constantly taking priority, leaving the Midland frustrated. Clearly there was a case for a third route from the North into London and during 1863 the MR was granted by Act of Parliament permission to build a line from Bedford via Luton. By the summer of 1868 construction had been completed and, pending completion of St Pancras station later that same year, passenger trains terminated at Somers Town (goods) platforms. The three termini from the North were within a mile, with the gothic splendour of St Pancras to be an enduring example of that age and of the style of the Midland. St Pancras station was the work of William Barlow and Sir Gilbert Scott with the erection of the roof entrusted to the Butterley Iron Company. Not content with a magnificent station the MR added a grand hotel. The Midland had style.

To negate a need for heavy payloads of coal to be dragged to the summit at Sharnbrook (milepost 59¾ between Bedford and Wellingborough) the Midland Railway built a less demanding deviation – Wymington. Here, at Souldrop, the tracks of the deviation can be seen at a lower level to the mainline upon which Jubilee 45638 (a rare visitor) is in charge of a Southbound express. 21 April 1960. (*Rail-online*)

On the lovely spring day of 21 April 1960 Britannia *Apollo*, 70015, hammers north. A blowing regulator valve will doubtless be 'booked' for fitters' attention at its home depot of Trafford Park. (*Rail-online*)

From an operational perspective the Midland now had, from the coalfields of the Erewash Valley, a well-engineered route into London with four running tracks (though not always immediately parallel) from Trent to South of Luton and later right into London. The reason that the tracks were not consistently parallel was that a ruling gradient of 1 in 200 (South) and 1 in 119 (North) had been set and restrictions would – over the climbs between Oakley and Irchester in each direction and also between Market Harborough and Kettering also in both directions – be unsuitable for the heavy coal trains that would be constantly on the move. To ease the flow of the coal trains and allow the express trains of their day a chance to achieve good speeds the freights were routed from Syston (North of Leicester) to Glendon (North of Kettering) and via a deviation from Irchester (South of Wellingborough) to Sharnbrook (North of Bedford). That still left a steady climb, at the ruling gradient, between Bedford and Leagrave Southbound, and unless momentum could be gained between Elstree and Radlett a difficult 5 miles to Sandridge (between Radlett and beyond St Albans) Northbound. Following years of frustration with the L&BR/LNWR and with the

GNR, the Midland now had an excellent main line with which to promote its various services which increasingly extended beyond pure railway travel to include hotels and shipping.

Leeds, Bristol, London. Coal, cotton, limestone, iron ore, iron and steel products. The Midland wanted more. It wanted a good route into Manchester and into a station other than London Road.

Earlier in this Chapter references have been made to a preference of surveyors for gentle gradients, river valleys and selection from options up to a route of choice for construction to be completed within a very reasonable timescale. For those involved with a route to Manchester the task would be a great deal more difficult, with the added challenge that other railways already well established in Lancashire would not welcome an advance by the Midland. The miners of Eastwood had to wait seventeen years for their line to Leicester; completion of a line from Ambergate to allow access to a new station at Manchester Central through parts of the Peak District would take until 1880; thirty-five years then hence forward. The route, though, was not conceived as a whole, but in sections with the initial impetus provided by the North Midland Railway which passed through Amber Gate/Ambergate, 10 miles North of Derby.

The Manchester, Buxton, Matlock and Midlands Junction Railway (MBM&MJR) issued in 1845 a prospectus which envisaged the construction of a line following a route surveyed by George Stephenson for a distance of 42 miles from a junction with the Manchester and Birmingham (M&BR) at Cheadle to, or near, Ambergate. The Act of Parliament was obtained in 1846 along with other Railways – the M&BR and the Midland Railway (MR) – having been empowered to subscribe towards the total capital cost. However, on the same day that the Act was obtained the M&B, the London and Midland Railway and the Grand Junction Railway merged to form the London and North Western Railway and, therefore, its previous position shifted towards protecting the L&NWR rather than working with the Midland as a joint major contributor.

The MBM&MJR had second thoughts about its preferred route and having repeated the statutory process in 1846/7 was – subject to having the necessary capital – enabled to build a line of very similar total distance though with a need for fifteen tunnels (with a total length of 6½ miles) and a ruling gradient of 1 in 100! It was a grand plan, but that was all it was. The promoters decided that what would be built was an 11½ mile line from Ambergate to Rowsley and that was opened in 1849.

In 1852 the MBM&MJR leased the line for a period of nineteen years jointly to the MR and the L&NWR. The MR had aspirations to push on towards Manchester, but the L&NWR showed no sign of interest in any such venture. The L&NWR owned 97 per cent of the equity in the Stockport, Disley and Whaley Bridge Railway (SD&WBR) and that Railway then proposed a new line to Buxton to follow the route that the MBM&MJR had failed to develop; this in effect negating thoughts the MR was quietly considering. However, the MR wanted to have running rights over the proposed new line to/from Buxton and in 1852 made a proposal to the L&NWR that a new section of line be built between Rowsley

This photograph is included to offer an insight into the demanding nature of engineering a route with acceptable gradients through the Peak District. Often the limestone cuttings would fill with exhaust smoke and steam and thus render the photograph worthless, but on this occasion the photographer was fortunate. (*Rail-online*)

and Buxton. The SD&WBR (effectively, of course, the L&NWR) advised that whilst they would be content for 'local' traffic to have running powers from Buxton to Stockport, they would not be minded to allow 'through' running. The MR plans were thwarted.

The MR needed to find an ally and found one in the form of the Manchester Sheffield and Lincolnshire Railway (MS&LR) who were in a disagreement with the L&NWR. That created an opportunity for the Midland Railway to successfully propose to parliament a route from Rowsley up the valley of the River Wye to Miller's Dale (some 10 miles) and then along a ridge to Chapel-en-le-Frith. The Act was obtained in May 1860 and construction started in September of that year. Of the 400 route miles covered by this book, this section is perhaps the most interesting as the scale of the engineering challenge was unsurpassed elsewhere.

Accordingly greater attention is given to the developments as the MR strived to attain its goal of Manchester and its lucrative trade. Objections from the influential Duke of Devonshire had already caused one divergence from the originally proposed route and

now the Duke of Rutland required a 1,058 yard tunnel to be cut and covered/bored under his land, one of eight tunnels along the new section. Bakewell received a fine station featuring stone and glass canopies over the platforms, an iron footbridge and a shunting yard. Thence via Hassop (station some 2 miles from the village), tunnelling under Little Longstone to the (total) 300 feet spans of Monsal Dale viaduct (which slipped in 1907–8), through Cressbrook and Litton tunnels (making three consecutive tunnels on curves and the last lacking any ventilation shaft) and finally over a new viaduct into Miller's Dale station. At Miller's Dale passengers seeking the spa waters of nearby Buxton were obliged to change trains.

Beyond Miller's Dale there was a need for two tunnels at Chee Tor necessitated by the flow of the River Wye around an imposing limestone spur, though with a further consequential challenge of then bridging Chee Dale and running the tracks along a narrow ledge. Then, after a triangular junction to allow traffic to/from Buxton in each direction (opened 1 June 1863) the tiny Blackwell Halt was installed. The line towards

This is Chee Dale, one mile north of Miller's Dale and 8F 48297 has plenty of steam for the continuing climb at 1 in 100/90 towards Peak Forest, 4 miles distant. Hereabouts the railway ran along a ledge with lovely views of it available. Note the dry stone walls, well-tended limestone ballast and safe walking route. (*W.D. Cooper 2029, Courtesy J. Suter*)

Although for the footplate crew of Jubilee 45649 *Hawkins* the Southbound climb to Peak Forest has been accomplished, the distant signal being at caution means that there is no chance of an acceleration towards Miller's Dale. The location is Great Rocks Junction and the train is the 8.55am Manchester-St Pancras. The turntable just visible in the bottom right-hand corner was used to turn pilot locomotives and also the Northwich based 8Fs, which worked 1,100 ton trains from the Tunstead crushing plants to production centres in Cheshire. (*E.R. Morten 2021, Courtesy J. Suter*)

Manchester then continued through Peak Forest tunnel and along Great Rocks Dale, eventually reaching the summit of the Derby–Manchester route at Peak Forest, 980 feet above sea level and having climbed 810 feet since Derby. The ascent having been completed, relief for the locomotive Fireman was immediate as a long falling gradient of the 6 miles or so to Chapel-en-le-Frith was very welcome, though for Drivers and Guards (in freight train brake vans) another challenge as runaways on the descent were a dangerous possibility. Along the way were two further tunnels including the longest on the line, the 2,984 yard Dove Holes where the portal at the ends is almost 100 feet higher/lower than the other. Whilst boring this tunnel a river was unexpectedly found requiring a diversion to be engineered. The tunnel suffered two later collapses; 1872 and a more serious one in 1940.

Chapel-en-le-Frith station was built on a half mile viaduct with the small town directly beneath and the line then continued on a wide, sweeping curve to reach Chinley, then a wayside halt (though later, from 1902, a middle of nowhere five platform station also serving

the 21 mile line along the Hope Valley from Dore which had opened in 1894). Beyond Chinley the line entered the Goyt Valley along part of which at Buxworth a landslip occurred in autumn 1866 causing further problems for the civil engineers and the building along a new alignment around the slippage (the original foundation having settled it was used from 1902 as part of the expansion which had also affected Chinley's relative importance). Services between Miller's Dale and New Mills briefly commenced (for freight, prior to the landslip) from 1 October 1866 with passenger services commencing from 24 June 1867. Manchester was now just 25 miles distant.

For the operation of trains over this most challenging section of railway please refer to later parts of this book (1959 concerning operations from Rowsley and in Performance Logs for passenger trains).

Manchester could already be reached via the Marple, New Mills and Hayfield Junction Railway (MNM&HYR), a joint venture between the Midland Railway and the Sheffield Company or, as it was known later, the Manchester Sheffield and Lincolnshire Railway MS&LR

becoming later the Great Central Railway. Construction had commenced in 1860 and the section from Marple to New Mills completed in 1865, well in time to receive MR services coming through from Derby from June 1867. The Midland had secured from the MS&LR a running agreement for access to the Manchester London Road station and services from New Mills had commenced on 1 February 1867 (with the start of 'through' services delayed by the landslip at Buxworth).

Despite having achieved an ability to run through services between Derby and Manchester (plus the exciting prospect of the completion of the new terminus at London St Pancras and services over the 190 miles between those two major trading centres), the Midland still did not have at Manchester what it really wanted. What it really wanted was unfettered access to a station, free from having to pay rent (to the MS&LR) and at risk of termination of the running agreement.

An opportunity for the Midland Railway existed in the proposed Manchester South District Railway (MSDR) which envisaged a new link between Throstle Nest and Alderley and was the subject of a flotation in August 1873. The MR (as a partner with the MS&LR and Great Northern Railway in what was the Cheshire Lines Committee) showed an interest in this proposed link which recognised the potential of the cotton trade and residential developments likely for the area. As, over a period of time two of the partners in the Cheshire Lines Committee showed less or no interest (MS&LR/GNR) the Midland took the opportunity to take sole control of the MSDR, effective from 11 August 1876. The new, 8 mile line was constructed between Stockport (Tiviot Dale) and gave the desired unfettered access to Manchester (Central) station, being the principal station of the Cheshire Lines Committee. Opened in part from 8 July 1877 it was completed as a fine train shed 550 feet long by 210 feet wide and with a roof arching to a height of 90 feet above track level in June 1880. The station facilities were enhanced from 1905 by the additions to one side of two additional platform faces.

The interior of Manchester Central station and Black 5 44861 (plus a pilot locomotive) has arrived with the 9.15am train from Nottingham to Liverpool. The train will reverse and be taken forward by a locally allocated locomotive, often a 2-6-4 tank. 31 May 1958. The station is now in use as a conference centre. (*Science Museum/National Railway Museum LMS 481*)

It had taken thirty-one years, but the Midland Railway now had a route from London to Manchester between two fine termini. By August 1880 twelve passenger trains were departing daily for Derby and beyond. A calling point of Didsbury on the MSDR acknowledged the actual development as forecasted in the 1873 flotation by serving the needs of the business community of South Lancashire (that continued through to the 1960s when the *Midland Pullman* made its one intermediate stop between Manchester and London at Cheadle Heath). In the late nineteenth century the Midland offered a through carriages service between Manchester and Southampton via Derby and Birmingham and that outlasted a similar service which linked with Bournemouth which ceased when the L&NWR agreed to attach MR carriages to its faster service to Birmingham via Crewe. Whilst the route distances between the Manchester and London of the two rival companies (L&NWR/MR) was similar at roundly 190 (dependent upon divergences en route) the

engineering challenges of the MR as far as Ambergate influenced a commercial decision to compete on end to end journey timings by running lightweight trains.

A later development was the useful connection with the New Mills and Heaton Mersey Railway, authorised in 1897 and opened in 1902. This, via a lengthy tunnel at Disley (3,866 yards at a demanding gradient of 1 in 102) offered the Midland a faster route which it decided to take and extended that preference in 1904 to include Cheadle Heath; this became known as the Disley cut off. Finally, a further useful link was added from 1906 to enable MR trains to access at Throstle Nest Junction the Cheshire Lines Committee route to Liverpool. How the MR competed with its rival L&NWR for the London-Liverpool transatlantic passenger trade is recounted elsewhere in this book.

It may be recalled that in 1852 the MBM&MJR (i.e. the Ambergate to Rowsley section) had been leased for a period of nineteen years to the MR and the L&NWR. The lease was due to expire in 1871 and the

This is the foot of Sheep Pasture incline on the Cromford and High Peak Railway. The gradient of the incline changes from 1 in 200 to 1 in 8 and wagons traversed the section by means of a continuous 'chain' arrangement. On the left wagons sheeted over and containing limestone await despatch onto the Matlock-Ambergate line at High Peak Junction and empty wagons await their turn to head up the incline. 16 May 1964. (*Bob Jones*)

MR through route to Manchester was again in some jeopardy. In full knowledge of the possibility the MR had promoted a branch line from Duffield (between Derby and Ambergate) to Wirksworth (opened in 1867) and had surveyed a route from there to Rowsley. In the event the MR was able to negotiate with the MB& MJR the sole possession of that Railway.

No review of lines in the Peak District would be complete without at least a passing acknowledgement to the Cromford and High Peak Railway. Potential routes were surveyed as early as 1814 and in 1824 a meeting was convened to consider the linking of two canals – the Cromford and the High Peak – by means of a 33½ route miles iron railway. The proposal to proceed enjoyed the support of influential backers and the necessary Act of Parliament was in place in 1825. The construction was tackled in two main sections; Cromford to Hurdlow (15½ miles) was in use by 1830 and from there to Whaley Bridge by 1831. This was no ordinary railway. Included over its entire length were nine inclined planes with eight (stationary) steam winding engines working with chains and one capstan operation, plus sections of

conventional railway though with gradients as severe as 1 in 14.

Passenger services commenced in 1838 with an outsourced contractor providing a horse-drawn coach between Cromford and Whaley Bridge once daily. From 1856 the C&HPR took over the service using a steam locomotive on conventional sections and passengers walking up/down the inclined planes. For all involved, two legged and four legged, the journey over a period of sixteen hours would have been taxing in the extreme. As alternative services to/from Buxton became available demand for the C&HPR passenger service dwindled and from the end of the summer 1877 ceased completely.

In 1861 the line had been leased to the L&NWR and that Railway absorbed it completely from 1877. This enabled through traffic to be taken from/brought into Friden for initial conveyance to/from Buxton. This living anachronism had a settled existence over some seventy years with wagon loads of limestone, silica sand, bricks and milk being the staple products, plus water for local hamlets. In 1963 the lifting of the rails

The daunting prospect of Middleton incline as seen from its foot. Power for the endless chain which drew up or let descend wagons was provided by a steam powered winding engine (which is still available to be viewed in a working preserved state and forms a feature along sections of the railway which are now a footpath and cycleway). (*Kidderminster Railway Museum 017104, Courtesy V. R. Webster*)

of Middleton incline severed the line and closure (in 1967) was an inevitability.

The final part of this summary concerns the important role of the Great Northern Railway (GNR) as it strove to make a foothold in the East and North Midlands. As already noted the GNR had reached Nottingham in 1852 and by means of its main line from Grantham towards Doncaster had 'tapped in' to the lucrative contracts for taking coal from the collieries of South Yorkshire. In North Derbyshire, North Nottinghamshire and South Yorkshire, the Midland and the Great Northern were in competition and of course their customers in London wanted the best rates. By the 1860s a state of confusion existed which was good for no-one. A 'coal rates agreement' provided a temporary solution until 1868 when, upon expiry only the GNR felt a revision was necessary. The matter was referred to arbitration which, after a protracted period, resulted in 1870 in a decision that no increase in rates could be sanctioned. The decision did not go down well with the GNR and that Company than entered a separate agreement with the Manchester Sheffield and Lincolnshire Railway to hand over coal trains at Retford rather than Doncaster and at a lower rate. This gave to the GNR a competitive advantage over the Midland with a consequential, but unsuccessful, objection by the latter. A price war emerged and, of course, benefitted neither combatant. The Directors of the Midland decided that such a state could not continue and from 1 May 1871 increased the rate for coal traffic from Derbyshire as handed over to the GNR at Nottingham. The GNR found such an arrangement to be commercially unsustainable and decided that they would build their own line further into the coal mining areas of Bestwood and the Erewash Valley and continue west to and through the very headquarters of the Midland empire at Derby.

The Great Northern (Derbyshire and Staffordshire) Act of July 1872 authorised construction of a new line from Colwick (where extensive shunting yards were established) through Daybrook, Bulwell, Kimberley, Ilkeston and Derby Friargate to Egginton Junction, connecting there with the North Staffordshire Railway Burton-on-Trent to Tutbury line, giving access to the brewery trade of Burton-on-Trent. The Act also made provision for a line from Kimberley to access coal traffic along a route via Codnor Park to Pinxton and to and beyond Codnor Park.

That is a great amount of railway history condensed into a single Chapter. If the Chapter has conveyed a sense of willingness in the 1835–1880 era to take advantage of railway technology, of a sense of competitiveness between railway companies and a sense of just how hard individuals applied themselves to attain their goals, that will suffice. The fact that the routes and characteristics of the 1880s were generally unchanged by the replacement of the multiple railway companies in 1923 by the four big companies (LMS, LNER, SR, and GWR) by two world wars and Nationalisation in 1948 that will help the reader with the next Chapter which sets the scene for the years of particular interest to this book.

FOOTNOTES

Much of the network of routes as described has continued in use up to the present day. Notable exceptions are the lines between Rowsley and Chinley, from Nottingham to Melton Mowbray, from Colwick to Burton-on-Trent via Derby Friargate, from Wigston (Leicester) to Rugby, the Pinxton branch, the wholesale changes along the Erewash Valley, and Manchester Central Station.

Much historic infrastructure remains publicly available:

- Section of the Cromford Canal
- Derwent Valley Mills
- Section of the Erewash Canal
- Cromford and High Peak cycleway/walking route
- Sections of the Rowsley – Peak Forest section opened for cycling/walking route
- The Duffield to Wirksworth railway is operational as the Ecclesbourne Valley Railway
- The Midland Railway Centre near Ripley includes examples of Midland Railway signalboxes, signalling and rolling stock
- Examples of some of the locomotive classes used on the routes of interest are to be found in the National Collection and privately owned, in use from time to time at heritage railways and on main line (Network Rail) excursions
- Manchester Central station remains in use as a convention centre
- St Pancras station/hotel has been extensively and sympathetically restored/re-opened
- St Albans South signalbox has been restored and open to visitors at particular times.

Chapter Two

Setting the Scene

As part of a programme of nationalisation to oversee railways, canals and road freight haulage in Great Britain (excluding Northern Ireland) the British Transport Commission was created by the post-war government and came into operation on 1 January 1948.

The main holdings were the networks of the four national, regional railway companies (the London Midland and Scottish Railway, the London and North Eastern Railway, the Southern Railway and the Great Western Railway) the assets of which had been very heavily called upon to support the war effort, with consequential under-investment in the infrastructure and equipment. The Commission also took over 55 other railway undertakings and fleets of privately owned wagons, 19 canal undertakings, 246 road haulage firms and the London Passenger Transport Board. This vast organisation, under the initial chairmanship of Sir (later Lord) Cyril Hurcomb had at one time 688,000 employees.

The Transport Act 1947 provided for the operation of transport services via five Executives; railways (including engineering workshops) docks (twenty-three) and inland waterways (including former railway steamer services), hotels (later British Transport Hotel and Catering Services, then British Transport Hotels), London transport and road transport (including Pickfords and hauliers in ordinary, long distance work for 40-plus mile trips; these latter were later re-organised as British Road Services). This structure provided for a period of stability whilst the country struggled with society-wide matters, rationing and a return to peace time.

A change of government (Labour to Conservative) brought with it the dismantling of the structure of the Commission and Executives, effective from 1 October 1953 and introduced a new Chairman, General Sir Brian Robertson. On 1 January 1955 the railways were re-organised on the basis of six Area Railway Boards, each of which had a wide measure of operational autonomy though under the overall supervision of the Commission. At the same date the government de-nationalised much of the road haulage sector and separate managements were introduced for docks and inland waterways and for hotels.

Turning now specifically to the railways, this was a dated system functioning reasonably well, though in urgent need of capital expenditure for a general re-equipping. Recognising this need the government made available later that year (1955) up to £1,240 million to be expended in the following areas:

	£m
Coaching stock	230
Freight stock	225
Electrification	185
Diesel power	150
Goods yards	140
Signalling	105
Way and works	105
Stations	55
Steam traction	10
Ancillary/support	35

Later in this book it will become clear how elements of the programme were developed and introduced, but for now the organisation of the railways will continue to be outlined.

The railways were organised into six Areas, or Regions as they were presented; (London Midland, Western, Southern, Eastern, North Eastern, and Scottish denoted in publicity material and on stations by colours maroon, brown, green, dark blue, tangerine and light blue respectively). This book is primarily concerned with arrangements and operations within the London Midland Region though with trains of interest passing to and coming from each of the other Regions.

The London Midland Region was organised into three train operating Divisions: the Midland, at Derby, in general terms London St Pancras to Leeds and Manchester Central via the East Midlands; Sheffield to Bristol via Birmingham and Gloucester; the Western, at London, in general terms London Euston to the West Midlands, Crewe and Preston to Carlisle, and Central, at Manchester for Lancashire and parts of Yorkshire, Cheshire.

The day-to-day operation of timetabled passenger and freight trains was described for staff in Working

Timetables with the fine detail of individual parts of routes contained in a Sectional Appendix. By these documents, for example, a locomotive Driver for a London (St Pancras) to Leeds passenger train would have a copy of the Working Timetable and the two Sectional Appendices applicable to the entire distance of some 200 miles. Years of travelling over the route would have given a Driver an intimate knowledge and 'feel' for the route and its idiosyncrasies. He and his colleagues (there being some 80,000 footplatemen in 1955) would need every ounce of that experience as they worked trains up to 85mph along track in 60 foot sections, with no automatic warning system, semaphore signals lit by paraffin, with cast iron brakeblocks interacting by friction on wheel tyres ... at all times of the day and night and in all that the British weather could offer. As part of his development through the grades of Cleaner, and Fireman, the individual would have learned much and upon qualifying as a Driver would have 'signed for the roads' he knew (to Leeds via Leicester, via Manton, via Nottingham, via the Erewash Valley, via Derby, via the Old Road to Sheffield/Rotherham, via Wath ...) and when 'booking on' for duty would also have been made aware of any temporary restrictions in place at

that time, for example a speed restriction due to colliery subsidence.

Once a journey was underway the safe passage of each train would be controlled by signalmen using a method of communication known as the telegraphic block. As an example, between Derby and Bakewell, a route distance of some 25 miles there were twenty-eight signal boxes, some though not all manned around the clock; others being open to allow movements at certain times into goods yards or sidings. Signalmen would also have the Working Timetable and Sectional Appendix, together with Notices of additional or revised workings. The actual progress of individual trains would, as may be applicable, be reported by signalmen to co-ordinating Control points and to stations.

With a need to keep trains moving it was necessary at particular signal boxes for the Driver of the locomotive to sound the whistle to indicate which route ahead needed to be pre-set (that is the points on the track to be changed as may be necessary). If we again take, as an example, the Derby to Bakewell section there was at Ambergate a divergence of routes. So, when approaching a preceding signal box (Belper Goods) the Driver would sound the whistle as follows:

This is North Junction at Ambergate with 8F 48185 taking a north to west track of the triangular layout of the station. The signals at the end of the two platforms shown are identical, all set at stop and, from left to right on each are for access to the down sidings, for the mainline towards Class Cross and for the divergence towards Pye Bridge at Crich Junction. To the extreme right edge of the photograph are signals for the mainline tracks which avoided the station. (*Rail-online*)

Heading for Chesterfield via Ambergate station	1 short	1 long	1 short
Heading for Chesterfield via Toadmoor tunnel	1 short	1 long	
Heading for Rowsley (Bakewell)	2 short	1 long	
Heading for Codnor Park	4 long		
Freight train stopping for water at Crich Junction	2 short	1 long	3 short

Similarly, a little further along the route, at Ambergate North Junction trains approaching had just three optional routes:

Belper via Ambergate station	1 short	1 long	1 short
Belper via Toadmoor tunnel	1 short	1 long	
Rowsley	2 short	1 long	

Further south, at Loughborough the whistle codes when approaching from the South were:

Heading for Castle Donington line	1 short	1 long	
Heading for Sawley Junction via Sheet Stores Junction	1 short	2 long	
Heading for Nottingham	2 short	1 long	
Heading for Sawley Junction via Trent station	1 short	1 long	1 short

Taken between Wigston and Knighton, South of Leicester this shows the daily working of empty milk tanks from Cricklewood towards Westmoreland and Derbyshire for refilling. In charge is Jubilee *Victoria*, a long term resident of Holbeck, Leeds. (*Rail-online*)

Heading South along the Erewash Valley at Doe Hill comes a lengthy relief to *The Thames–Clyde Express* hauled by Millhouses BR Standard Class 5 73067. (*Science Museum/National Railway Museum*)

The Working Timetable for a route took into account many varied aspects and influences upon operation; for example the gradients faced by locomotives, the weight of the train, the length of the train, the power of the locomotive expected to work the train, the need for both stopping and non-stopping trains at stations, the need for locomotives to be changed or to take on supplies of water, connections with other trains, exchange of vehicles between trains, loading of GPO mail, the number of platforms available at stations, potentially conflicting arrangements at junctions. Unsurprisingly, the Working Timetable for a particular section was not changed at a whim and during the early/mid 1950s varied for seasonality of certain traffics, but not for core services. However, the demands of the nation were such that it was necessary to issue Weekly Notices of Special/ Additional trains of one sort or another and Special Notices for others. Here are some of the passenger trains for which arrangements would be made without the Working Timetable:

- Day/half day/evening excursions for ramblers/well dressings/illuminations
- City or town holiday week excursions e.g. Leicester to Southport/York/London/Belle Vue/Scarborough on consecutive weekdays
- Sporting fixtures
- Military specials
- Scouting jamborees
- Miners' welfare specials
- Sunday school outings
- Trade specials, for example to Cadbury's, Bournville
- Circus moves
- Theatre/stage group moves
- Billy Graham Crusader tour trains
- Invalid specials for Lourdes
- Horse boxes as trains (County shows and military)
- Royal trains
- Pigeons for racing, particularly in the spring
- Enthusiasts tours.

The engineering for the railway through Belper was expensive due to cuttings and multiple bridges, occasioned it is said because that is what the owners of the Mills required. Here 9F 92049 is not hanging around and with steam to spare the Fireman is taking the opportunity to get some cold water into the boiler. (*Photographer unknown, Midland Railway Trust collection*)

Publicly timetabled trains of the era ran on weekdays and/or Saturdays and/or Sundays; those conveying travelling post office vehicles (of which more later in this section) ran every day. In response to the need for individuals and families to take a holiday, summer Friday nights and Saturdays witnessed additional timetabled trains, plus working timetabled relief and 'Q' trains (run as required) from the Midlands to the resorts of Norfolk, Lincolnshire, North Wales, Sussex, Hampshire, Devon and Cornwall. The timings of Midland line trains to/from St Pancras were set according to the weight of the train that would be expected to be hauled by a locomotive of a particular power classification. For example an XL Limit train would have a maximum weight of 300 tons (say nine coaches including a heavy catering vehicle) to be hauled by a locomotive of class six power. With any tonnage above 300, or the non-availability of a class six locomotive, the Driver could request the provision of an assisting locomotive, a situation that frequently arose. Slightly less demanding timings would be set for Special Limit trains which conveyed an extra one or two coaches (say 65 tons gross) and in this way standard, station to station timings could be advertised to the public, e.g. Leicester to St Pancras in 105 minutes. The gradient profile of the Midland route from St Pancras to Manchester (Central) was far more demanding – particularly over the section through the Peak District – than the alternative route from London (Euston) to Manchester (London Road) and consequently train weights on the latter route were greater and with many more powerful locomotives available. The typical loading of a St Pancras-Manchester train North from Derby would be eight coaches, sometimes with an assisting locomotive. There were seven express services (either XL or Special Limit) in each direction between St Pancras and Manchester (Central). To/from Leeds (incl Scotland/Bradford) /Sheffield (Midland) from/to London (St Pancras) via Derby/Nottingham and Manton/Erewash Valley and Trent/Leicester there were five services, with additions originating/terminating at Nottingham/Leicester/Derby, extended to Sheffield on occasions as demand required.

Hassop, 1 mile north of Bakewell was the location chosen by the photographer on this lovely spring evening. He was rewarded by the sight of Jubilee 45629 *Straits Settlements* being constrained by the need to observe a temporary speed restriction. The village of Hassop was a couple of miles away from the little-used station and the station was closed to passengers in 1942, although goods' facilities were retained until 1964. The former station buildings are in use today as a cycle hire facility and café for users of the trackbed which now forms part of the Monsal Trail. (*E.R. Morten 2096, Courtesy J. Suter*)

Along the cross country route there was on weekdays a total of up to three through trains terminating at either Sheffield or Bradford or York, and five terminating at Newcastle; the stations of origin being Bristol (eight), Birmingham (two), Cardiff, Worcester and Kingswear/Paignton one each, a total of thirteen. These were timed to less stringent requirements than applied to the Midland lines to London and tended to be heavier, with 12 coaches/400 tons not at all uncommon. There were additional services, including a Nottingham to Bristol train which ran via Worcester and took some seventy minutes to clear Tamworth following a 7.35am departure from Nottingham. Double heading of trains along this route was commonplace, with Gloucester to Sheffield and Birmingham to Bristol seeing regular employment of assisting locomotives. Locomotives from Bristol and Leeds would on certain trains work throughout between these points, but Newcastle bound (or originating) trains would exchange locomotives at Sheffield (plus York in the winter).

In addition to the faster services, there was an infrequent service of trains stopping at most, if not all, stations along a section; Derby to Manchester (25–30 stations dependent upon route) Derby to Nottingham (7), Derby to Birmingham (11 including a ticket platform at Saltley prior to arrival at the 'open' New Street), Derby to Sheffield (15), Nottingham to Sheffield (21) and Nottingham to Leicester (10). At the south end of the line to St Pancras was a passenger service originating generally from Bedford and was augmented during the early morning and evening to meet the surge in demand from workers heading to/from St Pancras/ Moorgate. From October 1956 British Railways offered just two classes of travel; first and second class, third class having been dispensed with.

Throughout the period being considered the civil engineers were striving to improve the condition of the permanent way and thus enable timings to recover ground lost during the war and post-war period. Whilst station to station times reflected the range of factors already introduced in this section – volume of various

As was usual for the time, the 6.42pm St Pancras-Sheffield via Nottingham was running with a tare tonnage which allowed the Driver of the train locomotive (in this case Jubilee 45590 *Travancore*) to request a pilot locomotive. A 2P 4-4-0 has been provided and the pair are setting off from Platform 7. The 2P (40567) was one of ten 4-4-0s allocated in 1957 to Kentish Town to provide such pilot assistance. 5 May 1958. (*Kidderminster Railway Museum 093035, Courtesy P. J. Lynch*)

Double heading of express passenger trains was a costly way of increasing the probability of trains that had a greater weight than allowed for in the timetable of reaching their destination on time. Here a Nottingham 2P lends a hand to a Holbeck Jubilee on the 10.40 Bradford–St Pancras train from Kettering. 40543/45658. 10 October 1957. (*Kidderminster Railway Museum 092977, Courtesy P. J. Lynch*)

A change of footplate crew at Nottingham Station East also provides an opportunity to replenish the water supplies in the tender tank of Kentish Town's Jubilee 45641 *Sandwich*. Shortly the train would be on its way via Edwalton to eventually rejoin the main line to St Pancras (via Leicester) at Glendon, North of Kettering. (*Rail-online*)

types of traffic, weight of train, motive power, gradients – it was possible where conditions were favourable to enjoy some exhilarating spells of fast running. Within the confines of the routes of interest and with XL timings between St Pancras and Leicester – where the first 75 miles were four tracks and expresses were sometimes unencumbered by slower moving trains – it was not unusual for a Jubilee Class 6 to cover the 20 miles between Luton and Bedford in a quarter of an hour and, in the 'up' direction, the 99.1 miles from Leicester could, on occasions, be achieved at an average of a mile a minute. Between Birmingham (New Street) and Burton-on-Trent a non-stopping passenger train could achieve a start to pass time of twenty-eight minutes for the 30.2 miles; this being the 'up' line (to Derby) in this case.

Fast station to station timings over long distances were facilitated by means of an ability of a locomotive at speed to pick up water from troughs laid between the rails over a distance of a few hundred yards. As early as

1904 the Midland Railway had realised the potential of this method and had installed troughs at Oakley (North of Bedford and 51½ miles from London) Loughborough (60½ miles from Oakley and 47 miles south from Sheffield via the Erewash Valley route) and Brentingby (near Melton Mowbray). The tenders of a Jubilee Class locomotive varied between a water capacity of 3,500 and 4,000 gallons and with water consumption of perhaps 30 gallons a mile, water would be required somewhere along their normal routes. Water capacities increased with the introduction of the British Railways Standard Class 5 and 7 locomotives. The method of operation was for the Fireman to lower into the trough from under the tender a scoop which would force water up into the tank; in the space of 20–30 seconds several hundred gallons being gathered. Timing was imperative and many a leading coach (and its unwitting passengers) will have received a wash. Double heading meant that only one locomotive could benefit, but in such cases the time spent at stations (replenishing the tank of the

To enable locomotive water supplies to be replenished without a need for trains to be stopped, the Midland Railway installed water troughs at Oakley, Loughborough, Brentingby and Wigginton (along our routes of interest). At the last named location, near Tamworth, 4F 44577 has a lengthy train including a portable container, but is not proceeding at a pace to enable it to benefit from scooping up water. The troughs at the various locations were a standard length of one quarter of a mile (400 metres) which at say 60mph (96kph) would allow the Fireman some 10-12 seconds in which a torrent of water would be cascaded into the tank before the scoop was raised and returned to its more normal position under the tender. (*Rail-online*)

other) would be greatly reduced. An additional water trough was installed later at Wigginton near Tamworth on the Derby–Birmingham line.

The timetabling arrangements and Regional boundaries/locomotive change points influenced the mileages that coaching stock and locomotives would achieve on a daily or weekly basis. Coaching stock rarely exceeded 400 miles in a day; for example London to Manchester return was 382. The weekdays and Saturday Cardiff to Newcastle service required two sets of coaches, with an individual daily mileage of just 312. It was a similar story with the Kingswear/Paignton to Bradford service, though in that case a Bristol based locomotive would work north to Leeds, returning the following morning with the same footplate and catering crew who 'lodged' overnight. The restaurant/kitchen car would need replenishing with gas and the entire train cleaned, reservation tickets placed and brought into

the station from the stabling point. Steam locomotives needed considerable attention to be disposed at the end of a run and to be prepared for the next. The carriages used on these services varied from timber, former London Midland and Scottish Railway and London and North Eastern Railway vehicles to the new all steel British Railways standard Mark I type introduced progressively from 1951. Summer weekends brought forward a vast range of the types produced by all four of the pre-Nationalisation companies.

That completes the scene setting for passenger services. Next, is freight.

With freight traffic – as with passenger – it is possible to classify the main types. In summary these were coal and coke full and empty, mineral (including iron ore, limestone, steel industry products and scrap) and general merchandise. Of these three types the tonnages carried nationally in 1956 were 162, 65 and 41 million respectively. Of the flows nationally, the highest density of coal and coke traffic was that originating and (wagons) returning (empty) along the Erewash Valley and the coalfields of Nottinghamshire and Derbyshire. This was an age of proud mining communities dependent upon a continuation of demand for the product from individual seams – suitable for industrial power generation, for coking, for domestic use, for railway locomotives – and of course a continuation of safe supply. Every photograph researched for this section illustrated wooden railway wagons and often proudly bearing the name of the colliery; Annesley-Bentinck, Babbington, Newstead, Gedling, Sherwood, Silverhill, Shire Oaks, Bolsover, Clay Cross, Cresswell, Newbold, Pinxton, Shirland, Pilsley, Silkstone … and many more. From a railway operation viewpoint this was challenging with a constant need for collecting and returns of wagons for marshalling into trains in the yards at Toton/Stanton Gate. Nationalisation of the railways had included a provision for the purchase of these privately owned company wagons and gradually the names faded and the wagons themselves were replaced. Within the concentrated area of perhaps 1,600 square miles, some 550 locomotives were allocated to depots at Kirkby-in-Ashfield (to which depot the electric light first arrived in 1958), Annesley, Kirkby Bentinck, Mansfield, Toton, Westhouses, Hasland, Staveley and Langwith. I shall also include Colwick as its role will become apparent in a later section.

Most of the wagons involved were 13 tons capacity, linked together by couplings, but with no method of braking except if a brake lever was manually depressed and pinned into position. Once formed into trains of up to eighty-seven loaded wagons (1,131 tons) the only method of braking was by use of a brake on the locomotive and its tender, with assistance from the Guard screwing friction brake blocks onto the 4/6 wheels of the brakevan.

The then widespread use of coal for domestic heating resulted in a huge demand peak between October and

Summer time brought with it a reduction of coal trains in some sort of motion and a consequent need to temporarily store rakes of wagons. Here in June 1957 a pair of 4Fs from Hasland (44162/244) have been busy – as have the shunters – along the Grassmoor line. (*Science Museum/National Railway Museum LMS 400*)

April from Leicester and south thereof, from Birmingham and the West Midlands for domestic coal and industrial coke (for gas making) with a consequential need also to return empty wagons. During the summer months wagons at collieries would be filled and form potentially mobile stockpiles. The operation was inefficient, an average round trip colliery back to colliery was of the order of 11 days and an average transit time 1½–2 days, both including marshalling into trains and being sorted again upon return. The period covered by this book just includes the final few months of operation of the last few in a remarkable class of locomotives known as Beyer Garratts. Thirty-three of these locomotives were built in 1927–30 for working heavy coal trains south from Hasland (near Chesterfield), Toton (between Derby and Nottingham) and Wellingborough and from Toton, west to Birmingham; also taking iron ore north from Northamptonshire for use in steel making. These locomotives can best be described as being two power units serviced from one boiler. They were allowed to take eighty-seven loaded 13 ton wagons and return up to 100 when empty.

In researching for this book I was pleased to listen to a former Fireman based at Toton who worked on these locomotives. He recounted how, once on the move south, his Driver would hope to save time by picking up water from the troughs at Queniborough rather than having to stop a little further on; the sensation of gaining the necessary momentum with 1,150 tons of train and the timing necessary to drop/lift the scoop clearly made a lasting impression. Coal (9 tons) for most of these locomotives was loaded into cylindrical bunkers which in theory would turn and trim the coal to where the Fireman could reach it; this being a very unusual facility for which the actual loading at depots resulted in coal getting everywhere around the outsides of the bunker and a theoretical complete turn becoming a 30 degrees rocking in each direction at best reality. One of the very few advantages of these locomotives from a Fireman's perspective was that when the cab door was closed the distance between the seat and a recess in the frame of the door allowed a relatively comfortable position to be taken; useful for the many times when lengthy delays occurred awaiting access to receiving yards at Washwood Heath (Birmingham), Wellingborough or Brent (North London). A final anecdote related to the regular Sunday morning arrangement whereby a group of perhaps ten footplate crews would be taken from Toton to Birmingham to work trains of empty wagons back to Toton ready for sorting and tripping to individual collieries.

The movement of heavy and consequentially lengthy trains of coal/coke was eased on the Midland line south of Toton by the availability for much of the route to Brent of four tracks and with divergences to avoid adverse gradients. The route to Birmingham was mainly two tracks from Trent as far as Water Orton, with side lines (loops) into which freight trains would be diverted whilst passenger or more urgent traffic was allowed to pass. Between Sheet Stores Junction and Stenson Junction and then in every loop and in a continuous line from Water Orton it was commonplace to have coal trains waiting for an opportunity to move. A shift of nine hours or more would often include a mileage of less than forty.

A vision of the future for coal traffic in trainloads was provided by a dedicated service between Shipley colliery sidings in Derbyshire and Stonebridge Park power station just north of London. High-sided steel wagons capable of carrying and discharging 40 tons of coal were conveyed three times each week in each direction, the trains running via Market Harborough and Northampton. Because Southbound they ran always at night, they were known as the Toton ghost trains; men from that depot working as far as Northampton.

Another development in the 1950s was the testing of a method of continuous braking systems on new, steel wagons with a capacity of 16 tons. The aim was to be able to control the train in the same way as applied to passenger train locomotives and coaching stock and once introduced would be a major step forward. Trials between Toton and Wellingborough /Brent with sets of up to seventy continuously braked wagons were held at various times during the early to mid-1950s. These trials brought to the Erewash Valley exotic power in the form of Class 7 pairs of Royal Scots (46117/54) and Britannias (70020/3 and later 70043/4 equipped with air pumps), interspersed by Class 5s 44667/45342 and newly introduced British Railways Standard Class 5s, 73030/1. For short distance trials L1 tanks were brought from Stratford, East London 67729/37. Later trials with BR Class 9 locomotives (which replaced the Garratts) took place and gradually the braking of many freight trains in whole or part by use of vacuum control became the norm and the option of air braking not then pursued.

For the period of interest, traffic flows of mineral and general merchandise along our routes are more straightforward where they are in identifiable train loads or distinguishable as part loads. For example, iron ore from Northamptonshire heading north-east and north-west, limestone from Derbyshire, stone from Leicestershire, beer from Burton-on-Trent,

Trials with rakes of mineral wagons fitted with vacuum brakes spanned several years and utilised various classes of steam locomotives including pairs of Black 5s, Royal Scots, Britannias, 9Fs and L1 tanks. Here a pair of 9Fs are so engaged and approaching Finedon Road near Wellingborough 92153/8. (*Colour-rail collection 19842*)

(seasonal) sugar beet into the Colwick Estates railway, chocolate from Bournville, steel billets/strip/sections from the North-East and Sheffield/Rotherham … For individual wagon loads (timber, scrap, sand, petroleum products, chemical, covered van loads, for example) there was no easy way of identifying point of origin/destination, but it was apparent from locomotive depot allocations and helpful advice from friendly signalmen. Even if the train was identifiable as going to Carlisle that was not an end of the matter for the operators. The history of the railways was such that Carlisle had a dozen small yards and sorting/dropping off/picking up/re-sorting was a time-consuming matter. In this section, livestock (cattle and sheep) and horse boxes (with or without groom) should be included although with horse boxes conveyance as part of a passenger train would frequently be arranged. There was also a considerable flow of perishable goods; bananas, other fruit particularly seasonal from Worcestershire, flowers and, most evenings/nights, fish from Hull/Scotland.

Milk was conveyed in bulk by glass lined, six wheel tank wagons and, following cleaning, the empties would be sent back from London (Cricklewood) as far as Carlisle to make the next loaded journey; at the more local end of the market milk churns would be conveyed by local trains to/from stations close to dairies.

In other categories of non-passenger traffic can be included racing pigeon specials, particularly from Scotland and the North-East (perhaps to Mangotsfield) and loading up to 18–24 bogie vehicles, the railways internal flows of vans and wagons between engineering workshops and depots, vehicles being returned from depots to those workshops for overhaul and returns thereof, and civil engineering trains of ballast stone, rails, cranes, tunnel inspection vehicles etc. A (thankfully) rarity was the sight of one of the breakdown crane trains stationed at major depots on the move to/from an incident.

Finally for traffic comes mails and parcels. There was in place an agreement between the British Transport

Commission and the Post Office with regard to a national scheme of mail train services, generally starting in the later afternoon or early evening. This provided for up to eighty travelling Post Office letter sorting vehicles to be conveyed nightly either within dedicated sets (for example Glasgow to London Euston) or as part of a timetable passenger service (for example Bristol to Newcastle). Where the sorting vehicles formed part of a timetabled train, the timings were dictated by inter-connecting mail services at particular stations. For example anyone expecting a quick Bristol to Derby journey would be sadly disappointed with a time of four and a quarter hours.

Along our routes of interest were mail trains between Bradford/Newcastle and Bristol, and between Lincoln and Tamworth; this latter station being a particularly busy nocturnal interchange point for mail from/to the Anglo-Scottish services. Another interchange was made between the Bristol to Newcastle train at Birmingham and one bound for Crewe (exchanges there for North Wales/Scotland) and later in the night when its equivalent service arrived at 1.57am there was an interchange of mails inbound from Scotland/North Wales/North West via Crewe. The cross-country trains were heavy; conveying three sorting vehicles in which Post Office staff worked, four storage vans for mail awaiting sorting or sorted awaiting transfer later in the journey, and five passenger vehicles. Nearly an hour would be spent at Birmingham whilst exchanges were effected and sixteen minutes at Derby, between 11.38 and 11.54pm. After the Westbound service from Newcastle had left at 12.43am the returning Tamworth-Lincoln mail train would be dealt with between 3.04 and 3.16am. The night's work would be completed when the 1.10am from Bristol arrived at 5.33am and the Post Office sorting vehicle was detached, thus completing a round trip to Bristol which had started with attachment of the vehicle at 8pm the previous evening to the Bradford to Bristol passenger service. In between these trains were parcels services, the 2.35am Derby to Nottingham worked by the locomotive that would later work the 7.35am Nottingham to Bristol passenger train throughout (of which more later). There was at the time under review a huge level of interest in predicting results in the Saturday programme of football matches between September and April; this was known as 'the pools' and coupons would need to be sorted and despatched under controlled conditions to Liverpool to be received there before 'kick-off'. Also in the time sensitive area of night traffic was the conveyance of newspapers from London and Manchester.

On six days/week and at up to 7,000 different locations the railway itself accepted, collected and delivered parcels for carriage by passenger or timetabled parcels trains, a historical accident of an overlapping service with that offered by the Post Office, who did not offer a collection service. The railways accepted parcels up to 224lbs (100kg), irrespective of size or shape. This was traffic that was increasing, an annual total of between 45 and 48 million bags of parcels post being handled by the railways nationally for the Post Office, with an additional 75 million individual consignments for railways service traffic.

Also of interest was the railway's own internal mail service whereby huge numbers of documents were sent in envelopes marked OCS (on company service) and addressed simply SM New Street (Station Manager Birmingham New Street) YM Bescot (Yard Master Bescot Yard) DOS Rowsley (District Operating Superintendent, Rowsley), MPD Derby 4 (motive power depot Derby). By these means, Bemrose printers at Derby would disseminate weekly thousands of Notices, flyers for excursions, timetables; stations would return to the Ticket Audit Office at Derby thousands upon thousands of clipped tickets and depots would send in documents for locomotives, carriages and wagons.

So much for the traffic. What about the motive power to haul the trains? For passenger services for our routes of interest steam motive power was provided, in the main, from:

Holbeck (Leeds)
Millhouses (Sheffield)
Trafford Park (Manchester)
Derby
Saltley (Birmingham)
Gloucester (Barnwood)
Barrow Road (Bristol)
Kentish Town (London)
Bedford
Leicester
Nottingham
Lincoln

For freight, the following could be added:

Burton
Toton
Hasland
Grimesthorpe (Sheffield)
Rowsley
Wellingborough
Cricklewood

Of these Burton and Wellingborough would, as will become clear, help out with summer weekend passenger trains.

Colwick (east of Nottingham) supplied power for passenger trains to/from Derby (Friargate) and for freight trains to Derby and Burton (via the former Great Northern Railway route) and to certain locations along the Erewash Valley.

Whilst each of these depots has an interesting and unique history, the following have been selected for detailed transitional review through the period 1957–63 inclusive:

Holbeck   power for services to London and Bristol routes
Millhouses   power for services to London and Bristol routes

Trafford Park power for services to London route
Derby   power for services to London, Bristol and Leeds routes
Kentish Town   power for Manchester and Sheffield/Leeds routes

For each of these, the starting point is the position at 1 January 1957 and is covered in the Chapter, Motive Power Depots and Motive Power.

First generation main line diesel locomotives were in evidence from time to time, particularly on the Derby to Manchester section. This arose because Derby was the designated Works for overhauls, modifications and, in conjunction with the Mechanical and Electrical Engineer, for testing of new equipment such as that for the heating of carriages by other than the traditional steam supply. The locomotives were:

Number	Power	Built	Configuration	Builder
10100	1600 HP	1951	4-4-4-4	Fell Developments
10000	1600 HP	1947	Co-Co	English Electric/ HA Ivatt
10001	1600 HP	1947/8	Co-Co	English Electric/ HA Ivatt
10201	1750 HP	1951	1-Co-Co-1	English Electric/OVS Bulleid
10202	1750 HP	1951	1-Co-Co-1	English Electric/OVS Bulleid
10203	2000 HP	1954	1-Co-Co-1	English Electric/OVS Bulleid
10800	827 HP	1950	Bo-Bo	North British Loco Co/British Thomson – Houston/ HA Ivatt

Examples of diesel electric, 350hp, shunting locomotives introduced in 1945 could be found working at yards at Derby, Toton, Saltley, Washwood Heath, Bromford Bridge, Nottingham and in the London area where up to fifteen could be found variously at Hendon, Cricklewood, Cadburys depot, Express Dairies sidings, Kentish Town, Cattle Dock sidings, Somers Town and St Pancras Goods.

Although Derby Carriage and Wagon Works has been producing lightweight diesel muliple units since 1954, such units were not deployed along over lines of route of interest and were seen only briefly on proving test runs around the Chellaston loop or the Wirksworth branch. The term lightweight arose from the work of the Light Weight Trains Commitee of the Raiway Executive between August 1951 and Spring 1952. In all 219 vehicles were built, including those based in Manchester (Longsight) and introduced between Buxton and Miller's Dale from October 1956.

Although Derby was the predominant locomotive works along the routes of interest, Bow Works (formerly for the North London Railway) overhauled locomotives from the London Tilbury and Southend section and beyond those a range of former LMS tank and freight types from 0-6-0 to 8F 2-8-0. The scale of operation was much less than that for Derby, which dealt with a wider range of classes though excluding the passenger types Patriots, Jubilees, Royal Scots and Britannias which were in the domain of Crewe. Locomotives heading to or away from attention at Bow could often be seen at Kentish Town although normally 'run in' from Devons Road depot. Kentish Town could also witness locomotives transferring between Neasden and Kings Cross, whilst if the area of observation was slightly widened to include Cricklewood, Southern Region based locomotives could be seen on occasions with inter-Regional workings.

Finally, some statistics about British Railways at the end of 1956:

- Route miles   17,800
- Locomotives, steam   17,527
- Locomotives, diesel and electric   680
- Multiple unit stock vehicles   5,392
- Coaching stock vehicles   49,293
- Wagons   1,102,607
- Staff   570,000
- Stations and sidings forwarding freight and those receiving coal   5,200
- Passenger journeys   1 billion (during the year).

As has been described, this was a twenty-four hours a day, seven days a week, every day of the year operation and in accordance within the Working Timetable. Also as described there was a need for consideration of short-term revised arrangements and in the planning to meet variable demand levels for traffic of different types. In 1907 the Midland Railway had recognised a need for some form of centralised control of trains by telephony. Following a trial at Rotherham the method was successfully extended to the most congested sections of that Railway (Cudworth to Toton) with District Controllers at five points. That resulted in a decision

One of the best vantage points to see plenty of action at very close hand near Derby Station was Five Arches bridge. A walkway allowed pedestrians to cross the River Derwent, railway workers to reach the Signal Works and cattle docks, and allowed free access to hordes of spotters and observers. For fear that I may get over excited and fall into the river, my parents banned me from this location. Not a hope; I am in the group actually trying to see something far more important than the Holbeck 2P and Black 5 on *The Devonian* which was obscuring our view. 40552/44813. 5 August 1958. Coal slacker pipes, cylinder drain taps open, coal off fall plates … all part of the thrill of being as close as possible to hundreds of tons of mechanical engineering passing within a few inches. Magic. (*Kidderminster Railway Museum 093024, Courtesy P. J. Lynch*)

For passenger services from Bakewell to Derby Rowsley had a small allocation of Compound 4-4-0s, including 40929. The locomotive is seen here departing from Derby with the 5.05pm to Bakewell, stopping at all stations except Nottingham Road and Duffield, which were served by the following 5.08pm Derby to Chesterfield stopper. The crew of the 5.05pm seemed to revel in a departure delayed by late running of the Bristol to York express which was booked to precede it from Derby and rarely could a Compound in the mid-1950s be heard elsewhere to such effect. Photographer unknown. (*Midland Railway Trust collection*)

to further extend the control system to over 1,500 miles and divide that into forty-two sections. Working 'books' were introduced for different types of trains showing equipment available at stations. Punctuality improved and the Midland Railway enhanced its reputation. Central Control was located at Derby and each day began with a telephone 'conference' between the Superintendent of Operations and his District Controllers at twenty-six locations. District Controllers were enabled to take decentralised supervision over all traffic in their respective area, though with a guiding overview from Central Control before significant alterations to train movements were implemented. The entire route mileage was thus continually monitored by a small staff, priorities assigned as necessary for fast passenger trains, train containing perishable goods, heavy freight trains, motive power and available rolling stock assigned and staff duty times pre-arranged. Over the following forty years that system of control was

extended more widely and became a norm. Its origins can be seen in the following outline of the organisations of the Divisional Operating Superintendent for the Midland Division of the London Midland Region based at Derby, during part of the span of time of interest in this book.

First, there was round the clock (three shifts of eight hours) staffing for the forward provision of motive power for both the Midland lines to/from London and the cross country line, for stock for all passenger trains on the London line, for freight trains on both the London and cross country route and for dealing with any mishaps.

On a two shift basis (6am to 10pm) was a Passenger Train Controller for all passenger trains on the cross country route. In support of the three shift operation were Controllers managing milk tankers, horse boxes, cattle vans and arrangements for conveyance of corpses and, in support of the two shift controllers, the provision of 16 foot wheelbase horse boxes/cattle vans for conveyance as part of the formation of a passenger train. On a single shift basis (normal office hours) would be individuals or teams concentrating upon needs to strengthen (i.e. arrange for additional vehicles to be added/detached) timetabled trains, pigeon specials, theatrical, livestock, agricultural show traffic, party reservations, Special Notices Weekly Notices drafting, arranging printing, proof reading, parcels loads, mails, newspapers, incident reviews from previous day, reviews of Guards' journals, wagon control, arrangements for invalids, catering and sleeping car requirements ... and more.

Close by was the Train Timing Office and the Inspectorate; this latter organisation having a responsibility for the standard of service by named trains (e.g. *The Palatine, The Thames-Clyde Express*), for following up complaints received and for inspection of rolling stock and equipment carried.

All of these activities required a great deal of clear communication. Telegraphy was used together with the use of code words to save space/time. Examples are:

CABBAGE	Do you agree to following?
EARWIG	Following is urgently required
CICERO	Special train(s) will run as under. Please advise all concerned
DEBRIS	I will advise you further
WALNUT	Make all necessary arrangements as far as you are concerned
SLATTERN	Cannot agree to your proposal
OHIO	Send on all speed
ARNO	Undermentioned Notice received

The 2.10pm St Pancras-Leeds/Bradford express has Jubilee 45639 (*Raleigh*) in sole charge as it awaits departure and will be followed a quarter of an hour later by a locomotive of the same class destined at least as far as Derby with a Manchester service 45622 (*Nyasaland*). (*Science Museum/National Railway Museum LMS 643*)

The Erewash Valley line between Trent and Clay Cross was inevitably affected by colliery works subsidence and caused the imposition of many speed restrictions. In this picture of the *Thames-Clyde Express* (Northbound with a Compound piloting between Leicester and Sheffield and Jubilee 45566 *Queensland*) there is evidence of subsidence and a need for speed to be restricted; all very helpful to a photographer with film and shutter speed concerns. 21 March 1957. (*Science Museum/National Railway Museum LMS 183*)

A clear evening resulted in the photographer heading for Avenue Sidings/Clay Cross in time to see an Edinburgh-St Pancras express with 2P 40436 piloting a Black 5 and overtaking 8F 48358. (*Science Museum/National Railway Museum LMS 19*)

Approaching Breadsall Crossing some 3 miles north of Derby is a Caprotti valve gear fitted Black 5, c1957. (*Science Museum/ National Railway Museum*)

The railway never slept and to work in Control was a totally absorbing occupation. The individual who kindly explained to me the foregoing organisational arrangements told me that on many occasions he would arrive for his shift complete with flask and sandwiches, became totally involved until a hand on his shoulder indicated that his eight hours shift was over … with flask and sandwiches unopened.

For the interested observer at a station or by the lineside this was … well, it was just wonderful!

Chapter Three

Motive Power Depots and Motive Power for the Routes

Along the lines of route of interest to this book were motive power depots supplying and maintaining locomotives for use on particular services; passenger, parcels, freight, shunting. Between Leeds/Sheffield and St Pancras thirteen or fourteen depots (dependent upon route taken) would be passed and between Sheffield and Bristol – again dependent upon route – up to eleven. Each depot had a history which would – and in some cases have – make in their own right articles or books and throughout the period under review (except Millhouses, Sheffield and Kentish Town which were closed at the end of 1961/62 respectively), added much to the then richness of the general railway environment.

The original motivation for this book was express passenger workings and for that reason the depots providing power for 'through' services (i.e. Leeds/ Sheffield/Manchester to St Pancras and Leeds/Sheffield/ Derby to Bristol/Cardiff) have been selected for detailed review. The depots are Holbeck (Leeds), Millhouses (Sheffield), Trafford Park (Manchester), Derby, Kentish Town (London) and Barrow Road (Bristol). Other depots and many freight workings receive due recognition – Nottingham, Leicester Midland, Bedford, Buxton, Saltley (Birmingham), Bromsgrove and Gloucester Barnwood – but I hope that readers will accept that the sheer scale of quantity of locomotives and workings involved caused a necessary restriction on

This is a view of the yard at Bristol Barrow Road depot with the position of the photographer being the coaling plant. Locomotives captured include two Jubilees (*Leander*, now preserved, and *Western Australia*, 45690 and 45568 respectively), 4Fs, a 9F, a Black 5 and a pannier tank. The electrification warning flashes on the locomotives suggest a date between 1960 and 1963. (*Photographer unknown*)

what could reasonably be included without sacrificing the main themes.

Excepting Trafford Park, the six depots of prime interest were essentially Midland in origin and to some extent each benefitted from the investment made in the 1930s by their then owner (the London Midland and Scottish Railway) to improve facilities for day-to-day maintenance, coaling and ash disposal plant. The Midland favoured roundhouses and at Holbeck, Derby, Kentish Town and Barrow Road were examples of such with, generally, twenty-four short stub tracks (sufficient for two small locomotives or one large one with tender) arranged around a turntable. Each stub could have an excavated and brick-lined pit to enable easier access under the locomotives for inspections, oiling/greasing and the changing of brakeblocks and springs. Millhouses did not lend itself to having a roundhouse

and was an eight 'road' (track), dead end straight shed. Trafford Park was exceptional as it had three railway Companies as joint occupants (the Great Northern, the Manchester Sheffield and Lincolnshire Railway and the Midland Railway), each of which had their own block of offices and was a twenty dead end, straight shed with the yard bounded on all sides by the railways it originally served. In common with several other London Midland Region motive power depots the electric light replaced gas lighting as late as 1958.

Each locomotive carried on the front of its smokebox a small cast plate carrying the code of its home motive power depot. These codes changed when British Railways Regional boundaries and responsibilities were revised and/or local reorganisations took effect within the Region. During the period covered by this book the following codes applied:

Leicester Midland depot yard with the scene dominated by the imposing coaling plant. The LMS invested heavily in the improvement of facilities at its motive power depots and such plant lasted to the end of the need to service steam locomotives. In this regard Leicester was a very late beneficiary; by BR in 1952. In view are an 8F, a Crab, a 2P and a 4F. (*Kidderminster Railway Museum 156489, Courtesy P. Strong*)

This is Bedford motive power depot yard where the local arrangement seems to have been for all locomotives to be placed to face north. The four-road straight shed sees an 8F quietly awaiting its next working. 24 April 1960. (*Kidderminster Railway Museum 006074, Courtesy W. Potter*)

B16 locomotives rarely visited Derby Midland, but here 61438 is on the turntable at 4 shed awaiting a suitable return working home towrds York. 31 July 1960. (*G. Morris*)

A photograph taken from the footsteps of the signal box at Millhouses depicts Jubilee 45573 *Newfoundland* working hard upgrade out of Sheffield. The train is passing the motive power depot and the seemingly ever present line of wagons which prevented a good view of the yard and its occupants. (*Rail-online*)

Trafford Park was a twenty-road depot originally shared by three railway companies. By the mid-1950s the star locomotives based there were Jubilees. Here *New Hebrides* and *Somaliland* (45618/28 respectively) are in residence at their home location. (*Rail-online*)

Taken from a rarely available vantage point, this shows part of the extensive yard and buildings forming Derby 4 shed. On the right are coal lines 1, 2 and 3, upon which twenty/thirty locomotives could be awaiting replenishment of supplies, c1960. (*G. Morris*)

Holbeck	55A
Millhouses	19B to 41C (1 February 1958)
Trafford Park	17F to 9E (20 April 1958)
Derby	17A to 16C (9 September 1963)
Kentish Town	14B
Barrow Road	22A to 82E (23 February 1958)

In terms of quantity of steam locomotive allocations at any one time during the period under review, Derby – with up to 131 – was the largest, though the vast majority were not for express passenger work. Millhouses, with an allocation in the mid-thirties was the smallest, though unlike Derby the majority were for passenger train workings. The extensive shed yard at Derby, always full of interest, with hour to hour changes of operational locomotives being augmented by locomotives having arrived for overhaul at the Works adjacent and those recently emerged as new construction or recently overhauled and to be 'run in' prior to being returned to their home depot. New and overhauled examples would tend to stand out in the crowd; freshly painted. Express passenger locomotives were painted in a dark bronze green, lined with orange and black; mixed traffic and many tank locomotives black, lined out with grey, white and red, leaving the majority a plain and usually dirty black. During the era under review the labour market was radically changed and the relatively unattractive, unsocial hours activity of the continuous railway operations plus the onset of dieselisation had a combined effect of reducing the number of new entrant Cleaners and an inevitable general worsening of external appearance of locomotives. I use the word general because there were exceptions and some depots continued to take a pride in their allocated locomotives; Nottingham (when it had Royal Scots and Patriots), Saltley, Barrow Road (Jubilees, Standard Class 5s and, later, Patriots) often exemplary and Holbeck examples were generally well turned out.

During the period under review certain classes of locomotives that arrived along the routes of interest were too long for the turntables at the depots and were turned via triangular junctions nearby; Millhouses using that at nearby Dore.

The overbearing characteristics for casual visitors to such depots – except Millhouses, which always seemed to offer a controlled calmness – was one of cramped, restricted space with a constant need for reorganisation of whatever was resident at the time, with other characteristics being a pall of smoke haze which hung above the depot (and often assisted locating it if on foot or with a coach party), coal dust, ash and cinders, noise, the pleasant aroma of smoke, steam with lubricating oil, gloom inside all buildings/roundhouses, leaking water from multiple hydrants and hoses, in winter fire devils to prevent external injector pipes from freezing, the warmth of the sand store (where wet sand was heaped around a constant fire prior to being put into the sandboxes of locomotives), the crashing of coal dropped from height into the tenders/bunkers of locomotives and always a goodly cross-section of working men going about their varied duties. Of course there was also the duty Shed Foreman and anyone found entering such premises without authorisation was liable to a verbal onslaught and threat of arrest. Unauthorised access was not for the young, faint of heart types and word of mouth communication on station platforms reliably advised that whilst Millhouses yard was easy, Kentish Town was easy at weekends and Barrow Road usually tolerant, Derby was impossible. I cannot comment upon Holbeck or Trafford Park as visits were made only as part of organised weekend coach trips to large conurbations. For a century and more, steam locomotive motive power depots formed a part of social history in a similar way to that for heavy, labour intensive industry such as the mines and the steel industry.

The changing nature of demands for the movement of passengers and freight, together with developments in industry and centres of production meant that British Railways frequently had to re-allocate locomotives to where they could be best deployed. External examples included the seasonality of production of food products, the siting of new steelworks or coal mines and internally the need for suitable power for the planned timetables. For these reasons and more the allocation of locomotives across depots was constantly reviewed and changes made on a weekly/monthly basis. For instance, in 1957 Barrow Road witnessed twenty-two changes to its allocation whilst in the same year Millhouses had fifteen changes and in the six months from July 1957 Derby had thirty-one. The extensive changes which affected all six depots of particular interest are available, though separate to this book.

For this book the consideration now turns to the needs of express passenger workings and certain other workings of particular interest. For the six depots the power classes are 5, 6 and 7, with a note for certain classes 2 and 4 where such locomotive types could find themselves deployed to double head (pilot or assist) another locomotive. Such instances would include trains timetabled to XL Limit or Special Limit schedules, but which in practice had necessarily been strengthened (additional carriages increasing the weight of the train) and therefore were beyond the capability of the assigned locomotive to keep to time, or on the cross country because of sheer weight of train and inability to maintain station to station timings. As will become clear in later Chapters, there was for several years a need for either more power Class 7 locomotives or a need for additional Class 5 locomotives to relieve aged Class 2 and 4 locomotives.

As a starting point, here is a summary by depot and year of the allocation of locomotives of power classes 5, 6 and 7 (no Class 8 were involved), plus classes 2 and 4 of the 4-4-0 type and the type 4 diesels which started to arrive in quantity from 1960.

Holbeck

Power Class	1/1/57	1/1/58	1/1/59	1/1/60	1/1/61	1/1/62	1/1/63	1/1/64
5 ex-LMS 4-6-0	18	17	17	17	16	14	14	8
5 BR 4-6-0	5	6	6	5	4	2	-	-
6 Jubilee	18	18	18	18	18	17	11	11
7 Royal Scot	8	8	5	5	5	-	-	-
7 Britannia	-	-	3	3	3	3	-	-
7 A3	-	-	-	-	9	1	1	-
2	3	3	3	3	-	-	-	-
4	4	4	2	-	-	-	-	-
Type 4 diesel	-	-	-	-	-	-	19	23

Notes: The allocation of the A3 type allowed the Royal Scots and Britannias to be used more extensively south of Leeds. A3s north to Carlisle. Holbeck also provided power for other former Midland routes to Lancaster, Morecambe, Heysham and Carnforth

Millhouses

Power Class	1/1/57	1/1/58	1/1/59	1/1/60	1/1/61	31/12/61
5 ex-LMS 4-6-0	6	6	-	-	-	-
5 BR 4-6-0	5	5	11	9	5	3
5 ex-LNER B1	-	-	-	3	1	2
6 Jubilees	10	12	12	12	12	12
7 Royal Scot	-	-	-	-	5	5
7 Patriot	-	-	-	-	2	1
2	1	1	-	-	-	-
4	4	3	1	1	-	-
Type 4 diesel	-	-	-	-	-	-

Notes:
The depot closed on 31/12/61 and remaining power as above was re-allocated to Canklow (as part of the Sheffield rationalisation)
All power classes and types could be found on routes to St Pancras and to Bristol

Trafford Park

Power Class	1/1/57	28/12/57	27/12/58	2/1/60	31/12/60	31/12/61	29/12/62	28/12/63
5 ex-LMS 4-6-0	3	4	4	7	5	5	3	4
6 Jubilee	4	7	-	-	-	-	-	-
7 Britannia	-	-	6	6	3	-	-	-
7 Royal Scot	-	-	-	-	5	3	-	-
7 Patriot	-	-	-	-	-	1	-	-
2	-	-	-	-	-	-	-	-
4	8	3	1	-	-	-	-	-
Type 4 diesel	-	-	-	-	-	-	-	-

Derby

Power Class	1/1/57	28/12/57	27/12/58	2/1/60	31/12/60	31/12/61	29/12/62	28/12/63
5 ex-LMS 4-6-0	11	16	16	1	8	4	8	15
5 BR 4-6-0	5	-	-	3	4	6	-	-
6 Jubilee	5	3	5	11	9	2	-	11
6 Patriot	1	1	-	-	-	-	-	-
2	5	7	6	-	-	-	-	-
4	4	2	2	1	-	-	-	-
Type 4 diesel	-	-	-	-	19	65	85	90

Kentish Town

Power Class	1/1/57	28/12/57	27/12/58	2/1/60	31/12/60	31/12/61	29/12/62
5 ex-LMS 4-6-0	18	18	18	11	10	8	-
6 Jubilee	13	10	16	8	8	3	-
7 Royal Scot	-	6	2	9	9	-	-
7 Patriot	-	-	-	1	1	-	-
2	-	8	5	2	2	-	-
4	-	2	-	-	-	-	-
Type 4 diesel	-	-	-	-	-	-	-

Notes:
The depot closed early 1962
All power classes and types could be found on routes to Sheffield/Leeds and Manchester Central

Barrow Road

Power Class	1/1/57	28/12/57	27/12/58	26/12/59	31/12/60	31/12/61	15/12/62	31/12/63
5 ex-LMS 4-6-0	7	-	-	-	-	-	-	-
5 BR 4-6-0	-	5	4	4	4	4	3	3
6 Jubilee	10	10	9	9	9	3	3	3
6 Patriot	-	-	3	3	3	3	-	-
2	2	2	2	2	1	-	-	-
4	-	-	-	-	-	-	-	-
Type 4 diesel	-	-	-	-	-	-	-	-

These statistics are 'snap-shots' in time and, as explained, revisions were made between the dates shown. For example, four Class 7 locomotives were allocated to Kentish Town for periods of 2/3 months in spring 1959 and one for two months in autumn 1959, three Class 7s were at Trafford Park for July 1958 and four Class 7s were allocated to Derby for summer 1961. Chapters for each year 1957–1963 inclusive will add more detail.

It is appropriate to place into context the totals of the power classes identified within the total allocation of a depot. Every locomotive required periodic examination and time out of service for such matters as the washing out of the boiler and checks as to the condition of the firebox; pistons, valves and motion. Such examinations followed either a mileage attained or number of steamings. Therefore, at any one time a proportion of the allocation would necessarily be out of traffic. Add to that an allowance for unforeseeable failures in traffic, the predictable calls for locomotives to be sent to Works for overhaul, the demands for additional trains to be worked and the consequences of the timetable having been set upon the basis of unattainable XL or Special Limit timings being met without pilot/assisting locomotives … and you have the situation facing the operators on 'anyday 1957'. The situation was not confined just to our lines of route of interest and elsewhere on the London Midland Region a huge increase in double heading of trains was a costly reality.

The total allocations of our six depots of interest was as follows:

As at (date)	Holbeck		Millhouses		Tr. Park		Derby		K. Town		Barrow Road	
	steam	diesel	steam	diesel	steam	diesel	steam	diesel	steam	diesel	steam	diesel
1/1/57	87	-	37	-	45	-	131	3	96	-	52	-
28/12/57					56	-			104	-	48	-
1/1/58	92	-	38	-			122	3				
27/12/58					54	-	112	15	102	-	52	-
1/1/59	86	3	36	-								
26/12/59											50	-
1/1/60	74	3	35	-								
2/1/60					51	-	84	38	91	-		
31/12/60					54	-	95	44	80	-	65	2
1/1/61	80	4	36	-								
30/12/61			35	-	41	-	69	77	51	-	45	3
1/1/62	56	4										
15/12/62					32	-	66	99	3	-	56	3
29/12/62												
12/1/63	44	24			37	-	56	104				
28/12/63												
31/12/63											45	-
4/1/64	31	30										

Individual Chapters for each year 1957–63 will explain the detail of changes as they occurred and why.

Statistics regarding average daily mileages achieved by particular classes of locomotive are not easy to find. However, one that did appear in a formal British Railways paper was that over a period of months in 1957 the Jubilees allocated to the London Midland Region averaged 272 miles per day in traffic and the average availability per locomotive over a period of 230 days was 72 per cent, or in presenting it another way each locomotive was, on average, not available on 64 days of the 230. On the Midland lines the average daily for a Millhouses Jubilee would be (based upon an out and home trip to St Pancras) of the order 320 miles, a Kentish Town example of the class (based upon a Manchester out and home working) would be 388, though a Derby–Bristol return would accrue 265. Another indicator of relative usefulness in a 24 hour period could be gleaned from mileages run by locomotives inbetween overhauls at Works. One of the two Britannia Class locomotives allocated new to the Southern Region ran just 52,289 miles over two years, whilst an example based on the London Midland Region ran 91,000 miles in 20 months and a Scottish Region allocated example accrued 139,000 miles in 33 months … and whilst the Southern locomotive was granted a General Overhaul, the other two received merely an Intermediate. The Chapter for 1958 adds further detail.

The seemingly simple expedient to solve the need for additional power by working locomotives more intensively foundered partly upon long-standing depot and crewing arrangements with turns/diagrams/workings vigorously upheld at local level.

The foregoing summaries provide an indication of the steam motive power available for the routes of interest at particular dates. The handful of main line diesels available from time to time (10000, 10001, 10201, 10202 and 10203) put in some useful work on the St Pancras–Manchester line and when available the Fell mechanical 10100 was also used until its demise in October 1958. In the period 1 January to 30 September 1957 those locomotives (including the Fell) were available for traffic for between 54 per cent and 70 per cent of the total of 273 days available. On the total number of days they were available the five accumulated an average each of a total of 91,000 miles. Therein lay a basis of the case for dieselisation; have a look back at the mileage statistics for the LM Jubilees … and I shall let the arguments begin!

The first production batch of diesels to arrive was the Metrovick 1200hp type 2 (D5700-19) which saw use in multiple (pairings) on St Pancras–Manchester passenger trains from 1958. That type was followed by an initial batch of ten Peak class BR/Sulzer 2300hp type 4 (one of which was rated at 2500 hp), but it was not until the second and third production batches of that type appeared from Derby and Crewe BR Workshops that widespread changes to timetables and locomotive workings could confidently be planned and then introduced. Full details are included in the Chapters covering the years 1957–1963 and also include the introduction of diesel multiple units.

Chapter Four

1957: Meeting Increased Demand, but at What Cost?

For its supplies of oil in the 1950s the United Kingdom had a high dependency upon freedom of movement of shipping through the Suez Canal. In autumn 1956 an uneasy political situation between Egypt and the UK plus France deteriorated to such an extent that the European allies embarked upon ill-advised direct, military action. The potential for that action to quickly escalate across the wider Middle East alarmed America plus the United Nations and the latter instructed the UK and France to desist. The consequences of the action that had taken place included the scuttling along the length of the Canal of forty-seven ships, effectively severing traditional supply routes and necessitating alternative routing of available shipping. In the UK, restrictions in the form of the rationing of petroleum products was imposed nationally from 7 November 1956 (and lasted until 14 May 1957).

As part of the response of the government, British Railways was required to provide additional services, both passenger and freight. To assist this effort, the government acceded to the request of the British Transport Commission for men in footplate and certain operating grades on National Service to be relieved of that duty.

The impact of petrol rationing upon passenger journeys was quickly apparent; on the railways 8.2 million more passenger journeys were made in December 1956 compared with the equivalent month in 1955. The strengthening (i.e. adding carriages) to normal, timetabled trains was widespread across the Regions, with an inevitable consequence on the London Midland Region of XL and Special Limit timed trains exceeding the weight limits for (on the Midland Division) motive power classes 5 and 6, with a resultant demand for double heading. The Christmas/New Year holiday season required the provision of additional relief services and thick fog in the days leading to Christmas added to a general picture of a system struggling to cope. Although new steam locomotives were being built the types and rates of production were insufficient to make a significant difference; a total of 191 due in 1957.

For freight there was an opportunity for the railways to regain traffic lost in part due to a strike in 1955 by most footplate staff and in particular from the rapidly increasing number of C Class licenced road hauliers – of which there were more than one million – created as a result of the Transport Act 1953. New, overnight rail services such as a Hendon–Cheadle (for Manchester and Liverpool markets) and a Nottingham–Somers Town (St Pancras) were introduced and with supportive publicity attracted both new and returning old business.

The volume of traffic to be moved was relentless and on Saturdays (and for FA Cup match replays, on Wednesday evenings) trains for football supporters could add considerable demand. For example, on 26 January specials run included twenty from Peterborough to Huddersfield (ten via Stamford, Melton Mowbray, Nottingham and Derby), four from Birmingham to Middlesbrough and five from Sunderland to Birmingham.

Even though during 1957 private car ownership increased by 7½ per cent, there was for British Railways a 7 per cent increase in passenger miles and journeys. The direct comparison between June 1956 and June 1957 showed an increase of roundly 16 per cent and suggested that at the start of the summer timetable (14 June) the railways would have a continuing, exceptionally busy time. In parallel to the period of fuel restrictions, the Civil Engineer for the Midland main lines from St Pancras had largely completed a programme of upgrading the permanent way, thus enabling an acceleration of timings for passenger services. The Signal & Telecommunications Engineer was also heavily engaged on preparatory work for the resignalling of the section from St Pancras to Carlton Road Junction. This entailed work in stages leading to the introduction of a new power signal box at St Pancras (which replaced three manual signal boxes), colour light signals between Carlton Road Junction and the terminus and the installation of a 70 feet plus signal gantry upon which signals controlled the daily movement of some 320 trains. There had, though, been no allocation to the Midland Division of locomotives with a higher power classification than 6. For the three Operating Divisions of the London Midland Region the requirement for the provision of additional locomotives to power the weight of the trains in an effort to maintain the public timetable was roundly over 80 per cent above that for the equivalent period of 1955.

As will be recorded later in this Chapter, the demands for motive power and the maintenance of such, called for some extraordinary measures for Summer Saturdays passenger traffic, but for now we will stay with the acceleration of timings for the Midland Division.

There was a desire to have (or return to, if revisiting earlier times) regular, 'clock face' departures Northbound at 00.15 and 00.25, with semi-fast services to Leicester, Nottingham and Derby as well as express trains to Sheffield, Leeds/Bradford/Scotland and Manchester. The main day time departures from St Pancras were:

Time	Destination	Note
7.25 am	Manchester	
7.55 am	Manchester fast	*The Palatine* (due 11.45 am)
9.15 am	Edinburgh via Melton	*The Waverley*
10.15 am	Glasgow via Leicester	*The Thames-Clyde Express*
10.25 am	Manchester	
12.15 pm	Sheffield/Leeds/Bradford	
12.25 pm	Manchester	
2.15 pm	Sheffield	
2.25 pm	Manchester	
3.15 pm	Sheffield/Leeds/Bradford	
4.15 pm	Sheffield	
4.25 pm	Manchester	
5.05 pm	Sheffield/Leeds/Bradford	135 mins to Derby
6.33 pm	Derby	
6.42 pm	Sheffield	124 mins to Nottingham
6.50 pm	Manchester	

On what is generally thought to be the first occasion upon which a Clan Class locomotive ventured to St Pancras (15 June 1957) 72009 (*Clan Stewart*) was photographed just after having departed from Kettering whilst working the 10.30 Bradford-St Pancras express. (*Kidderminster Railway Museum 092948, Courtesy P. J. Lynch*)

The chronic need in 1957 for the Midland Division of the London Midland Region to have additional Class 7 locomotive power was answered in part by the allocation of six Royal Scots. One of the six, 46110 (*Grenadier Guardsman*) would not normally have needed the assistance of a pilot locomotive (here Black 5 44775) and the reason for its deployment on the 12.25pm St Pancras-Manchester was probably to simply return it expeditiously to Leicester. The train was photographed in October 1957 near Kettering South Junction. (*Kidderminster Railway Museum 085576, Courtesy P. J. Lynch*)

The timetable offered a welcome return to pre-Second World War, mile a minute timings between St Pancras and Kettering (72 miles), Leicester (99), Nottingham (via Edwalton) (125). Of note were the five daily day time services to (and also from) Leeds. Coming south, there were similar improvements. Express trains from Manchester departed at 7.25, 8.55 and 10.25am and, in the afternoon at 12.25, 2.25 (*The Palatine*), 3.25 and 4.25. Also catching the eye was the 7.05am from Sheffield (8am from Derby) timed at 138 minutes for the 128½ miles non-stop to St Pancras from Derby; a showcase job for a Millhouses Jubilee. As an aside the name palatine relates to the rose of Derbyshire and gave the county a named train as for Lancashire (red rose) and Yorkshire (white rose). For reasons that will become apparent later, the routing of the noon Bradford/Leeds to St Pancras train via Derby is also noteworthy.

Whilst considering these (relative) improvements it is worth recording here that the Midland Railway first

introduced systemic 00.25 minute departures and their 2.25pm crack express from Manchester offered dining and Pullman carriages whilst some forty-five years later the British Railways equivalent could muster no catering whatsoever. The Midland Railway certainly had a style that a nationalised industry would struggle to match let alone better. On alternate Saturday afternoons in 1912/13 one of the Cunard Shipping Company's mail ships (either *Mauritania* or *Lusitania*) sailed from Liverpool to New York. As a connecting service the London and North Western Railway ran a train from London Euston, departing after breakfast time. By contrast the Midland set out to attract the American clientele by offering on the Friday evening from the Grand Hotel at St Pancras a non-stop dining carriage express to Liverpool and accommodation at the Company's newly refurbished Adelphi Hotel. Compound Class locomotives with large tenders worked this train of seven carriages via the Peak District and Cheshire Lines Committee route to Liverpool, completing the journey in less than four hours. Style, choice, competition, enjoyable travel ... what could 1957 offer?

From Sheffield and Manchester through passengers to London certainly had choices. The former Great Central Railway via Nottingham, Leicester and Rugby was available from Sheffield (Victoria) to London (Marylebone) and offered a more plentiful catering service, whilst from Manchester (London Road) the former routes of the London and North Western Railway via Stoke-on-Trent or Crewe and Rugby was available and with catering. Later in the book the effect of the electrification of the L&NWR route will be discussed in some detail, but in terms of comparative journey times between the two routes in 1957, there was little to choose, with best times of around three and three quarter hours. For now a comparison between the Midland and Great Central routes illustrated a duplication which – apart from those passengers motivated by food on the move rather than time for the journey – favoured the Midland.

Departure from Marylebone for Sheffield Victoria	Departure from St Pancras for Sheffield Midland
10.00 am	10.15 am
12.15 pm	12.15 pm
3.20 pm	3.15 pm
4.50 pm	5.05 pm
6.18 pm	6.42 pm

If the analysis is widened to include the former Great Northern Railway route from London (Kings Cross) via Retford the 8am service would have a passenger in Sheffield in three hours and seven minutes, just shading the timing of the 9.15am from St Pancras. Even as early as 1957, the relatively weak position of the Great Central route for through passenger services to/from London was starkly clear, just as its potential for freight services should have been equally clear.

This book is also concerned with developments along the cross country route between Bristol and Leeds/York/Newcastle and in terms of timetabling in 1957 few changes were made. *The Devonian* (Bradford–Paignton) Westbound no longer called at either Droitwich Spa or Worcester (Shrub Hill) and despite a later departure from Bradford was still into Bristol at 3.47pm. In the opposite direction *The Devonian* continued to take an unusual route (for Midland Division trains) out of Bristol via Stoke Gifford and the Westerleigh curve; this being to allow drivers' route knowledge when working Summer Saturday trains from Devon/Cornwall which avoided Temple Meads station and emerged near St Philip's Marsh.

The Lickey incline had seen a change to motive power. Arriving from the Western Region a batch of pannier tank locomotives (8402 from Cardiff Canton being the first) soon settled in and replaced the Midland jinties which went to either Saltley or Newton Heath. The latter shed staff may have been surprised to find their new charges equipped with an extra fusible plug, though they probably would be unaware that the tubeplates were an extra 1/8″ thick. The handle reversers on the 84XX made adjustments on the climb more difficult, but in other respects they were well received. The 0-10-0 banker 58100 was cut up at Derby Works on 8 and 9 April 1957. Whilst its replacement (9F 92079) was in the works at Crewe various other 9Fs stood in for periods of a week, their large, high sided tenders being difficult to coal from the stage at Bromsgrove and that was the reason 92079 had swopped its high sided tender for a BR1 type off 92009.

There was, until the summer, a pleasant working for a 4-4-0 with the three carriages morning train from Bristol to Gloucester where they were formed into the larger portion of the Newcastle bound train which originated in Cardiff. However, for the summer timetable, that heavy Cardiff–Newcastle train was run in two portions. The Bristol portion ran ahead and changed locomotives at Sheffield, whilst the Cardiff portion – some thirty minutes behind the Bristol portion – had a locomotive which worked through from Gloucester to York, just as in the winter timetable. Bristol/Gloucester to Birmingham passenger services were confidently entrusted to Compound 4P 4-4-0s.

Returning now to the theme of operational developments during the year, the demands on motive power for the accelerations along the Midland lines out of London, the unabating demand of passengers and the approaching twelve week seasonal high peak period from mid-June was necessitating the consideration of a new option. For summer weekend traffic and stock retained at West Country and other resorts between weekends, a large volume of additional services was operated and in many cases started on the Friday nights.

A lovely railway picture full of interest and showing to good effect the signal gantry adjacent to Derby Junction signal box of 1892 vintage. Class 9F 92049 runs into Derby over Five Arches bridge with what was probably the Saturdays only Scarborough-Kings Norton service, which it will have brought from Rotherham. (*Rail-online*)

Impressive, certainly and at the time quite a thrill for all involved; the face of the Fireman seems to confirm that. Summer 1957 was the first year in which 9F 2-10-0 freight locomotives were deployed on summer passenger trains. I'll wager that this was the Scarborough or Filey – King's Norton getting into its stride out of Derby and will soon be raising the echoes through Pear Tree and Normanton. Saltley's 92051 is complemented by 2P 40416. 3 August 1957. (*Kidderminster Railway Museum 092937, Courtesy P. J. Lynch*)

For these services coaching stock was not a particular problem: thousands of carriages were held in reserve. Locomotive power was a problem. The questions were: 1) is the locomotive equipped with a vacuum brake, 2) is the type of locomotive passed for the proposed route? 3) is the type of locomotive capable of hauling and stopping the designated gross weight of the train? and 4) do the footplate crews know the class of locomotive? If four 'yesses' applied the motive power controllers would have a chance. Two of the questions related for the first time to the potential use of Class 9 2-10-0 locomotives, recently built and introduced for heavy freight work from depots such as Wellingborough, Leicester and

Toton. Such locomotives would be available on summer weekends and once their use was officially sanctioned, the London Midland and Eastern Regions (later also Western Region) lost no time in arranging extensive and successful utilisation.

Observing operations on Summer Saturdays was a particularly pleasurable experience. Opportunities to vary locations were eagerly sought and accepted whilst the 'show' unfolded. Along the lines of route of interest to this book were locations where as many as ten 9Fs could be (and were) seen; Derby, Birmingham and Sheffield being of particular interest. Here is a non-comprehensive random list of observations during that summer.

Date	Working	Return	Locomotive
10 July	Leeds–Paignton	-	92057
	Scarborough–Birmingham	-	92104
	Desford–Blackpool	-	92052
2 August	10.10 am Leicester–Bristol parcels	-	92126
	1.37 pm Derby–Bristol parcels	3 August	92137
3 August	10.30 am Leicester–Paignton	-	92126
	6.40 am Leicester–Paignton	-	92106
	11.05 am Leicester–Paignton	-	92048
	? Sheffield–York	York–Sheffield	92024
5 August	8.25 am Leicester–Scarborough	-	92024
	8.15 am St Pancras–Nottingham	-	92080
	? Leicester–St Pancras	-	92121
10 August	6.50 am Sheffield–Blackpool	2.55	92077
	8.10 am Sheffield–Blackpool	2.20	92055
	8.50 am Sheffield–Blackpool		92050
	9.50 am Leicester–Blackpool	2.15 (to Desford)	92107
	1.38 pm Bristol–Newcastle		92049
	2.40 pm Bristol–Birmingham/ Leicester		92133
	- St Pancras–Sheffield (addtnl)		92137
11 August	- St Pancras–Sheffield (addtnl)		92142

It is quite possible that on 10 August as many as a dozen 9Fs were engaged along our routes of interest and together with the 2-6-0s from Burton and sundry 0-6-0s from other depots the watching public had a wonderful time. Note also the number of trains that conveyed families to popular destinations; three departures from Sheffield to Blackpool, three from Leicester to Paignton. In that era industry would shut down for holiday fortnights and generate huge surges of demand; the hosiery and footwear industry of Leicester, the steel works of Sheffield, the railway and Rolls Royce works of Derby ... and so it went on.

With all this passenger traffic, the potential for late and disturbed patterns of running was ever present. To assist operating and station platform staff throughout the London Midland Region, locomotives carried a board mounted on the front of the smokebox onto which the identification code for the particular train was pasted. Additionally most regular, timetabled passenger train carriages carried route information, for example and probably one of the longest in the country CARDIFF–NEWPORT–GLOUCESTER (EASTGATE)–BIRMINGHAM (NEW STREET)–YORK–NEWCASTLE, although on occasions a set of carriages would find itself confusing everyone by announcing itself as a STARLIGHT SPECIAL. The use of identification boards on locomotives was often misunderstood by casual observers as indicating a special or additional train. In fact, the three digit numeric code with a prefix letter either M (Midland lines), W (Western lines), C (Central lines) or P (special parcels train) was applied also to regular timetabled passenger trains which if they ran in portions had a suffix /1 or /2.

Timetabled trains used the block 1–499, even numbers for 'up' trains, odd for 'down'. The up Devonian was 240, down was 251. Along our lines of route the following blocks were allocated:

690-800   Manchester Central–London St Pancras and vv

811-868   Derby–Bristol and vv

869-893   To North Eastern Region

894-914   From North Eastern Region

930-999   To/from Regions other than North Eastern

These identifications were swept aside from 1961 when a four digit national code was adopted and is summarised in the Chapter for that year.

The timetables for the winter of 1957/58 showed no significant changes to the pattern of services established for the summer. The big development at the London end of the Midland line was the arrival in early October of six Class 7 Royal Scot locomotives, sourced from four Western Division depots and transferred on loan with some reluctance. The arrivals at Kentish Town had wider benefits for the Midland line in that Nottingham received from 14B three Class 6 Jubilees and Derby two of the same Class albeit that one was a returnee after being away for a few months. Predictably and correctly the Class 7s worked XL Limit Manchester and return services (340 tons allowed for a Class 7 to Derby and 300 tons on from there to Manchester) dispensing theoretically at least with a need for the double heading of eight trains a day for which an assisting locomotive had latterly been the norm. The order of preference for assisting locomotives would be Class 5 (of which Kentish Town had a stud of 18) and then Classes 4 and 2 respectively (2/10) and the regularity with which the 4s and 2s were turned out indicated that all was still not well.

On the cross country route the (7.40am Kings Norton) 8.05am Birmingham-Newcastle Special Limit

One of the six Royal Scot Class locomotives transferred in 1957 to the Midland Division of the London Midland Region was 46127 (*Old Contemptibles*) with its attractive and unusual nameplates. Like the others 46127 had attained a high mileage since its previous general overhaul and once its stint on the Midland Division was complete it entered Crewe Works. Here it is outside the Paint Shop and has also been fitted with automatic warning system equipment and a cab speedometer. (*Photographer unknown*)

timed train was booked to run start to stop at Burton-on-Trent (30 miles) in thirty-three minutes and with the return service offering a saving of thirty-one minutes due to better pathing from Wath Road to Chesterfield, and omitting its previous stop at Burton.

Interest for the general observer at the lineside or at a station was consistently high – almost all station based photographs include someone or a group of individuals simply enjoying the environment – with shunting of carriages and parcels vans by the (or even one of the) station pilot locomotives, arrivals, departures, changes of locomotives, crew changeovers and a chance of a quick look on the footplate, water supplies being replenished, platform Inspectors and train Guards urging action, confused passengers seeking directions … and always it seemed, someone carefully noting down the numbers of the locomotives. At that time it was a very popular attraction, supported by the availability of books providing full listings, names where appropriate and technical details and others which omitted much superfluous detail, but replaced it by a listing of the motive power depot to which each

locomotive was allocated. For regular, keen observers the interest lay in something that was in some way out of the ordinary or – if around Derby – a newly built locomotive, fresh out of the Works and very soon to be dispatched to a far flung shed and unlikely to be seen locally for many a month. At mid-year Derby Locomotive Works completed the construction of its final new steam locomotive and the total of 2,941 (since 1851) was reached when British Railways Standard Class 5 4-6-0 73154 was out shopped and dispatched to work in Scotland. The Chapter in this book entitled Motive Power Depots and Motive Power includes references to the passenger train locomotives allocated to the depots which normally supplied power for trains through Derby. Therefore, the Holbeck, Millhouses, Kentish Town, Trafford Park and Barrow Road Jubilees, for instance, were deemed common, the Holbeck Royal Scots not so and anything emanating from, say Carlisle or Newton Heath would be of particular interest as a 'cop'. Anything Scottish was beyond expectations with popular belief that two Royal Scots (46102 and 46121) had never been seen in

One of the D16/3 Class 4-4-0s that replaced the D11/1 Class on Lincoln-Nottingham-Derby passenger workings was 62571. June 1957. (*Science Museum/National Railway Museum LNER 504*)

public! Derby was fortunate in as much as trains from Lincoln would bring in Eastern Region locomotives, necessitating either the purchase of a separate book listing locomotives with numbers beginning with 6 or entering the few that appeared as a personal list in the London Midland Region book. During the course of the year locomotives of Class D16/3 replaced the five D11/1 type that had been regular visitors (62660, now preserved, 62663/6/7/70). The Lincoln based locomotives were used on two daily diagrams (Sux), one of which involved an entertaining shift as south end station pilot at Derby.

Such was the high level of interest that a separate Chapter entitled 'You'll Never Believe What's Been Through!' has been included and identifies unusual and interesting sightings and occurrences in each year, 1957–1963. Football specials, diversions, locomotives out of their normal homeland, visitors from other Regions … much of it is there and if you have more then let's be having it!

During the course of the year the investment in traction and rolling stock as part of the 1955 Modernisation Plan started to become readily apparent. Examples included an extension on Sundays from 10 March of diesel multiple unit services between Grantham and Nottingham (Victoria) to include Derby (Friargate) by what were additional services, the introduction from 3 June of multiple units on the Bedford to Northampton line, from 16 September along the Crewe to Stoke-on-Trent and Derby line and from 7 October all daily Miller's Dale to Buxton passenger services. As a consequence of the latter development 0-4-4 58083 was withdrawn. Other steam revisions included the arrival at Leicester of four BR Standard Class 4 4-6-0s intended to eliminate the use of Compounds on their last regular passenger duty to St Pancras, although the daily piloting of *The Thames-Clyde Express* between Leicester and Sheffield remained. As an indication of difficult times yet to be faced, seven Compounds were taken out of the store elsewhere on the London Midland Region and prepared for a re-entry into traffic. Early in the year Wellingborough had received a batch of four diesel mechanical shunting locomotives for work in the extensive yards there. In addition to the six main line diesels seen from time to time along the Midland line, particularly south of Derby, 10800 was used in April on Rugby to Leicester passenger services

and in October Brush, Loughborough turned out the prototype type 2, D5500, the first of a successful Class that would eventually total over 200. Other investment developments included the fitment of vacuum brakes to 25,000 existing freight vehicles and to 6,000 new 16 ton capacity mineral wagons, with an intention to extend the programme in 1958 to all newly built freight vehicles plus 80,000 existing. Whilst not yet affecting the routes of interest to this book, the installation along 105 miles of tracks between London (Kings Cross) and Grantham and to 2,000 steam locomotives of an Automatic Warning System (which audibly indicated to the driver whether a signal passed was clear or indicating a need for caution and with a need for a timely reaction to the latter) was a welcome development. The menace of rolling mist, of fog and smog caused the necessary use of Fogmen. Such men would be positioned at particular signal locations and place upon the track an explosive detonator which would be activated by the leading wheelset of a passing locomotive and thereby warn the Driver of another signal perhaps 300 yards ahead. For a Driver, with assistance from his Fireman at certain locations where sighting could be influenced by curvature or infrastructure, to safely bring a train over say 200 miles in poor visibility was testimony to sheer professionalism, route knowledge and absolute concentration evidenced by red-rimmed eyes obvious to any passenger who paused to think as they rushed by the locomotive with a muttered 'ten minutes late again'.

Nationally, 591 fitted (i.e. vacuum braked) freight trains were run on weekdays (300 more than before the War) and in recognition of the commercial potential for containerised movement of trainload traffic British Railways had a stock of 35,000 containers and was adding to that inventory.

During the year Melton Mowbray station became Melton Mowbray Town and Coxbench (on the branch between Little Eaton Junction and Ripley) was closed to all facilities.

Penultimately for 1957 there was a downturn in general economic activity which affected the volume of general merchandise to be moved. However, in mid-December the weekly tonnage of coal moved was – at 3.834 million tons – the highest weekly total since 1948.

On Christmas Eve the up *Palatine* was hauled into St Pancras by a pair of Compounds … Happy Christmas!

Chapter Five

1958: Motive Power Needed for the Midland Lines: Steady State on Cross Country

Early 1958 events included some re-arranging of the British Railways' Regional organisation structure in as much as it affected our routes of interest. The boundary between the London Midland and the Western Region was at Barnt Green (10½ miles the Bristol side of Birmingham New St) and with the latter Region taking responsibility for motive power depots including Bromsgrove (21C to 85F), Gloucester Barnwood (22B to 85E) and Bristol (Barrow Road) (22A to 82E). The Sheffield District of the Eastern Region took control of the Midland line north of Chesterfield (Midland)/Horns Bridge and several motive power depots including Millhouses (19B to 41C). The former Great Northern lines in the Nottingham area, including the line to Egginton Junction via Derby (Friargate) passed from Eastern Region to London Midland Region control. Whilst seemingly not being of specific relevance to our routes, the former Great Central line south from Heath (near Chesterfield) passed from the Eastern Region to the London Midland Region and, with it, responsibility for future timetable planning and strategic direction as a route which, as has already been noted as offering a declining, comparative, through passenger timetable, was actually of significance. From a train operating perspective the effect on our routes of interest was greatest on cross country. The Western Region authorities would advise their London Midland Region contemporaries when through trains approached Barnt Green, having regulated their progress to that point, whilst from the York/Leeds/Sheffield direction the London Midland Region would normally be advised when the train was at or approaching Horns Bridge. Derby, Midland Division Control would advise the Western/Eastern Regions as progress was made by trains. This, of course was a far cry from how the Midland/ LMS/ early British Railways had organised themselves, but Regional Boards, devolved decision making and some commercial freedom to secure traffic was the order of the day. Interestingly, the Eastern Region opted for a unified line of route control for their (former Great Northern) main line to the North as far as Grantham (105 miles) which passed through three Districts whilst

the London Midland opted for purely geographically based Divisional managerial control. The weakness of the latter was best evidenced by arrangements for what could have been a unified, planned and controlled fast freight route – the 80 miles from Annesley to Woodford via the former GC/ER route – being discarded in favour of diluted responsibility across three Divisions.

At the motive power depots of interest (Millhouses and Barrow Road) the locomotive allocations remained unchanged as did the Workshop responsible for overhauls and, initially, for the provision of spares. The replacement for any locomotives withdrawn before the end of 1959 would also be the responsibility of the previous Regional 'owner'. In practice, motive power continued unchanged, albeit that it was strange to see Jubilees sporting Eastern and Western shedplate codes.

The build programme for new traction in 1958 was for 428 completions, of which nine was carried forward from 1957. Included in the programme were a first British Railways order for Derby Locomotive Works for main line examples (apart from 10001, delivered in 1948) and an order for electric locomotives to be built at BR Doncaster Works; all other main line units were committed with private contractors. Making up the total were 257 diesel shunting locomotives, of which 184 were to be produced at a total of five BR Workshops.

Within the 1955 Modernisation Plan a provision of £10 million had been made for steam locomotive development work. Some of the Regions were keener than others; double blastpipes/chimneys assisted the Kings and some of the Castles of the Western Region whilst the A4s and many of the A3s of the Eastern Region were similarly treated, with pleasing results in day to day operation. The London Midland Region – with a relatively low total stock of Class 7 power compared to the Eastern – trialled the potential from a programme of fitting double blastpipes/chimneys on more Class 6 Jubilees, but did not proceed. I have assumed here that the capital cost of re-building the 30 Merchant Navy Class locomotives and many of the 110 West Country/Battle of Britain Class locomotives of the Southern Region had been separately budgeted and, similarly, also the experimental fitment to ten BR Class 9F 2-10-0s of a feed water heating drum principle, based upon work successfully undertaken for the Italian State Railways by Dr Piero Crosti. The BR experiment was facilitated when the batch of locomotives was built at Crewe and involved the secondary use of exhaust gases to heat water prior to it being injected into the boiler. This resulted in the smoke from the firebox being expelled via a port (longitudinal chimney) on the right hand (Firemans) side of the boiler and exhaust steam injectors to convey more water to the boiler. The potential benefit lay in the need for less coal to maintain boiler steam pressure. Even if deemed a success it is difficult to see how the application could have been extended to classes other than certain BR Standards and how a return on capital cost would have been computed given the likely future lifespan of steam. The ten locomotives (92020-29) were based at Wellingborough and on weekdays were deployed on coal trains between there and Brent/Cricklewood and at weekends in the summer also on passenger trains, taking them to Bristol and York. Between September 1959 and June 1962 the equipment was removed from each of the ten locomotives, after which they worked conventionally though without smoke deflectors.

Another trial involving the 2-10-0s along part of one of our routes of interest was the fitment to three of the Class (92165-7) with a Berkley Mechanical Stoker. This involved the controlled feeding of coal from the tender into the firebox by means of a rotary screw, allowing coal to fall into a channel where the screw mechanism would transfer it to a point where the Fireman could operate steam jets to direct the coal onto the bed of the fire. This was not a new concept to British Railways as Merchant Navy 35005 had such a stoker for a period and in 1955 consideration had been given to fitment to the Princess Coronation pacifics. In theory it sounded like a beneficial, labour saving device for long runs (the intention here being overnight Birmingham/Carlisle/Glasgow heavy, fitted freight trains with the same Fireman working through as far as Carlisle, but the practicalities involved having a supply of suitable coal. Unlike South Africa – where such devices were used successfully with locally produced screened and washed, high density steam coal – the Whitwick and Blidworth 'variables' unscreened, loaded into partly emptied common user wagons and then having been tipped into the bunker of the mechanised coaling plant at Saltley were discharged from some height into the tenders of locomotives. Then, with an ample dousing to keep down the dust/fines this mixture frequently produced a solid face of black composite which needed

encouragement, ideally before the hopper and screw mechanism became clogged. Resorting to hand firing through a small opening above where the firehole doors would have been was extremely taxing for even a physically fit and able Fireman who, over a shift of some eight hours, not only had to go further back into the tender to bring forward the theoretically self-trimming coal, but had on many occasions to shovel and lift/fire through a smaller than normal opening in such a way as to maintain steam pressure. The later part of the journey included the Settle-Carlisle section including its 15 mile drag up to Blea Moor summit. Many an evening must have included a quiet 'thumbs up' between the crew as Ais Gill was reached. It was not long before the coal for the three locomotives was being specially prepared or supplies of 'trebles' sourced especially for the diagrams. The principle of the benefit from such stokers was proven elsewhere, but with the policy of British Railways to take from the Coal Board coal at a price and a quality commensurate with that price the true potential in the UK was never realised. It was also a pity that given the difficulty with the coal an option to fit a steam coal-pusher at the rear of the bunker (as with the tenders of the Princess Coronation Class and certain BR Standard classes) was never pursued. Officially, the experiment was deemed to have been a success, but the equipment was later removed.

Class 9Fs from Saltley were entrusted with three, late afternoon fitted freight trains from Water Orton (7 miles East of Saltley) and coupled together the three would be readied for departures at 4.45pm (Glasgow), 4.55pm (Carlisle) and 5.05pm (Leeds). In quick succession these trains with up to fifty-five vans of 12 ton capacity used to pass the author 3 miles north of Derby between 5.30pm and 6.30pm with the Glasgow being booked non-stop to Sheffield to where it was routed via Dronfield and paused for water. These trains were both impressive and a good advertisement for British Railways' ability to move train loads overnight at speeds up to 50mph … in this case including perishable fruit and vegetable traffic from Worcestershire/Herefordshire, carpets from Kidderminster and the vast panoply of general merchandise from the West Midlands/Black Country conurbation. The locomotive on the Glasgow train was replaced at Carlisle and with the crew also being due to be relieved there at 11.46pm; a 7¾ hour shift of 225 hard miles with no overtime, but an excellent mileage bonus payment. The return working for the locomotive and men (having lodged) was the 4.03pm ex-Carlisle, with the locomotive/crew due on Saltley depot at midnight. The crew was rostered to do the return trip twice each week. On only two occasions did I see the

Number 92167 was one of the three 9Fs to be fitted with a Berkeley mechanical stoker and was regularly engaged on early evening departures from Water Orton to Glasgow/Carlisle/ Stourton; fully vacuum fitted trains of up to fifty-five vans. On this occasion the train is being worked through Derby station rather than via the goods lines, an indication that it is either the Glasgow (booked non-stop to Sheffield) or the Carlisle (booked to call at St Mary's yard for additional vans). Above the train and to the left of the locomotive is London Road from which a fine view of the motive power depot could be obtained. (*Photographer unknown, Midland Railway Trust collection*)

three mechanical-stoker fitted locomotives working the three trains in question. Included for interest is an extract from the Saltley crew roster book.

Such trains as just described were vital to the railways … fast reliable services with traffic over a distance of say 300 miles where the economies of scale of the operation could offset the incremental costs of individual collection/delivery times to/from depots not faced by competing road hauliers. The position of the railways has to be placed into context. At that time only 7 per cent of the 7,000 freight trains operated daily by the London Midland Region were fitted with continuous brakes. It was, therefore, unfortunate that as part of the government's need to scale back on public expenditure programmes the timetable for the fitment of brake cylinders and ancillary equipment was one of the areas to suffer; others included station improvements, the rate of production of new coaching stock and delayed commitment of follow-on production orders for type 2 diesel locomotives.

The early months of 1958 witnessed a general improvement in timekeeping along the Midland lines to St Pancras compared to what had been a dire last quarter of the previous year. Double heading with

4-4-0s was common place and even the Royal Scots on occasions appeared south of Derby with assistance provided, though such was always an alternative way of working an unbalanced locomotive back to its home depot. The six Royal Scots were not, though, the best examples of the class and could be seen on Derby shed far more frequently than their London-Manchester through workings would have suggested should have been the case. Nevertheless, the Western Division wanted them returned and as quickly as alternative arrangements could be made.

The summer timetable in June took into account the introduction (in April) of diesel multiple unit services along the Lincoln-Nottingham-Derby and Birmingham-Nuneaton-Leicester routes, although a few passenger and mail services from Lincoln/Nottingham to Derby remained steam hauled and happily brought with them the sight of Class A5 pacific tank locomotives allocated to Colwick depot (GN depot East of Nottingham). Despite the excessive demands upon motive power and the difficulties in the early part of the past winter, no significant changes were made to the services to and from Sheffield and Manchester although the previous fast 6.42pm St Pancras-Nottingham and Sheffield service had its weight increased and ten minutes added to its schedule. The bigger changes along the routes of interest were to be found on the cross-country route. *The Devonian* in each direction was speeded up by twenty-five minutes 'down' and seventeen minutes 'up'. The

8.35am from Bristol no longer called at Cheltenham Spa and was extended to York whilst the later service (10.30am) between the same points was accelerated by twenty-eight minutes.

BR LM REGION **MIDLAND LINES** BR 358/5

Freight Engine Workings Commencing 12 June 1961
Enginemen's Workings Only   Saltley – Sheet 146

			Book On am	Book off am	H.M.
TURN 809			2.55	11.55	9.0
	ENGINE PREPARED by Turn 1011				
	Saltley M.P.D. 3.10 am LE CpldMX	D			
3.23am	Water Orton 3.50 EF (D)	D	(349)		
11.30	Carlisle P.B. Jn				
	RELIEF 11.30 am for Carlisle	D			
	London Rd by 12A Turn 73				
	REST	D			
			pm	am	
TURN 810			10.37	7.41	8.12
	RELIEVE* from Kingmoor M.P.D.		11.35	8.52	9.17
	12A Turn 194 at 11.30 pm (FSX)				
	12.15 am (SO)				
	Carlisle D. Hill 11.32 pm EF (C)	FSX	(349)		
7.25 am	Washwood Heath–LE	MSX			
7.31	Saltley M.P.D.				
	Carlisle D. Hill 12.20 am EF (C)	SO			
8.36	Washwood Heath–LE	SO			
8.42	Saltley M.P.D.				
	RELIEF on arrival				
TURN 811			am	am	
	RELIEVE* from Kingmoor M.P.D.		1.45	10.11	8.26
	12A Turn 196 at 2.35 am				
	Carlisle D. Hill 2.40 am EF(C)	Sun	(349)		
9.55 am	Washwood Heath–LE	Sun			
10.1	Saltley M.P.D.				
	RELIEF on arrival				
TURNS 812-814	NOT USED				

Notes added for this book (from top):

LE – light engine(s)
EF – engine first
*H.M. – hours minutes
SX – Saturdays excepted
(349) – thought to be relevant page of Working Timetable

Cpld – engines coupled
D – daily
(C) (D) – classification of train
FSX – Fridays and Saturdays excepted
MSX – Mondays and Saturdays excepted
SO – Saturdays only

In the down direction eighteen and sixteen minutes were saved off one Bristol service from each of one train from Bradford and York.

Whilst the latter savings may seem insignificant over a journey of some 200 miles, the need to have trains on the move rather than awaiting lax departure times can be evidenced by a review of services Westbound through Cheltenham (Lansdown Road) at lunchtime on a Summer Saturday. For Birmingham (New St)-Bristol line traffic just one curved platform face was available with a water crane at the far end acting as a magnet to attract any passing steam locomotive crew(s); whilst one locomotive taking water would not be too much of a problem, two, with an attendant need to draw forward the train 20 yards or so, would be and frequently was. Drawing forward was a problem with curvature of the platform causing sighting difficulties for the platform staff, Guard and locomotive Drivers. Trains routed via Camp Hill and Kings Norton may not have taken water since the troughs (if available) at Wigginton East of Tamworth (67 miles) so Cheltenham was always a popular spa. The use of 9F 2-10-0s and BR standard Class 5s with tender water capacities of up to 4,725 gallons helped, certainly compared to the lower capacities of some of the Midland /LMS tenders still in use. Delays here would cause a potential backing up of following services. The 12.30pm departure to Bristol (ex-Bradford) was frequently double headed and any need for both locomotives to take water placed the timekeeping of the following trains at risk.

Not only at risk locally; with four of the trains destined for Bournemouth via the difficult Somerset and Dorset route with its single track sections and crossing points, the need for timekeeping was of constant concern.

12.30 pm	Bradford–Bristol
12.40 pm	Cleethorpes–Bournemouth
12.51 pm	Sheffield–Bournemouth
1.09 pm	Worcester–Gloucester
1.17 pm	Bradford–Bournemouth
1.40 pm	Newcastle–Paignton
2.03 pm	non-stop
2.08 pm	Manchester–Bournemouth
2.20 pm	Sunderland–Bristol
2.30 pm	Newcastle–Cardiff/Bristol
2.40 pm	Bradford–Paignton/Kingswear

New services that summer included examples of a commercial venture by British Railways to attract the long distance car driver and his or her family. The arrangement included the car being placed into covered trucks/vans formed as part of the train and the passengers conveyed overnight in sleeping berth compartment carriages. One service ran overnight in each direction twice weekly between Newcastle/Sheffield and Exeter and another was introduced to run between Sutton Coldfield and Stirling, offering places for up to eighteen cars, eighty-four sleeping berths and a train of seven carriages plus up to nine covered vans for the cars. These trains extended already popular services between London and Scotland. The Sutton Coldfield service left at 9.35pm (Sundays and Wednesdays) with

an Aston depot locomotive which was booked to go as far as Carlisle via Burton, Derby and Leeds. The return service ran south on Monday and Thursday evenings. Although Aston men worked the Northbound train to Derby it was Derby men who worked the return (with Conductor from Burton), leaving around 4am, shunting the stock into the bay at Sutton Coldfield and heating the carriages until the passengers had departed, then empty coaching stock to Duddeston, light engine to Aston shed, bus to New Street and home for lunch. This train proved to be popular and as the weight was increased the need for Class 6 and then Class 7 locomotive power brought it to greater prominence, light summer evenings allowed a glimpse north of Derby. However, it was the return workings that brought some exotic traction to the Midlands and had the bush telegraph working overtime … more later. Further north, at Sheffield Millhouses illicit visits became more frequent on Tuesdays, Thursdays and Sundays. The reason for this was that the Glasgow (St Enoch)-London (Marylebone) car-sleeper service did not call at Leeds and the Scottish or Carlisle locomotive worked through to Beighton Junction, before spending the day on Millhouses depot awaiting that night's return working.

The London Midland Region – Midland and Western Divisions – continued to experience a need for double heading. The basic conflict was between publically timetabled XL and Special Limit trains with their respective weights, the need to strengthen such trains to move the volume of expected and actual travellers and the need for costly double heading due to a lack of Class 7 locomotive power. As previously noted the Western Division wanted returned the six Royal Scots sent across the previous autumn. The needs of the Western Division were deemed greater than those of the Midland – at least for now – and the need to find suitable Class 7 traction for the latter resulted in a wider consideration, extending beyond the Regional boundary. It is conjecture on my part, but it is likely that the meeting when held would have considered the needs of the London Midland Region in total rather than the Midland Division in isolation. Clearly, if a solution could be found for the Western Division, with its main lines suited to heavy, pacific locomotives of Class 8 power, then the transfer of some of the Class 7 Royal Scots and Patriots would be more palatable. To achieve such a position a Commission headquarters decision would be necessary … no Region would willingly make available to another a sizeable fleet of front-line locomotives. At what must have been a very interesting meeting it is likely that a table of comparisons between the classes of locomotives the LM Region had at its disposal together with classes of locomotives that potentially could provide a solution would have been available. A listing would have included the following, plus possibly one or more of the Eastern/North Eastern Region pacific classes.

Class	Wheel Arrgmnt	Driving Wheel F Ins	Weight T cwt	Length F Ins	Coal Tons	Water Galls	Cyls	Route code
Ex-LMS 5	4-6-0	6 -	125 5	63 8	9	4000	2	7
Jubilee 6	4-6-0	6 9	134 4	64 9	9	4000	3	8
Royal Scot 7	4-6-0	6 9	137 13	65 3	9	4000	3	9
Patriot 7	4-6-0	6 9	123 9	62 9	9	4000	3	9
Coronation 8	4-6-2	6 9	161 12	73 10	10	4000	4	9
V2 7	2-6-2	6 2	145 2	66 5	7.5	4200	3	9
West Country 7	4-6-2	6 2	132 13	67 5	5	4500	3	?
M Navy 8	4-6-2	6 2	151 4	71 8	5	6000	3	?
Britannia 7	4-6-2	6 2	143 3	68 9	7	4250	2	8

Note: Length rounded to nearest inch.

The railway and enthusiast press of the time suggested that an approach had been made to secure all thirty of the Merchant Navy Class, but that such an approach had not been acceptable. In 1948 there had been a programme of exchanges of locomotives of the four pre-nationalisation companies for trials and comparisons of performance over given routes. As part of this programme, three West Country Class locomotives were involved in trials and on the London Midland Region included the St Pancras-Manchester route. For the trials the locomotives were paired with LMS style tenders with water scoop apparatus and a higher coal capacity than the West Country's own scoopless and low coal capacity versions. The performance of the trialled (Southern) locomotives on the St Pancras-Manchester via Derby route was deemed to be unexceptional in any way. The design of the tender used by the Southern locomotives was influenced more by a need for water rather than coal, with the latter limited to five tons. A rough trip from St Pancras to Manchester with delays en route could have exposed such a limitation, but we will probably never know whether this was a factor in the consideration. The wider conclusions from the trials included that the West Country Class had a boiler which was well capable of producing steam to meet requirements and marked highly in comparison with other locomotives trialled, though to produce the steam the locomotives were comparatively hungry for coal and thirsty too. The ex-Southern locomotives also seemed to perform better when crewed by men from their home depots who understood the steam reverser and how to finely adjust the settings of it. Whether or not any reference was made in 1958 to such outcomes is not known by me, but no move of any Southern Region Class 7 or 8 took place.

The next practical move involved the consideration of using V2 2-6-2s, of which thirteen examples had been taken into LM Region stock resulting from the boundary changes of 1 February 1958. The V2s were heavy – very heavy over the centre and trailing driving wheel axles – and the Regional Civil Engineer would need to be consulted. Two trials were arranged: on Sunday, 16 March 60855 was sent over from Neasden and was tried out over various points and crossings in the vicinity of St Pancras station and the following Sunday the same locomotive plus one carriage travelled from Cricklewood to Wigston (3 miles south of Leicester) stopping along the way to traverse various points, crossings and check platform edge clearances (the Midland having erred in building stations on curved alignments). As no further V2s were seen it can be safely concluded that the civil engineering constraints, and/or capital cost outlay requirements precluded further considerations.

What next? Although the fifty-five Britannias were only some two tons lighter than the V2s they had the advantage of having an extra axle to reduce the average axle load and were not subject to the same onerous level of route availability restrictions. Because of the planned, early dieselisation of the Great Eastern line services between London (Liverpool St) and Norwich, the obvious first calling point was for the twenty-three examples successfully allocated since 1951/2 to that route. For good reasons the Great Eastern line management was favourably inclined towards its Britannias and had planned a post-dieselisation cascade of power from the Norwich line to accelerate services to/from Clacton. The good reasons included the high mileages accrued in revenue earning service between major repairs. Whilst plying the 124 miles each way between London and Norwich 70012/38 achieved in their first three years 321,000 and 336,000 miles respectively. An average of 2,000 miles a week equated to five return St Pancras-Manchester workings and would suit well the needs of the Midland Division. It was suggested to the ER management that the ten Clan Class locomotives – a less powerful version of the Britannia and Class 6 rather than 7 – may be adequate to meet the needs of the Clacton services and agreement was reached that a trial would be arranged. Clan 72009 duly arrived. The Stratford crews soon reported the inadequacy of the Class 6 versus their 7s and the trial was deemed a failure. Number 72009 was returned north to Carlisle.

The options having been explored and the results considered the practicality of operating the Western and Midland Divisions through the fast approaching summer timetable required decisions to be taken. The decisions taken were that six Britannias would be transferred to the Midland Division; one from the Great Eastern line (70042), the two former prestige examples based on the Southern Region (70004/14) and three from the Western Region. The Western Region was so keen to help it actually sent four examples (70015/7/21 and one that was returned unused, 70016). Number

70016 was placed on the front row of the shed yard at Derby and hundreds came from far and wide to appreciate its powerful profile. It was also decided that two additional Britannias would be transferred from the Scottish Region (70053/4) to Holbeck, thus releasing for more use south of Leeds two Royal Scots (46103/33). However, until this latter move could become effective the Western Division was prevailed upon to let four of their Royal Scots stay longer on the Midland Division (46157 went to Camden, 46127 went to Holyhead and later 46110, which stayed at Kentish Town whilst the other three went to Trafford Park, went back to Crewe North. The final three, 46116/31/52 later went from Trafford Park back to Camden).

In the railway town of Derby word of the arrival of the Britannias spread like wildfire. On the first, fine Saturday morning of the summer timetable there was at Breadsall Crossing 3 miles north of Derby a surprisingly large gathering of fathers and sons plus others who were interested in the development. It was at that location that I spent most of my spare time. The down *Palatine* due to pass at around 10.30am was confidently expected to produce a Britannia, but we were surprised and certainly impressed when *Apollo* (70015) sped past on the 8.55 up from Manchester. My Dad quickly said to me 'It's not a Brit' as the *Palatine* was heard in the distance; the acceleration of the three cylinder locomotive gave way to the sight and sound of *Sierra Leone* (45627) as it made its way, right on time. The gallery was largely unimpressed and drifted away leaving the regular attendees to our usual

The external appearance of *Arrow* (70017) suggests a date of summer 1958 and shortly after arrival at Trafford Park for Midland line duty. Here it has BR Standard Class 5 73126 as an assisting locomotive on *The Palatine*, 7.55am St Pancras-Manchester. The Britannia should not have required assistance but as the 5 was Patricroft based it is possible that it was being worked home expeditiously. (*Colour-rail 19879*)

A clean Britannia at Derby and a Trafford Park allocated one at that! It is 70021 *Morning Star* and leaving for St Pancras with an early evening express from Manchester. The hordes of spotters on Hulland Street footbridge, on the station platforms and on the train support a conclusion that this was August 1958, a couple of months since the Britannias arrived, on the day the Loco Works was open. (*Photographer unknown, Midland Railway Trust collection*)

vigil. The only time I saw more people there was one damp March evening in 1957 when the strictly 'Not for Publication' Notice of a Royal Train movement from the Manchester area to an overnight stop on Trent North Curve seemed to have received scant regard and generated a large attendance. The train was hauled by a pair of Jubilees, both with a small Fowler tender, one of which was *Prince Rupert* (45671) and the other thought to be *South Africa* (45571). For that movement there was no attendant publicity, though the following day a pair of smartly turned out Kentish Town Black 5s took the train to an official engagement at Sudbury (Staffordshire). At risk of disturbing the flow of this section about the introduction of the Britannias, there is a story about the Royal Train on that March night that deserves to be recorded. The two Jubilees having been detached at Derby the local depot provided power for the few miles to Trent where the train was to be stabled overnight on the north curve. Having completed that task the locomotive returned light engine to Derby, leaving to another Derby locomotive and crew the task of providing steam to heat the carriages and their important occupants. Derby had several 4F locomotives fitted with steam-heating apparatus and one of these

was provided in the capable hands of Driver Reg Beardsley and Fireman Geoff Morris (about whom more later in this book). This was to be as boring a shift as could be imagined and Special Instructions included that under no circumstances should the crew leave their locomotive. Sometime early in the shift Fireman Morris needed to respond to a call of nature and having climbed down off the 4F found suitable cover. He had strayed too far; a fact reinforced by the heavy hand of the law. The civil and British Transport Police were present and it was one of the former who effected the 'snatch' and would have none of the (very plausible it has to be said) explanations as to 'who' and 'why'. Geoff Morris was arrested and taken by road to Long Eaton police station. His plea for the police to 'phone Derby 42764 (4 Shed Office) was ignored as they preferred another more complex procedure. Eventually Geoff was told he was free to leave. Any chance of a lift? Not a chance! With no knowledge of Long Eaton except the railway geography Geoff found a recognisable railway location and followed the track to Trent, thence to the north curve, the train, the 4F and a highly amused Driver Beardsley. Of course it did not end there and banter and mirth in the messroom at 4 Shed knew no bounds.

The Britannias were certainly impressive and no doubt the professional operators hoped they would reduce the need for double heading and increase route punctuality statistics. In fact, things did not start well. Within a few days of arrival 70014 parted company with its tender and train and managed to do this at 60mph whilst between Hazel Grove and Cheadle Heath. This was not a unique occurrence, 70012 having done the same on the Great Eastern line in 1957.

On 17 June 70014 (*Iron Duke*) commenced a daily, weekday diagram involving the 7.55am down from St Pancras to Manchester, the *Palatine*, with a return working to town at 4.25pm with the same Kentish Town crew. The locomotive completed the diagram on the 17th and 18th, but on the 19th it parted company with its tender and train. This extraordinary occurrence was not, however, unique as 70012 had done the same in 1957 near Bethnal Green on the Great Eastern line out of Liverpool Street. The then coupling arrangement between the engine and tender was a bar as used also on certain Southern Railway classes and threaded to allow a large nut to be turned and effect a union. What had happened was that the thread had been sheared and the union destroyed.

Quite by chance the Midland Line's Divisional Operating Superintendent – Mr James Burge – was a passenger on the train and during the following day he recounted to the then District Inspector at Rowsley – Mr John Heydon – the story of what had occurred. Later, for interest, Mr Heydon wrote down the story and his son Patrick (also a long-serving railwayman) passed a copy to me. The following is a summary of what Mr Heydon recorded and uses the first person context of Mr Burge's account.

'Travelling on the down *Palatine*, 7.55 St Pancras–Manchester, just past Hazel Grove signal box, there was a sudden, full application of the brakes and we came to a stop in mid-section. Looking out of the window there was not a sound except for larks singing overhead. Sensing something was seriously wrong and seeing the Guard looking out at the rear of the train, I told him who I was and jumped out of the train onto the up line to investigate. The hairs on my neck stood up seeing the tender on the train, but no engine.

I ran forward to Bramhall Lane signal box where a speechless signalman pointed towards Cheadle Heath. The local ganger was sitting at one end of the signal box, also shaken and I realised just what had happened and why the engine and tender had parted company. I told the ganger to walk back from the rear of the stationary train towards Hazel Grove signal box and look for part of a large bolt which coupled the engine

to the tender. This bolt had sheared in half and was later found.

Having spoken to Cheadle Heath South signal box the signalman confirmed that having an express on the block an engine only was standing at the South Home signal. I told the signalman what must have happened and told him to try and move the engine from the Down Main line into the sidings.

At Bramhall Lane the local trip engine (usually Heaton Mersey class 4F 0-6-0, but on that day an 8F 2-8-0) was shunting in the Up sidings. This was used to go to the front of the disabled train. On the way the Fireman said 'how can we possibly couple to the tender of the *Palatine*?' On arrival at the train we looked around and, by good luck, found a coil of old signal wire on the line side. This was used to secure the assisting engine to the tender. Sending the Guard back to 'pull the strings' to release all the brakes on the coaches, we were able to move the train which was on a falling gradient of approx 1 in 100 between Disley Tunnel and Bramhall Lane signal box.

After the tender was detached and shunted into the sidings we proceeded with the train to Cheadle Heath South signal box. On arrival we stopped opposite the *Iron Duke* where the Driver and Fireman were throwing out the fire. The Kentish Town train men wanted to change over with the Heaton Mersey men to work forward to Manchester Central with the Class 4 freight engine, but 44112 which had appeared to take forward the *Palatine*, but I would not allow this as the Heaton Mersey men knew the road into Central and the London crew must have been shaken up by such an experience.

The Kentish Town Driver told me that seeing a gap appearing between the engine and tender, thinking the train was catching up with him, he opened the regular and shot forward, but was able to bring the engine to a stand at Cheadle Heath South Home signal.'

Just a few notes of explanation may assist. Having severed its connection the vacuum that was keeping the brakes of the train carriages off was destroyed, the brakes would be immediately progressively applied as referred to by Mr Burge as a full application and bringing the train to a halt. The Driver of the locomotive would have gradually stopped his engine by putting it into reverse gear thus applying steam into the cylinders to restrain forward movement. Pulling the strings on the carriages would disable the brakes and allow the replacement locomotive to create new vacuum pressure and having done so would be in full control. The signalman referring to having a train on the block meant that it was within his signalling section, albeit that the engine was some way forward of the tender and train. The ganger was a track worker. The enginemen throwing out the fire was essential as no further water could be injected into the boiler and serious damage to the firebox could quickly have resulted. Locomotive 40067 was used to shunt 70014.

All of the Britannias were then fitted with a different type of drawbar, safety links between the engine and tender and a Klinger valve which enabled the Driver to retain braking power in the highly unlikely event of a recurrence.

From a maintenance perspective it was decided that the six locomotives and (short-term) the three Royal Scots would be allocated to Trafford Park rather than at the Southern end, whilst Trafford Park's Jubilees would go to Kentish Town. Given that Longsight depot was close to Trafford Park and had fitters who knew both new classes, plus a developing adverse labour availability situation in the South, this made logical sense. Trafford Park though did not seem to have any spare members of staff in the category of Cleaner and the front line

locomotives soon became grimy and worse. In the time that Britannias were on the Midland it is ironic that the only one to emerge looking as it should was 70004, one of the two former Stewarts Lane locomotives to be entrusted with the Golden Arrow Pullman service to Dover. In August 1959 70004 was displayed at the Open Day at Derby Locomotive Works.

It took a while for the observers to work out the daily diagrams of the Britannias and early attempts by the author included a chance identification of something else of interest. The 4.25am from St Pancras to Manchester was due out of Derby at 8.12 and the author calculated that he could see this, return home and still be at school on time. The first attempt produced a blank as the trip working to Wirksworth making its way along the down slow line completely blocked out a view of the 8.12. The attempt the following morning looked like heading the same way (the signalman having closed the gates once for the passage of two trains, rather than twice), but the brake van of the freight just cleared in time to

For display at the 1959 Open Day at Derby Locomotive Works an effort was made to clean Britannia Class *William Shakespeare*; any residual grime being transferred to the clothing of un-supervised spotters who undertook a forensic examination of the locomotive. Note on the lower retaining strap for the smoke deflector the route indicating disc/lamp bracket as would have been displayed by this locomotive when allocated to the Southern Region. The two initially allocated to the Southern Region were not fitted with water scoops. Both 70004 and 70014 later worked on the Midland Division. (*Rail-online*)

see part of the engine and tender of the 4.25. Not a Britannia, but a Longsight Patriot was a fine alternative. A friendly platelayer who had been in the cess ahead of my position offered the helpful advice that it was *E.C. Trench*. Subsequent forays produced other members of the Class (45508/15/20) and clearly this was part of a Longsight diagram involving relief of the locomotive that worked the 4.25 as far as Derby. However, it was not then a Britannia turn and after further observations and advice from the signalman the all important information was that it soon would be:

4.25 am	St Pancras–Manchester	2.25 pm return
7.55 am	St Pancras–Manchester	4.25 pm return
10.25 am	St Pancras–Manchester	5.55 pm return
12.25 pm	St Pancras–Manchester	12.05 am return
7.25 pm	Manchester–St Pancras	4.25 am return

Up to 390 miles and five out of six available for traffic seemed to be the plan. In the short time that the three Royal Scots remained on the Midland line they worked turn and turn about with the Britannias. The diagrams most regularly seen (7.55/4.25 and 10.25/5.55) were adhered to and time-keeping north of Derby was generally good. Once the final Royal Scot had gone to Camden the reliance upon the Britannias increased, but their availability was clearly less than expected. The incidence of double heading of passenger trains south of Derby was still high with the aged 4-4-0s still being called upon. The two final Royal Scots in the jigsaw (46103/33) did not arrive (at Kentish Town) until November 1958.

The well-to-do burghers of Buxton had noted the arrival of the Britannias and lobbied for one such to be used on the morning and evening trains to/from Manchester.

If the Manchester route was struggling for cleanliness, on occasions the public face at least of the cross country route could hardly have been better presented. Bristol Barrow Road depot had an allocation of Jubilees – ten of them – and four Standard Class 5s, also 4-6-0, and around that time the staff there were turning them out in a very smart external condition. The sight of 45682 *Trafalgar* at the head of *The Devonian* with the Western Region set of Mark 1 coaches in chocolate and cream livery made a lasting impression; there was a sense of real pride in the job. The Barrow Road crew worked with the locomotive through to Leeds and then lodged overnight prior to working home the following morning on a (Bradford) Leeds-Bristol passenger working which had them home a full twenty-four hours after leaving. There were less attractive rosters;

how about the 10.30am Bristol-Newcastle to Derby, lodge, and back with the 2.10am Derby-Bristol parcels. One train that I imagine that Barrow Road men would not look forward to working was the 5pm Bristol-York passenger as far as Birmingham New St. This was the return working for the Derby locomotive off the 7.35am Nottingham-Bristol and on too many occasions it was Derby's sole Patriot 45509 *The Derbyshire Yeomanry*. That locomotive had a reputation quite unlike any other and none of the Derby, Saltley and Barrow Road men I have spoken to over the years had a good word for it. The locomotive did not carry any name until 1951 when it was re-allocated from Newton Heath (which received a Jubilee in return) to Derby and named at Derby station. (Also of interest Royal Scot 46112 was named *Sherwood Forester* at a 1949 ceremony at Nottingham). For far too long 45509 lingered at Derby for no logical mechanical reason. Number 45509 would commence a weekday diagram with the 2.35am Derby-Nottingham parcels, then it would stand and provide heat for the carriages forming the 7.35am passenger train to Bristol which it would work throughout. By the time the crew for the 7.35 booked on and located their locomotive the odds would be that the fire was well and truly clinkered and most of the normally relaxed journey to Derby would be spent trying to pull it around. By the time the train reached Tamworth (usually just after 9, see later) the Driver would have requested assistance forward from New Street, hence the comments from Saltley men that the Bristol line relief locomotive was usually called upon daily to assist a locomotive short of steam. On a daily basis I am sure Barrow Road would have dropped the fire in preparation for the return. When 45509 reached Derby it was relieved and went on shed to await its call for the 2.35am.

I also had cause to curse 45509 because for a day at Tamworth the train of choice from Derby was the 8.12 (the 7.35 from Nottingham). The first train my pals and I wanted to see at Tamworth Low Level was the 7.46am from Crewe, known locally as the 9 o'clock stopper and a regular Princess Coronation Class working. The 9 o'clock stopper was actually due away at 8.56am and if the Nottingham train was on time at 8.49 everything was fine. With 45509 we never did see the 9 o'clock stopper!

In September 1958 quiet celebrations were held in offices, canteens and messrooms along the Bristol route as the news passed that 45509 had been re-allocated to Newton Heath depot and was unlikely to trouble anyone again. How ironic that a little later Barrow Road was allocated three of the same class.

Tamworth, with Princess Coronation Class 46240 *City of Coventry* making haste in mid-afternoon with the London Euston bound Royal Scot denoted by its tartan styled headboard. Above the third carriage is the bridge carrying the Midland line between Derby and Birmingham New Street. It was such scenes that daily in school holidays brought hordes of spotters who were obliged to find viewing positions away from the platforms. (*Rail-online*)

The month after 45509 headed to pastures new, disaster in the form of fire engulfed Fell diesel 10100 which was disturbing the peace at Manchester whilst awaiting working the 12.05am departure to Derby/ St Pancras. The oddity was officially withdrawn in November. By November the Britannias were mostly conspicuous by their absence in Works and with poor time-keeping and double heading again at high levels it may not have been pure coincidence that some of the Jubilees still paired with the smaller, 3,500 gallon Fowler tender tenders received the Stanier 4,000 gallon type from 8F 2-8-0s. Not only could time be saved in replenishing water supplies, the Stanier design afforded a more comfortable and slightly less draughty journey for the footplatemen. Little was seen of Royal Scots 46103/33 and newcomers were more in the form of the first few of the twenty 1,200hp diesel electric locomotives being built by Metropolitan, Vickers Electrical Co Ltd at Stockton, the first of which had been delivered to Derby

in July and since joined by others at a rate of one per month. These locomotives worked in pairs on express passenger trains between St Pancras and Manchester (and occasionally on Sheffield/Leeds/Scotland bound services as far as Nottingham or Derby) and singly between Derby and Manchester. Whilst welcome, a maximum permitted speed of 75mph was not going to help pull back the minutes lost, say, north of Leicester. Several of the Class were planned to be required to work in pairs on overnight freight services in each direction between Hendon and Glasgow (of which more later, in 1959) and initial trials commenced in the autumn.

The winter timetable for the Western Division of the London Midland Region gave notice of the need to make allowance for the preparatory work in connection with the electrification over several years of the former LNW routes from Manchester (London Road, later Piccadilly) to London (Euston) via Stoke/Crewe then Stafford and both directly along the Trent Valley to

Rugby and via Wolverhampton/Birmingham/Coventry, thence via Bletchley and Watford to London. A generally applicable introduction of an additional twenty minutes between London and Manchester meant that for the first time it was faster from London to Manchester via Leicester/Derby/Matlock. For anyone keen on studying timetables there was also a service from London (King's Cross) to Sheffield (Victoria) and even with a change of train there, a passenger could be in Manchester sooner than via an equivalent later departure from London (Euston). The important business communities of both London and Manchester would look to British Railways for at least a continuation of a level of service they had enjoyed and therein lay a need for the overall performance of the Midland line to be lifted and then consistently maintained.

Planned Sunday engineering works extending into Monday mornings on the Manchester-Crewe line created an interesting Sunday afternoon service from Manchester (London Road), which was routed via Stoke-on-Trent, Egginton Junction, North Staffs Junction, Stenson Junction, Sheet Stores Junction and then non-stop up the Midland main line to St Pancras. This tortuous journey of four hours and fifty minutes gave an arrival into St Pancras at 10.10pm, and with no catering facility. The train was a Longsight Class 7 locomotive and crew working, a Derby Driver travelling to Stoke to act as Pilotman over the lengthy section forward from there for which the Longsight men were not passed. This working soon attracted attention and in its early weeks brought onto the Midland Britannia 70032, Royal Scot 46111 and Patriot 45536. Such workings would later become a daily event known popularly around the East Midlands as 'the diversion', on which subject there will be more later.

Three other developments are worthy of particular note. Without fanfare or ceremony the first BR Derby built 1,160hp diesel-electric, four axle D5000 had been outshopped in late summer and entered traffic in mid-September on the mid-morning Nottingham-Liverpool passenger service which it worked at least as far as Manchester, returning with the 2.30pm ex-Liverpool.

The new order of things – at least for a while – as a pair of Metrovicks (D5700/1) take what was probably the 4.25pm St Pancras-Manchester North away from Wellingborough, c1960. (*Colour-rail 32368*)

Here is the Fell Developments mechanical marvel 10100 in its final livery of dark green with orange, black, orange, lining and red coupling rods. That dates the picture (taken as the train approaches Belper from the Manchester direction) as 1957/8. The locomotive caught fire at Manchester Central and was withdrawn that same month of October 1958. (*Photographer unknown, Midland Railway Trust collection*)

In autumn construction had begun at BR Derby C&W Works of thirty four-car diesel multiple unit trains for introduction during 1959 on suburban services between St Pancras and Bedford. Track improvements to allow passenger traffic over all four tracks to be available were occupying the Civil Engineer and the capital outlay also included provision for building and equipping a new maintenance facility at Cricklewood.

Finally, and in response to the concerns of the business community, news emerged of new Pullman, high speed diesel unit trains to be operated along the Midland route from St Pancras to Manchester.

At a national level, total passenger traffic receipts for 1958 were within £1m of the comparative (Suez influence) figure for 1957, with improvements month on month between August and the end of the year. The spread of diesel worked services nationally had reached 19 per cent of that for steam. Confirming what all observers had noted, piloting of steam services on the London Midland Region had increased by 25 per cent compared with in 1957. Total receipts for freight were £29.5m less than for 1957 and overall the working deficit for the year was £48.1m compared with £27.2m in 1957. Before the accountants start asking questions, let us move on into 1959.

Chapter Six

1959: A Need to Adapt; the Diesels Arrive, but to No Great Effect

Simplistically, the economic success of a railway depends upon a flow of traffic for which customer payments exceed costs. A railway has a high fixed cost base and once that level of cost has been reached a profit starts to accrue. For British Railways the analysis of performance was generally based upon operating results (that is earnings less the cost of generating those earnings) before the addition of central charges and interest upon capital invested.

As noted for 1957 and 1958 the operating losses had been £27.2m and £48.1m respectively. Whilst a direct comparison between the two years was difficult due to the Suez crisis, it was clear that a decline in economic activity of heavy industry – particularly iron and steel – had largely influenced the drop in freight receipts that accounted for the majority of the working deficit. In categorised areas of freight – coal and coke, and general merchandise – the reduction for BR was worse than general UK economic activity; 8.4 per cent (BR) compared to 7 per cent nationally and 19 per cent (BR)/13 per cent respectively. For the iron and steel industry the railway would feel the effect of the downturn at all three stages of production; raw material flows to steel works, semi-finished product from steel works to centres of industrial production, and finished goods.

Competition from road hauliers was also intensifying and a network of motorways between major centres of population was to be developed. The first 61½ mile section of the M1 linking London and Yorkshire was to be opened in November 1959 and in addition to other planned motorways a network of by-pass roads to avoid city and town centres was to be developed. Some traditional markets for railway traffic had been damaged by the strike in 1955 by some footplate staff, with fresh fish from the East Coast ports a good example of a traffic flow of great interest to road hauliers. There is no doubt that BR was aware of the advances all around them and their responses included a move to containerisation, an extension of freight trains fitted with continuous vacuum brake systems, through organisational changes to allow commercial decisions to be taken at a lower level than hitherto, a drive to improve time-keeping and transit times and cutting variable costs wherever possible. Examples of varied freight operations will follow, but for now there is a relevance in considering a wider perspective.

Political minds were starting to focus on what the future may hold for the railways. The scale of the capital investment programme (the 1955 Modernisation Plan) was such that when interest and central charges were added to the operating deficit the total deficit was £90.1m. It was time for the Modernisation Plan to be reviewed and for variable costs to be cut. The re-appraisal of the Plan was undertaken by the British Transport Commission and the output of that re-appraisal shaped the strategic way forward for the period to the end of 1963. The re-appraisal was published in the form of a Government White Paper and included a reference to the need for a wider consideration of the question of the curtailment of loss producing passenger services. The debate was of national interest and moved into the political arena. In the report the Chairman of the Commission – Sir Brian Robertson – outlined plans to speed up work on the electrification of the Western Division of the London Midland Region lines south of Manchester/Liverpool/Crewe and to include the Wolverhampton/Birmingham/Coventry/Rugby loop within an end timescale (subject to further review) of 1964. Such developments would inevitably impact upon the need for alternative services along the Midland Division route from St Pancras to Manchester. Other proposals with a bearing upon our routes of interest included an intention to virtually eliminate steam traction from the Midland main line south of Leicester, and also in the Bristol area, from 1963 and, as part of a proposed 10 per cent reduction in total route mileage (though without any closure of any main lines), the London Midland Region would propose to close the following:

- Kettering–Cambridge (closed 13 June 59)
- Wellingborough–Higham Ferrers (closed 13 June 59)
- Bedford–Hitchin
- Bedford–Northampton

- Rugby–Wigston (Leicester)
- Uttoxeter–Macclesfield
- Derby (Friargate)–Egginton Junction
- Pinxton–Kimberley East

Note: Monsal Dale station was closed from 10 August 59

On a wider perspective were proposals to:

- introduce a planned reduction in traffic levels along the former Great Central route.
- install new connecting tracks to facilitate new traffic flow routes for iron ore traffic between the Midlands and South Wales steel works.
- increase by 1,300 track miles the total to be controlled by colour light signals.
- extend the automatic warning system (track/ locomotives) to give a total route mileage so covered to 1,800 (excluding the Western Region which had an automatic train control system).
- reduce the fleet of steam locomotives (by 6,000 to 11,500), carriages (by 7,000 to 35,000) and wagons (by 250,000 to 750,000).
- reduce the number of workshops to be retained (by 10, to 22).
- increase the fleet of main line diesel locomotives (to 2,300) diesel multiple units (to 4,000) and a virtual elimination of shunting by steam locomotives.

Someone, somewhere was guarding the £10m set aside in 1955 for steam locomotive developments and following in the footsteps of Dr Piero Crosti and the representative of the Berkley Stoker Corporation came Dr Giesl Gieslingen with a proposal (successful as it turned out) to extend the use of his oblong ejector beyond the Talyllyn Railway and National Coal Board to include a BR Standard locomotive.

The new build programme for 1959 still included steam locomotives from BR Swindon (as the final examples). The number of new main line diesel locomotives in 1959 (excluding any due in 1958, but not completed) was to be 223 of six different types from six private contractors plus BR workshops and 316 shunting locomotives of four different types from seven BR workshops and four private contractors. In parallel BR Doncaster Works had completed the first of a (then) projected total of thirteen 2,500hp electric locomotives (E5000) for use on the Southern Region.

So much for the future, let us return to the reality of 1959 and a review of varied freight operations along the Midland main lines. For some time BR had been developing the idea of conveying containers overnight

between London and Glasgow; the principles being that customers would pack goods up to four tons into one (or more) containers which would then (within a given area/radius) be collected by (BR) road, taken to a railway point, loaded onto a flat-bed wagon, conveyed as a part of a train load overnight, unloaded and delivered by road (BR) to the end customer. The economy of scale of a unit of up to twenty-seven purpose modified wagons (550 tons gross) over a distance of some 400 miles at speeds of up to 75mph, to give a rail journey time of ten hours, would offset the incremental time/ cost of the extra handling compared with a road haulier. The appeal of such a service for time sensitive perishable goods became the thrust of the marketing initiative.

From an operational perspective this would be the longest non-stop run (301 miles from Hendon to Carlisle) of any BR freight train and was planned to be worked by pairs of the new Metrovick 1200hp locomotives. Trials had been arranged for autumn 1958 and these having proven the arrangements the new service was to commence in each direction over the night of 15/16 March 59. In addition to the wagons – fitted with roller bearings – the trains conveyed a three-axle van for the Guard and would rejoice in the name *Condor*.

The crewing of the locomotives predominantly involved Kingmoor (Carlisle) men who would complete two round trips a week for 1,200 nocturnal miles to/ from Hendon. Kingmoor men (Driver and 'Fireman') also worked the Carlisle – Glasgow Gushetfaulds leg, though sometimes Polmadie (Glasgow) men had a turn. When not on the *Condor* they could find themselves on various steam turns including the infinitely more challenging runs over the Settle and Carlisle and up and over Beattock Summit. In the event of a failure of the diesel locomotives the provision required two Class 5 power steam locomotives to be used throughout and a failure of one diesel required a Class 5 to be placed between the functioning diesel and the train. The need for a total steam substitution first arose on 8 April, from Dent through to Hendon. Thereafter, the use of steam continued from time to time and if the load on the night was less taxing the use of one locomotive would be authorised. From the South the train ran Mondays to Friday nights (departing 7.23pm, due Glasgow 5.15am in time for the markets) and Southbound on Mondays to Thursdays (7.50pm/5.40am) and Sundays (7.35pm/5.40am).

It took some time for customers to come forward to use the new service. Whilst loadings fell away (particularly during the Glasgow Fair season) for a while, the service eventually became very successful and benefitted from the conveyance of traffic brought over from Continental Europe via Transfesa wagon loads to South London. The *Condor* brand name was also used on a similar venture between Birmingham and Glasgow, though the concept was overtaken from 1964 and *Condor* named services withdrawn.

Having recorded the most advanced form of freight handling on offer from BR, the balance of perspective can be restored by reference to operations elsewhere which were towards the other end of the spectrum.

The majority of freight trains were loose coupled, slow moving between yards (for example Wichnor to Rowsley), between points of origination and end users (for example colliery to power station) or as local trips (for example Derby to Wirksworth). The ownership of yards could be traced back to the original owning company (in the case of this book mainly the Midland Railway) with movements between them perpetuated via exchange sidings where wagons from individual owning companies would be segregated and sent on their way. Similarly the workings from motive power

depots could be traced back and over many parts of BR things generally had not changed a lot over forty years or more. Rowsley yard and motive power depot between Matlock and Bakewell in rural Derbyshire provides a good example of how traffic was worked. Facilitated by its policy of connecting its networks, the Midland Railway had a route out of the Erewash Valley (via Condor Park, Crich Junction and the newly opened triangular station at Ambergate from 1876) to the Derby to Manchester line through the Peak District to the lucrative industrial and domestic markets of Lancashire. The coal mined in Lancashire was bituminous and whilst ideal for certain applications there was a demand for other types for use at the cotton mills, chemical works, engineering works and locomotive fuel and for domestic consumption. Add to that raw materials such as iron ore and limestone and finished products for export from Liverpool (Manchester via the Ship Canal from 1894) and the potential for the Midland Railway will become evident. In 1877 an extensive yard was developed at Rowsley for receiving Southbound

A favoured location for photographers was Duffield, 5 miles north of Derby. On this occasion the photographer was in position early in the morning for the 7.40am seven non-corridor carriage train from Bakewell to Derby hauled by smartly turned out Fairburn tank 42053 of Rowsley shed. Note in particular the immaculately maintained shoulder of ballast. (*Rail-online*)

traffic. Additionally for Northbound traffic, fourteen dead end sidings were laid and into which were placed wagons initially sorted into trains for individual railway companies (for example the Lancashire and Yorkshire, the London and North Western Railway) as well as for the Midland. To provide motive power the facilities for locomotives were greatly enhanced and from 1878 the railway community of part of Rowsley was very much in business; a burgeoning business at that and one which provided a better living wage for those employed than that for the alternative, steady state employments of quarrying and farm labouring on the estates of the Dukes of Rutland and Devonshire plus others. Over a period of thirty years the small village of Rowsley grew threefold in terms of population.

The motive power depot at Rowsley had been further developed in 1926 to accommodate up to fifty-nine locomotives (up to twenty-four inside the covered straight building) and that maximum was reached during the Second World War; Rowsley in rural Derbyshire was judged a less probable target for

bombing and, therefore, was used more extensively for marshalling, crewing and despatching trains. Following the end of the war, the yards were further developed and could accommodate 1,545 wagons.

Some 12,000 wagons were received, marshalled, sorted and sent on their way each week. Unsurprisingly the destinations of Northbound traffic were dominated by the needs of industrial Greater Manchester and Lancashire; Gowhole (exchange sidings near Buxworth), Buxton, Brindle Heath, Stockport, Longsight, Belle Vue, Heaton Mersey, Phillips Park, Warrington, St Helens and further west to Edge Hill and the docks at Garston. Additionally there were departures and arrivals also from London (Somers Town/Brent), Birmingham (Washwood Heath), Wichnor Junction (between Burton on Trent and Tamworth) and Derby (including timber for the steam winding engines along the Cromford and High Peak section). Loaded trains also passed through without calling into the yard; these being from Chesterfield, Codnor Park and Derby directions, including heavy trains of iron ore for Garston

When the Compounds were withdrawn one of the successors in title to the passenger services was Fairburn 2-6-4 tank 42228. Here it is drawing stock into the up platform at Darley Dale. Evidently the Fireman did not believe in temporary placement of a headlamp. (*Photographer unknown, Midland Railway Trust collection*)

and output from the coal mines of Nottinghamshire. Rowsley had only two passenger trains for which they were required to provide power; the 6.25am Darley Dale- Nottingham and 7.40am Bakewell-Derby (plus a Saturdays Only train popular with followers of Derby County).

The number of locomotives allocated to Rowsley depot at 1959 totalled fifty-one and included classes deployed on shunting the yards, for use on the Cromford and High Peak section, for the two passenger train services and for assisting freight trains up the demanding gradient to Peak Forest. That left seven Class 6P/5F Crabs, five Class 8F and 20 Class 4F (plus two aged 2F tender locomotives which worked 'pick up' freight services generally to Derby).

In a continuous 24 hour operation Northbound departures totalled around twenty-five and Southbound a dozen. Of the Northbound departures around 20 per cent had at least a proportion of the total number of the vehicles fitted with continuous vacuum brake equipment and 75 per cent required an assisting engine in the rear as far as Peak Forest (summit). In addition some Northbound 'through' trains also needed assisting with either a pilot locomotive or at the rear. For the operators the seven Crabs and five 8Fs were gold dust. However, the Crabs were assigned generally to the two London trains (a two-day cycle) and just five 8Fs was about a dozen too few. What was needed was either more 8Fs or mixed traffic Class 5 (either LMS or BR Standard types), but as has been explained earlier in this book, Class 5s as available were required to assist timekeeping of express passenger trains. So ... much of the freight work was entrusted to the 4Fs with 3F assistance and the limestone walls echoed to the Derby roar as the men in the Heaton Mersey link earned their money the hard way. Apart from three short sections totalling roundly 1,000 yards the 14 miles from Rowsley to the summit had an adverse gradient of at best 1 in 100/102 and at worst, 3 miles at 1 in 90, including six tunnels. Returning south, the challenge for the men and their locomotive was even more demanding; 16 hard miles from Cheadle Heath, seven being at 1 in 90/91 and the acrid Disley Tunnel at a continuous 1 in 132. Tell those men about the glamour of steam and they will tell you another story or two.

Loads for freight trains with particular motive power classifications were prescribed in a Loads Book (similar to that explained earlier for XL and Special Limit passenger trains), but it seems a reasonable bet that whomsoever authorised the content for 4Fs did not fully appreciate the characteristics of the Rowsley-Cheadle Heath section. Northbound, forty-four minutes were allowed (start to pass) Rowsley Down Sidings to Peak Forest North with a Class D freight (partly fitted) and fifty-six minutes Southbound (start to pass) Cheadle Heath South Junction to Peak Forest North. These timings were frequently exceeded due to any one or several factors including railhead conditions. Ideally 4Fs would not be allocated to Class D freights, but idealism had no place.

The management were of course alerted by poor timekeeping and consequences arising. For example, if the 12.50am to Ardwick endured a poor run up the hill, the following 1.10am to Walton would suffer, similarly the 2.50am Brindle Heath followed by the 3.05am Heaton Mersey or, later in the morning (when parcels/passenger trains were around) the 9.16am Ancoats followed only five minutes later by the 'through' Agecroft. Trials were arranged and resulting from them, the loadings for a Class D with a 4F were reduced by two loaded wagons to twenty-six Northbound and twenty-four Southbound.

At that time Rowsley had 125 or so men passed to drive and had a similar number of Firemen, organised into four links; passenger, London, Heaton Mersey and Birmingham plus four other links. I 'take off my hat' to every one of them.

As at 1959, two-thirds of the original 33 miles of the C&HPR remained intact, from High Peak Junction (between Ambergate and Cromford) to Harpur Hill. Those 22 miles included three inclines; Sheep Pasture (this having been formed in 1857 between Sheep Pasture and Cromford), Middleton and Hopton, the first two of which were inclined plains involving endless chains and the latter was more conventional. The statistics concerning these inclines are remarkable when considering that main line four-wheel wagon loads of traffic were being handled.

Incline name	Gradient: 1 in _	Length of gradient yards	Method of operation	Power
Sheep Pasture	9 to 8	1,320	Endless chain	Winding
Middleton	8.25	770	Endless chain	Beam engine (1825)
Hopton	20 to 14	200	Conventional	Locomotives (two)

Over a route distance of 5 miles the line climbed over 1,000 feet. For the conventional incline at Hopton two locomotives were necessary and the load upgrade was restricted to five wagons plus a brakevan.

In this generally inaccessible area, the main traffic was limestone from Hopton, Hoptonwood, Middleton and Longcliffe quarries, firebricks and building bricks from Friden plus local produce and, perhaps strangely for an area characterised by above average rainfall, water for domestic use at hamlets along the route and by the locomotives working the various sections.

For working purposes, the line was in two sections. The first section was from High Peak Junction to beyond Friden worked by locomotives sub-shedded (from Rowsley) at Cromford Wharf/Yard (one), Sheep Pasture (one) and Middleton (two), the latter because of the need for two locomotives on the Hopton incline. The other section – between Parsley Hay to near Harpur Hill – formed part of the Ashbourne to Buxton 'main line' (the C&HP having been leased in 1861 to the London and North Western Railway for 999 years, with complete amalgamation from 1887) still worked by locomotives from Buxton with roots back to the L&NWR days.

Between Middleton Top and Friden there was (in 1959) one train a day (Monday to Friday); the pilot locomotive being detached at Hopton Top to shunt the quarry sidings in the area whilst the train locomotive took the train forward with stops to shunt and add/detach wagons as necessary prior to arrival at Friden. At Friden the train was taken forward by a 'main line' locomotive to Buxton. At that time there were three weekday freight trains between Buxton and Ashbourne. The C&HPR train locomotive then returned from Friden with wagons ex-main line train and again after shunting/adding/detaching, joined up at Hopton Top with the morning's pilot locomotive for the return to Middleton Top. On Saturdays the arrangement was amended to allow the C&HPR train locomotive to work through to Parsley Hay where traffic for Ashbourne was taken forward by a train from Buxton along the 'main line'. As water capacity of the locomotive along the C&HPR was low additional supplies were available from tanks at Longcliffe. The 11 miles from Old Harpur to Ladmanlow were closed to traffic in 1954.

Locomotives in use in March 1959 were sub-shedded from Rowsley (to which they were returned for washouts of boilers and maintenance) and at that time one of the former North London Railway 0-6-0 tank locomotives survived (58850). For many years, four such locomotives had been the mainstay of the fleet but relatively recent withdrawals had seen 58862 (1956) and 58856/62 (1957)

replaced. Number 58850 was withdrawn in September 1960, but at the time of interest was supplemented by one Kitson built 0-4-0 (47007 at Sheep Pasture) and any of the J94 0-6-0 tank locomotives (68006/13/30/34) at Cromford and Middleton Top, whilst others were being attended to at Rowsley. (Refer also to The Human Element regarding the J94s.)

Bank Holiday weekends in the spring/summer and the local tradition of dressing (flower pageantry) wells brought visitors and interest from far and wide to the 'main line'. Over the weekend of 9 and 10 May 1959 an excursion was run on the Saturday from Derby (Friargate) via Tutbury and Uttoxeter to Ashbourne and thence to Thorp Cloud and Tissington and on the following day an excursion went through from Derby (Midland) to Buxton, calling at all stations from Ashbourne. In what was an attractive area for walkers, ramblers and hikers seeking to flee the industrial cities and towns the area was a traditional destination for special trains from Stockport, Manchester, Nottinghamshire and Leeds/Bradford. At that time there were many who wished to commemorate the freedom to roam mass trespass that had occurred in April 1932.

The C&HPR was an anachronism. Assets depreciated by 1860, plant and equipment made to last, low track maintenance costs, inaccessible to road competition … Conjure if you will with economic methods of working, reason for the railways operating deficit and profitability of wagon load traffic!

In more populated areas than the White Peak wagon load and part wagon load traffic enjoyed by the railways almost as a perceived right was coming under increasing commercial pressure from road hauliers. There was also some 'cherry picking' in that haulage contracts won by road often resulted in the less attractive flows being passed by the hauliers onto the railways which were obliged to accept such as a common carrier. All the more necessary then for the railways to secure and develop bulk trainload coal and mineral traffic. The development by the Central Electricity Generating Board of its network of coal-fired power stations surely presented an opportunity for the customer (CEGB) and supplier (Coal Board and BR) to work together to produce and implement better logistical arrangements. Amongst the power stations being developed were Willington A (1957), Castle Donington and Hams Hall C (1958) and Drakelow B (1959), all being within 20–40 miles of the Erewash Valley. Apart from the continuing tendency of the National Coal Board to use railway wagons as a storage facility and the highest priority for short supply vacuum braked fitted wagons being assigned to other routes, the third part of the planning – the layout of railway facilities being installed at new power stations – did not show any visible signs of progress. So, each weekday around eight to ten, loose-coupled coal trains would make their way along the route from Kirkby and Toton towards Birmingham (Washwood Heath) where, between Stenson Junction and Kingsbury (excepting Burton, sidings at Wichnor and a loop at Elford), the route was characterised by two tracks only. Willington was served by trips out of Denby (Ripley branch) worked by Derby locomotives and men. The scope for improvements was vast.

To round off this review of some freight operations reference can be made to two interesting workings through Market Harborough, though not involving the Midland line. During 1959 a new service brought a Doncaster based 9F along the GN/LNW joint line from Bottesford with a Wednesdays and Saturdays excepted train, 10.36am from Rossington to Willesden (North London). There was no booked return working for the locomotive, but there was a Willesden-Colwick (Nottingham) empty wagon train which was used, replacing the need on occasions to use the Colwick locomotive that brought in a train to Welham Junction (east of Market Harborough on the GN/LNW joint line) or vice versa, depending upon timescales and operational requirements.

So there we have it; the new of *Condor*, the old but still functional in a rural community setting Cromford and High Peak, the uneconomic movement of train load freight nearly everywhere, the huge opportunity for the CEGB/NCB/BR to work together to good future effect and competition intensifying. The one thing that was inevitable was something that the railways had not seen a lot of since 1948 … and that was change, massive change.

Returning now to our mainstream considerations along our lines of route, the early months of 1959 provided evidence of change starting to take effect. Passenger trains between St Pancras and Manchester were hauled turn and turn about by either steam or diesel locomotives, the latter generally in pairs and of one of two types; the 1,200hp Metrovicks which continued to be delivered at a rate of one per month and early examples of the BR Derby built 1,160hp (D50XX) series (which were destined for the Southern Region and for the Western Division of the LM Region.) On occasions it would be a combination of steam plus diesel. How many diagrams, how many Drivers/ Instructors/Inspectors/Passed Firemen at each depot to be trained on different forms of new traction, what contingency plans needed to be in place … the challenge. The disposal/stabling/preparation/examination/fuelling/

maintenance of diesel locomotives at steam locomotive depots with ash, coal dust and soot ever present was less than ideal. There was, of course, no history upon which to base a prediction of the level of consumable spares to be held, let alone capital spares such as main generators and any failure would need to be considered against a potential warranty claim on the manufacturer. And then there was the weather.

Local passenger services from Bedford to Northampton and Hitchin had been identified as being ideal for diesel unit operation. However, snow and ice in early 1959 saw a reversion to steam and two locomotives brought in from Skipton to act as 'stand-by'. It was not a case of any locomotive will do and problems with the new technology continued throughout most of the year before new BR Derby and Metro-Cammell diesel multiple units allowed some stability to be found.

In February the Northampton-Market Harborough line reached its centenary.

Spring 1959 cannot be allowed to pass without a reference to football special traffic. The early months in each year always included keeping an eye on Saturday football fixtures and particularly for the then very popular annual Football Association Cup knock-out competition. In that competition teams who were not in the main League could enter and progress to the point when the League teams would enter the competition. By the first Saturday in January sixty-four teams were in 'the draw' and by luck a non-League side could find itself playing a team such as Liverpool or Arsenal. Successive 'Rounds' at three weekly intervals would reduce the number of teams to 32/16/8/4/2 at which point the FA Cup Final would take place at Wembley in early May. In 1959 two teams along one of our routes – Nottingham Forest and Luton Town – reached the Final. Nottingham Forest – the eventual winners – were drawn in the third Round to play away at Tooting and Mitcham F.C. and by all accounts were fortunate to draw 2-2. Having won the replay and then beaten Grimsby Town, a fifth Round match at Birmingham on 14 February was next. Ten special trains ran, the four routed via Derby (Friargate) having B1s and the others having either Black 5s or Crab 2-6-0s. Two replays were required prior to the sixth Round match at home to Bolton Wanderers. That produced (on 28 February) four Newton Heath allocated Black 5s, all of which worked through and interesting though that was the real interest of the day was heading through Nottingham and along the Erewash Valley.

In fact the 1959 cup ties had not produced for the Midlands anything particularly outstanding. On 28 February that all changed. Norwich City of the lowly

FA Cup Final day, 2 May 1959 and a need to transport thousands of supporters of Nottingham Forest to Wembley. In addition to six Midland lines timetabled services, twenty-three specials were run and of that total seven went either via Trent and Leicester or via Edwalton to Kettering and thence (with the flow enhanced by specials from Luton) to St Pancras. Royal Scot 46158 (*The Loyal Regiment*) had charge of one of the trains and is seen shortly after leaving Nottingham near West Bridgford. (*Science Museum/National Railway Museum LMS 741*)

Third Division (South) was having a run of success that was beyond the realms of probability with wins against Manchester United, Cardiff City and Tottenham Hotspur. For their match at Sheffield (United) four Norwich B1s and one borrowed from Cambridge brought through excursions routed via Peterborough (East), Stamford, Melton Mowbray, Nottingham and the Erewash Valley via Trowell. Seven more trains were routed via Tuxford and Retford (six with K3s). In celebration I purchased a copy of the Ian Allan *Eastern Region* book. Norwich City continued to find unlikely success and following success in the replay, was drawn to face Luton Town in the semi-final at White Hart Lane, London. Following yet another draw the few supporters of Norwich City who were not by then penniless travelled to Birmingham the following Wednesday on five specials routed via Peterborough (East), Market Harborough, Rugby and Coventry again with Eastern Region B1s throughout. From Luton came more familiar motive power in the form of Black 5s. Luck ran against Norwich and so it was Luton Town that faced Nottingham Forest (who had beaten Aston Villa in the other semi-final) on 2 May 1959.

For the F.A. Cup Final, twenty-three specials and six ordinary trains ran from Nottingham and its surrounding districts; thirteen specials along the Great Central route, three via Grantham to King's Cross, seven via the Midland line plus the six ordinary trains to St Pancras. Motive power was sixteen B1s, three Royal Scots and two Jubilees with the rest in the hands of Black 5s. On such days motive power and stock would be specially arranged; in this case Immingham and Saltley locomotives transferred. Nottingham Forest 2, Luton Town 1.

On such days change was effectively disguised or, for the myopic, unlikely to disturb matters too

Awaiting their assured fate and at Chellaston Junction near Derby on 9 June 1960 are some of the eighty or so locomotives similarly positioned around Derby. 41857 43241/584/881/939 58065 42341. (*Kidderminster Railway Museum 018715, Courtesy W. Potter*)

much. But close to Nottingham change was palpably demonstrable. Within a two mile radius of Derby station the total number of stored and condemned steam locomotives had reached eighty; standing variously at St Andrew's Yard, Spondon Junction (Chaddesden line), in Chaddesden sidings, alongside the Birmingham line towards Pear Tree and around the Locomotive Works yard. Amongst them was 2F 0-6-0 58246 the last surviving Johnson Midland round-top firebox example complete with Salter safety valves. Whilst all of the locomotive types were locally familiar, new to many though only briefly was a sad procession of ex-Lancashire and Yorkshire Railway 2-4-2 locomotives, eight of which were cut up at the yard of Albert Looms Ltd., Spondon. Two locomotives of this Class (50646/50) had been used in 1956 on Wellingborough-Higham Ferrers trains.

Quietly sidelined at Wellingborough awaiting a decision on the retention or removal of the Crosti equipment were half of the locomotives so fitted.

One steam locomotive that could have been amongst the eighty was, however, seeing out its time in fine style. Compound 41157 which was a familiar sight on the Manchester-Derby line had been re-allocated in summer 1958 from Trafford Park to Lancaster (Green Ayre). There, its duties included a two-day diagram which took it to Leeds and may well have included the booked Leeds-Bradford final leg of *The Devonian*. Having been returned to Trafford Park it found itself as that shed's final Compound on duties to Derby/ Sheffield, before being spotted at Lincoln in January 1959. A few days later it worked the 7.45am Worcester to York passenger train as far as Sheffield. In the spring it was used between Birmingham and Ashchurch and Evesham before a final fling as a pilot on St Pancras services from Derby. In its final year it remained working from Derby and was condemned in May 1960 owing no one anything.

After the efforts of 1958 to secure for Midland main line services additional power Class 7 locomotives, to reduce the incidence of double heading and the dependency upon 4-4-0s rather than 4-6-0s for such pilot duties, it is appropriate to review the motive power position. Taking the five main depots (Kentish Town 14B, Trafford Park 9E, Derby 17A, Millhouses 41C and Holbeck 55A) over the period January 1958 to the very end of 1959 and by

Who would have thought that this was once a front line, express passenger train locomotive of a type referred to as Crimson (Lake) Ramblers? Sadly down at heel and long past its glory days, Compound 41157 with a local stopping service to either Sheffield or Manchester. Date unknown, but prior to its withdrawal in 1960 the locomotive did enjoy something of an echo of better times; the text of the Chapter for that year includes full details. (Photographer unknown)

adding the totals of classes 5, 6 and 7 at each depot at January 1958, 1959 and at the very end of 1959 gives totals of 138, 139 and 136 respectively; Class 7 only fourteen, sixteen and twenty-three respectively. Over the same period the totals of 4-4-0s was reduced by twenty-six, 14B seeing a net reduction of eight, 9E three, 17A eight, 41C three and 55A four. There was also some re-distribution of locomotives with 17A ending 1959 with eleven Jubilees (plus six for the year), but a reduction in Class 5s (minus thirteen), allowing more trains than previously to be single headed whilst being expected to maintain the timetable. Taking specific dates carries with it an inherent danger of missing significant variations in the interim. That was the case in 1959 and in particular affected Kentish Town. During the year there were five instances of Royal Scot Class 7 locomotives being re-allocated, but staying for periods no longer than three months.

46130 in February and again October, out May and December
46148 in March, out May
46154 in May, out July
46158 in May, out July

Note: 46160, 46139 and 46140 arrived in October, November and December respectively.

The review for 1959 also needs to record that diesel developments elsewhere on the LM Region allowed in November the allocation to Nottingham of four Royal Scots and one Patriot Class 7. This included the locomotive *Royal Scot* itself which was given special attention by the Cleaners whilst each of the newcomers assumed a well-cared-for appearance. Those arrivals further lifted the stock of Class 7 power along the line

This is the first of two pictures taken of Jubilee 45615 *Malay States* and included to show how quickly the external condition of working steam locomotives could deteriorate. In this picture the locomotive is shown on a June day in 1959 having just emerged from Great Rocks tunnel. At that time the locomotive had just been re-allocated from Kentish Town and away from the Midland lines, to Newton Heath, Manchester. (*E.R. Morten 363/2, Courtesy J. Suter*)

Poor availability of the Britannia Class locomotives resulted in 45615 being retained for much of the summer. However, by 10 August 1959 it was clear that the Cleaners at Kentish Town no longer had a responsibility for the locomotive and the effect is self-evident as it approaches Miller's Dale. (*E.R. Morten 371/7, Courtesy J. Suter*)

from twenty-three to twenty-eight; the Midland main line had never had it so good.

It is possible that the short-term allocations were to cover for planned non-availability of Britannias, but given the difficulties being experienced concurrently by the Western Division of the LM Region 'possible' could easily have been 'probable'.

During the course of 1959 the total number of type 2 (and later type 4 2,300hp) diesels increased. This resulted from the delivery of Metrovick 1,200hp and BR/Sulzer 1,160hp as follows; a gradual process that led to particular turns being used for crew familiarity (for example one daily return St Pancras to Manchester trip increasing to three, Derby to York, Derby to St Pancras ...) as well as assignment daily of two pairs of Metrovicks to Condor freight duties. The deliveries were:

Metrovick 1,200hp		BR/Sulzer 1,160hp			
D5700	8/58	D5000	9/58)		2/59
D5701	9/58	D5001	11/58)		2/59
D5702	10/58	D5002	12/58)		1/59
D5703	11/58	D5003	12/58)		2/59
D5704	11/58	D5004	12/58)		2/59
D5705	12/58	D5005	1/59)		2/59
D5706	12/58	D5006	1/59)		2/59
D5707	12/58	D5007	1/59)		4/59
D5708	1/59	D5008	3/59) all to		4/59*
D5709	1/59	D5009	3/59) Southern		4/59
D5710	2/59	D5010	3/59) Region		4/59
D5711	2/59	D5011	4/59)		5/59
D5712	3/59	D5012	4/59)		5/59
D5713	3/59	D5013	4/59)		5/59
D5714	3/59	D5014	5/59)		5/59
D5715	4/59	D5015	6/59)		6/59
D5716	6/59	D5016	6/59) all to		6/59
D5717	6/59	D5017	6/59) Crewe		6/59
D5718	7/59	D5018	7/59) South		10/59
D5719	10/59ø	D5019	7/59)		10/59

Ø D5719 awaiting components   * loaned to Toton in 5/59 then to 17A in 10/59

BR/Sulzer 2,300hp

D1	9/59
D2	10/59 (experimentally uprated to 2,500 hp)
D3	10/59
D4	10/59
D5	11/59
D6	12/59
D7	12/59

Additionally it needs to be recorded that the first of a production batch of four car diesel multiple units destined for St Pancras to Bedford services started to emerge from BR Derby Carriage and Wagon Works.

Much of this Chapter has been concerned with the developments along the Midland main lines from St Pancras and therefore there has been little mention of the cross country route between Leeds/Sheffield and Bristol. In fact, little changed. Barrow Road 82E had received in late 1958 three Patriot 4-6-0s in original form and, except for a few weeks in February/March, these worked turn and turn about with the Jubilees (the fleet being reduced by one, 45663, which was re-allocated to Derby in 1958) and together with four BR Standard Class 5s continued throughout 1959. The three 2Ps continued to see action as did Gloucester's Compound 41123 as a pilot engine.

The 12.48pm York to Bristol train became a train to watch out for as this produced on occasions an Eastern Region B1 working throughout.

The growing number of diesels did not affect workings west of Birmingham, although the 8.05am (7.40 ex Kings Norton) Newcastle train became in May/June a useful out and home turn from Derby to York for pairs of BR/Sulzer type 2s. Which leads us in to a consideration of aspects of the summer timetable arrangements.

The Sutton Coldfield to Stirling overnight car-sleeper service had proved to be popular in 1958 and with bookings for the 1959 season being healthy the decision was taken to increase the maximum number of cars to be conveyed from eighteen to twenty-four. This gave a train of six passenger carriages plus up to ten car carrying vehicles which was still well within the capability of an Aston Class 6 which was due to work through to Carlisle. It was motive power for the return working that seemed to cause problems; mid-June saw Carlisle Kingmoor Jubilees and a Clan working throughout and as the season progressed almost any available Class 5 or 6 4-6-0 from any depot between Aston and Carlisle could be deployed, with an additional possibility of Class 7 power Southbound.

The summer season proper again brought forth 9Fs in large numbers to assist on passenger trains. By this third summer of such activity the pattern was well established and along our routes of interest only really unpredictable south of Leicester. On successive Saturdays 1, 8 and 15 August the totals seen at work on trains originating at and through Derby was eight, eight and ten respectively. For example on the 15th:

92102 9.20am Filey–Kings Norton
92114 Relief Sheffield–Bristol
92138 12.00 Scarborough–Kings Norton
92152 7.30am Newcastle–Paignton
92155 7.45am Paignton–Newcastle
92157 12.00 Leeds–Bristol

During the daytime on that date seven of the Bristol Jubilees were hard at work together with two of the Patriots and BR Standard Class 5s and on such days along the cross country route it seemed as though change was something of vague interest only to others elsewhere. It seemed that way also north of Derby where the Midland line to Manchester and Sheffield (via Ambergate) swelled the volume of traffic; the only real surprise was a pair of Metrovicks on the 4.25pm St Pancras–Manchester. Had

The restoration of Compound 1000 and its availability for hauling special trains necessitated positioning moves from and back to Derby. Here it is heading for St Pancras with Jubilee 45569. (*G. Morris*)

I been observing that month at say Leicester it would have been a different picture that emerged. For the August Bank Holiday Saturday there was a concentration of available type 2 diesels in pairs and singly on passenger trains to/from St Pancras to Derby/Nottingham, plus the use as relief trains of some of the four car diesel multiple units (ex-Derby Works) in pairs to Leicester/Nottingham/Derby. On a Saturday there was a Leicester to Nottingham passenger train that could catch out unwary passengers and delight platform staff of a certain disposition when faced with impolite enquiries. 'This is the Nottingham train?', 'Yes, it's going to Nottingham, sir'. And it did via Market Harborough, Northampton, Wellingborough, Kettering and Melton Mowbray! The incidence of double heading was consequently much reduced and with it the need for 4-4-0s. In fact the preserved and restored in Midland Railway livery Compound 1000 made its first trial run from Derby on the 13th whilst at the far end of the spectrum sister locomotive 41101 painted yellow, red and black in the colours of the *Daily Mirror* newspaper (for an ill-advised Manchester-Blackpool sponsored excursion) arrived at Derby for prompt scrapping.

Apart from the appearance on some Summer Saturdays of a Southern Region Standard Class 5 at, or north of, Birmingham the stand-out item of interest that summer was one witnessed by very few people. In the early hours of 25 August, Jubilee 45585 plus two coaches and a track condition recording coach worked a high speed test train between St Pancras and Manchester Central. The train was timed to pass through Leicester in eighty-four minutes (99 miles), Derby in under two hours and reach Manchester in three hours and a quarter. The return was made in the early hours of the 26th August with a schedule of three hours ten minutes. The reason for these runs was part of the planning for the introduction of a high speed diesel service for business travellers from Manchester. The preparatory work for electrification of the former L&NW routes from Manchester (London Road) to London (Euston) via Crewe (and via Stoke) had resulted in a deceleration of all passenger services. That was of concern to the business community at each end of the route which was well represented by the Chambers of Commerce. Through the 1950s there had been an excellent dining car service, at 7.55am from Euston

A month prior to introduction into revenue earning service the two six-car *Midland Pullman* units were undergoing regular training runs for staff. Here one of the units, complete with traditional oil tail lamp, is heading under the fine signal gantry at Derby Station North and will shortly pass over Five Arches bridge. (*Kidderminster Railway Museum 018717, Courtesy W. Potter*)

to reach Manchester (with a portion also to Liverpool from Crewe) in three and three quarter hours – *The Lancastrian*. Coming up, the morning service from Manchester – *The Mancunian* – departed at 9.45am, ran non-stop with an arrival in Euston at 1.05pm. A second service from Euston departed at 9.45am – *The Comet* – due into Manchester at 1.15pm. The return journeys from Manchester were at 4.10pm and 5.35pm and from Euston at 5.40pm. Each of these principal expresses conveyed two restaurant cars and *The Mancunian* conveyed two kitchen cars (one a kitchen occupying the entire length of the carriage and the other offering space for diners). The deceleration of these services by up to forty-three minutes (public timetable) did not go down well with the business community and with the electrification through to Euston expected to need five years to completion, they looked to the British Transport Commission for a response.

The response was in the form of diesel units (two) offering a projected journey time of just over three hours to Pullman standards of catering with meals to

be served at all 132 seats in the six, air conditioned, double-glazed windows, carriages equipped with a Public Address System. The service would be first class only and in the morning would leave from Manchester (Central), call to pick up at Cheadle Heath and then run non-stop to St Pancras, with a return service in the early evening. Each unit was effectively two identical halves and were to be built at the Saltley (Birmingham) works of Metro-Cammell Ltd with an expectation of entry into service in autumn 1959, in time for the winter timetable changes. The build programme slipped and testing locally commenced in October and then, extended to include Derby to Luton and return, with a sixty-two minute timing between Leicester and Luton.

The main feature of interest in the winter timetable was the diversion from the L&NW route to part of the Midland route of several additional passenger trains. These followed the normal route to Stoke-on-Trent, but then diverted via Uttoxeter to North Staffs Junction, Stenson Junction, Sheet Stores Junction and then along the Midland route via Leicester to St Pancras with a

In early 1959 at Nottingham Midland the changeover from steam to diesel is apparent as Class A5 tank 69820 sees out its remaining time between Lincoln and Derby whilst a new diesel railcar awaits its next duty. B1 61142 has the Birmingham–Cleethorpes express. (*Science Museum/National Railway Museum*)

Pilotman (from Derby) conducting the Driver from Stoke. On weekdays the trains involved were the noon and 11.58pm from Manchester (London Road) and on Sundays the 9.40am and 1.55pm services. In the return direction the weekday trains were the 1.55pm (to London Road) and 1am St Pancras to Manchester (Central) and on Sundays the 10.35am and 5.25pm which were routed into Manchester Central (to enable track possessions to be undisturbed).

By far the most watched train in the Derby and Leicester areas was the 1.55pm Sunday Southbound train which became known locally simply as 'the diversion' and generally produced a Longsight depot Britannia. Probably only staff saw it, but the 1am from St Pancras was actually routed via Derby and then non-stop to Manchester Central, due 5.24 am.

Elsewhere in timetable changes, early examples of the BR Derby built four-car diesel multiple units had begun off-peak service running from 28 September between Bedford and St Pancras. Full service introduction was due to commence on 4 January 1960 and the fleet was to total thirty units. The timetable as projected and anticipated showed 44 services daily between Bedford (30), Luton 88 (50), St Albans 100 (79), Elstree 45 (30) and St Pancras.

Further north and from 2 November diesel multiple units replaced steam on local services between Sheffield (Midland) and Nottingham (Midland) via Chesterfield. On the same date the services along the Oxford-Bletchley-Bedford-Cambridge route were re-organised and became worked by BR Derby lightweight twin-car units. During the year Napsbury and Ampthill stations were closed.

In what was a year of exceptional levels of interest, I am conscious that the cross country route has received scant attention. It is possible that some items of interest may be found recorded separately in the 'You'll Never Believe .....' Chapter.

Chapter Seven

1960: Change Proves to be Difficult

The planned introduction from January 1960 of a completely re-cast timetable for services between St Pancras and Bedford was reliant upon completion of preparatory works and the availability of a new fleet of diesel multiple unit trains.

There was an operational requirement for the working of passenger trains on the up goods lines between Bedford and Harpenden and for passengers to be able to join/alight from new platforms at Flitwick, Harlington, Leagrave and Luton. Further, the timetable called for higher speeds between stations along the former goods lines, requiring re-ballasting and drainage works. The Civil Engineer had completed those works, as had the Signal and Telecommunications Engineer to meet the required arrangements. The first of a production batch of thirty four-car diesel units had emerged in May 1959 from BR Derby Carriage and Wagon Works and been sent to Cricklewood to enable Driver training. From 28 September up to eight units had been in use on certain off-peak services. A new maintenance facility at Cricklewood was being built/staffed.

The diesel units were of steel construction and each consisted of two vehicles equipped with two Rolls Royce eight-cylinder engines developing 238hp plus two intermediate trailing cars one only of which had a lavatory facility. There were no gangways between the vehicles. Seating was provided for up to 350 passengers and access to the 'open' seating area was via multiple side doors; a similar arrangement for access/egress to that currently applying to steam hauled suburban coaching stock sets.

The flows of varying traffic between Bedford and St Pancras would be a challenge, particularly to co-ordinate movement of loose coupled, partially (vacuum brake) fitted and fully fitted freight trains with the diesel units along the former dedicated goods lines and the need also for the 'fast' lines to be just that. Revisions to express train timetables were minimal, with the one of significance being the re-timing of the down *Robin Hood* service to Nottingham moved to 5.30pm and its former path amended to be used by a semi-fast to Leicester at 4.35pm. A few other expresses had stops at Bedford/Luton amended to suit the wider need. In addition to the diesel units there were respectively for passenger trains, parcel trains and freight trains on weekdays some thirty, seven and sixty up trains and thirty-two, six and forty-three down to be accommodated within the timetable.

Full service introduction from 11 January 1960 with up to twenty-six of the thirty units did not go according to plan. The range of faults which caused the problems with the units included electro-pneumatic control valves, compressors, final drives and braking defects, all of which required skills found at a depot/main works or manufacturer rather than at a station with a Driver at the far end of his knowledge and confidence base. The four spare units were called into service, but the levels of availability and reliability were such as to interest the national press and require alternative measures to be taken. As with all new technology not fully proven in a harsh and unforgiving environment – here, automotive technology was facing steel wheel on steel rail rather than a less demanding interface – causes needed to be identified, alternative solutions considered, manufacturers consulted, specifications revised, materials ordered and a programme of rectification arranged. Meantime there was a service to be maintained. The immediate operational need was met by the transfer from the Blackpool area of two-car units built by Metro-Cammell Ltd and BR Derby which went into service between Kentish Town and Barking, thus releasing any available four-car units for the Bedford line. However, there were still insufficient four-car units, so two morning services reverted to steam locomotive plus suburban carriages. Eight Metrovick diesels were transferred from Derby to Cricklewood and fitted with equipment to enable them to take conventional trains through to Moorgate. Together with similar locomotives in use in pairs on the *Condor* services, the consequence was that the St Pancras to Manchester trains again became almost exclusively steam hauled.

Whilst technical solutions to the problem were being moved from 'potential' to 'preferred option' and contractual obligations were being discussed, reliability and availability continued to give cause for concern and at the end of February twenty-two of the thirty sets were out of service. As one consequence the north-west of England suffered further when the first four-car sets built with British United Traction (a joint commercial venture between bus industry giants AEC and Leyland) 230hp engines destined for services between Manchester Central and Liverpool Exchange/ Central found themselves at work 150–200 miles south. A second consequence was that new build work at BR Derby C&W Works was postponed whilst attention was concentrated on modifying the 'power train' of the ailing units. A similar problem had arisen with units built by Cravens with Rolls Royce engines; the common factors being the final drive and the integrity of the system for rail rather than road applications.

April saw further transfers of units; in came four-car units originally for working out of Marylebone and back to the Blackpool area went the Metro Cammell and BR Derby two-car units. From 11 April the Metrovicks were replaced by steam between Luton/Kentish Town and Moorgate.

In parallel, new diesel parcel units – four single-car units – had also been causing concerns and three were returned to BR Derby for rectification work.

The shuffling of stock to support the high profile St Pancras to Bedford service continued with the temporary transfer to Cricklewood (four) and Trafford Park (two, though hardly equipped to maintain them) of the thirteen two-car units only recently introduced onto the Wrexham-Chester-New Brighton service. In return that service received new two-car units of which only one was powered and therefore proved inadequate. So, the status quo was quickly restored and the under-powered failures to perform from Wrexham went to a more suitable section around Llandudno Junction. At the same time the Manchester to Liverpool sets were released to return (and went via Derby Works where the first-class accommodation was fitted) and were replaced by further sets originally destined for the Marylebone services.

In the third week of June the Metrovick diesels were back at work on the Moorgate services (including through trains from Harpenden and Luton) and more Marylebone sets arrived. Even so Cricklewood depot was hard pressed to cover its twenty-nine daily diagrams from the forty-one sets it theoretically had available.

Despite all of the shifting of scenery and props the travelling public kept turning up for the performances and the first six months of diesel unit operation saw

On the third day of public service operation the *Midland Pullman* sets out from St Pancras for a non-stop scheduled run to Cheadle Heath, thence Manchester Central. 6 July 1960. (*Kidderminster Railway Museum 117439, Courtesy Millbrook House*)

a 20 per cent increase in the number of passengers travelling. Operational confidence in rectified units increased through the summer months and by the time of the approach of the winter timetable the passengers were able to feel the benefits extolled in the publicity a year previously.

Whilst on the subject of multiple unit diesel trains an update in regard to the *Midland Pullman* is appropriate. The projected January 1960 start of the service was delayed, though in the case of these trains it was an industrial relations problem that caused the delay. The matter to be resolved related to the potential employment of Pullman Car Company staff for the provision of the dining services to all 132 first-class passengers. However, by early February trial running commenced in the Manchester area and high speed running trials were then conducted along the Bedford to Luton section.

On 21 March one unit was employed on a demonstration run between Cricklewood and St Albans for the Minister of Transport – Mr E. Marples MP – and during the day he was shown other examples of the new order and how dutifully the public finances were being expended. The accompanying press quickly noted that amidst the fine decor and facilities of the *Midland Pullman* the train did not 'ride' as smoothly as expectation would reasonably anticipate.

Introduction into public service commenced on 4 July 1960, with a departure Southbound at 8.50am and, after picking up further passengers at Cheadle Heath, ran non-stop to St Pancras, due at three minutes past noon. A fill in trip to Leicester was then made (12.45–2.10pm return at 2.33 and into St Pancras at 4.10pm) prior to the return north at 6.10pm, due into Manchester Central at 9.21pm. The timings for the Southbound run included fourteen minutes recovery time and Northbound eleven. The significant thing about the Leicester run was that it provided – at 70mph – the fastest point to point average speed on British Railways. Fast though it undoubtedly was, the service failed to attract more than the train timers, the curious and the very few first-class travellers wishing to go to Leicester at that time of day. For the winter timetable the fill-in turn was cancelled and as a consequence the expensive asset stood for seven hours as an idle liability awaiting the return north. An additional hour in the layover time would result from an earlier departure from Manchester (from 2 January 1961) at 7.45am to arrive into St Pancras at 11am; for the Manchester business community a three and three quarters of an hour journey to London via the Peak District, with silver service at seat catering in an air conditioned environment was the sort of response from British Railways that the Chambers of Commerce had requested. However, the train in motion did not provide the smooth ride that could also have been expected and travelling technicians had a field day with contemplation of too closely coupled heavy gangways and the interface between the power car bogies and the Brown Boveri sprung drive. The three similar Pullman units supplied as eight-car sets to the Western Region were exhibiting similar ride characteristics even on the carpet between Paddington and Bristol/Cardiff. Reliability of the *Midland Pullman* was at the highest level and in the early months of service no failure occurred. Loadings rose from respectable to very healthy, no doubt as word of mouth advised that the Midland route offered a saving of fifty minutes compared with the L&NWR route.

The protracted introduction of D1-D10 had concluded in March, but rather than being sent to the Western Division of the London Midland Region they stayed close to home. September 1959 had seen some trial running of early examples between Derby and Manchester, then into service in October on the 7.25am Manchester-St Pancras and 2.25pm back. By November D6 and D7 were around, but the winter 1959/60 saw little use of any of the Class. The follow on production run (D11–D137) was deferred whilst electrical transmission package policies and locomotive weight concerns were addressed. The Civil Engineer needed convincing of their ability to safely negotiate obtuse crossings and he having been convinced the London Midland Region quickly put in place a plan to utilise the locomotives (at least) during the summer on the Western Division rather than the Midland. In April and May all ten locomotives were despatched to Camden (North London), Longsight (Manchester), Edge Hill (Liverpool), Crewe and Upperby (Carlisle) for Driver training and introduction into revenue service.

For the Midland main line and cross country the summer – almost unbelievably after the great efforts made to push forward diesel operated services in August 1959 between St Pancras and Derby/Nottingham – looked almost diesel free. The Metrovicks were either helping out locally from Cricklewood, on *Condor*, or laid up out of service. The BR/Sulzer 2s had gone to the Southern Region and the ten BR/Sulzer 4s were on the Western Division. The diesel influx to both the Midland main line and cross country would not start until the production batches of BR/Sulzer type 4s, 137 in total and to be built at BR Derby Works and BR Crewe Works, started to become available.

Change and new diesels were, of course, all pervading but for a while they could be thought of rather as a distant war, a long way away.

As at 1 May 1960 there were 547 main line diesel locomotives resulting from orders placed with eight builders (English Electric, Brush, Associated Electrical Industries, North British Loco Company, Metropolitan Vickers, Birmingham Railway Carriage and Wagon, Beyer Peacock and BR in conjunction with major sub-contractors), a construction programme for the year of 950 new locomotives (of which 3 were steam, 65 were main line electric, 359 diesel shunting and the balance main line diesel). BR had settled upon a method of categorising power availability into five; five being the most powerful and limited at that stage to an authorised build of twenty-two 3,300hp (Deltic) locomotives for the East Coast Main Line route out of Kings Cross to replace fifty-five steam locomotives.

The changing nature of demand for public transport, the financial performance of British Railways and the capital investment programme were each attracting political attention. On 10 March 1960 the Prime Minister, Harold Macmillan said in the House of Commons 'First, the industry must be of a size and pattern suited to modern conditions and prospects. In particular, the railway system must be remodelled to meet current needs, and the modernisation plan must be adapted to this new shape.' In other words perhaps, the railways are no longer appropriate for the current and future needs of the country and the capital to be invested must be directed to where maximum benefit will be derived.

All very good, sensible sentiments, but for now observers along the routes of interest settled down for another summer timetable season of wondrous attractions. Let the show begin!

Between May and October 1959, twenty-six 2,000hp English Electric build diesels had entered service at Camden (six), Crewe (seventeen), Longsight (two) and Upperby and had been (largely) successfully introduced to diagrams along the routes of the Western Division of the London Midland Region. That level of introduction had a consequential and beneficial effect on the availability of Class 7 steam locomotive

Rebuilt Patriot Class 45514 (*Holyhead*) spent only a few months working on the Midland lines and is seen here in 1960 just south of Syston on the up fast line and making haste for Leicester. Hereabouts Drivers were assisted in their task by three aspect colour light signals, very useful in an area characterised by mists and Trent Valley fog drifting around. (*Kidderminster Railway Museum 018708, Courtesy P. J. Lynch*)

power for re-allocation to the Midland Division. That allowed in late November 1959 Nottingham to receive an allocation of four Royal Scots and one Patriot (although one of the Scots was officially on loan from Holbeck) to bolster its then allocation of seven Jubilees and take on principal express workings. Next in line to benefit was Leicester (Midland) which received in January 1960, four Jubilees (of which, two from Nottingham) to which was added one more in March (from Nottingham) and another for a month from mid-June.

However, the big step forward was with the Class 7 power. As has been noted previously re-allocations were a fairly regular occurrence for some depots and therefore definitive allocations at a particular individual date are difficult to pin down. However, as at mid-July 1960, the Midland Division depots at Holbeck, Millhouses, Trafford Park, Kentish Town and Nottingham boasted thirty-seven power Class 7 locomotives of three different types:

Britannia: 70004/14/5/7/21/31/2/3/42/4/53/4
Patriot: 45514/32/6
Royal Scot: 46100/3/9/12/3/7/23/30/1/2/3/9/40/2/5/7/
8/51/7/60/2/4

Also of note was that Holbeck had at that time six ex-LNER A3 Pacifics (later increased to nine) which were deployed north of Leeds and therefore released the five Royal Scots and three Britannias for more work south to St Pancras and very occasionally towards Bristol.

Add to this the Jubilee and Patriot Class 6s at Barrow Road and Derby as well as the depots with Class 7 and the following applies; sixty-six locomotives in total as follows:

Patriot: 45504/6/19
Jubilee: 45557/61/2/4/5/6/8/9/70/2/3/5/6/7/85/9/
90/4/7/8
45602/5/7/8/9/10/1/2/4/5/6/8/9/20/2/6/7/8
/39
45641/8/9/50/1/4/6/8/9/60/2/4/7/8/75/82/
3/5/90/4/9
45712/25/39

For the sake of the record, Trafford Park did not at that time have any Class 6 locomotives, but did have responsibility for eight Britannias. Also for the record the Midland lines to St Pancras depots were down to just three 4-4-0s (two 2Ps and one 4P) and double heading was (apart from when avoiding a light engine path) almost totally confined to pairs of 4-6-0s.

Apart from Barrow Road (some), Nottingham (particularly 45532, 46100/12) Kentish Town (longer term resident locomotives) and Holbeck (particularly the Royal Scots and most Jubilees) the external appearance of most locomotives left much to be desired, with Trafford Park consistently losing any available supplies of cotton waste (even in Lancashire!).

All 103 of the classes 6 and 7 locomotives carried names. Splendid names ... *Iron Duke, Apollo* ... some that commemorated acts of great bravery by railwaymen ... *Private W. Wood V.C.* (from Stockport, awarded the Victoria Cross for conspicuous valour and initiative during the Battle of Vittorio Veneto in 1918) ... countries, provinces and states of the British Empire ... *Canada, Australia, New Brunswick, Tasmania, Malay States* ... great seafarers ... *Raleigh, Hawkins* ... battleships and battles ... *Amethyst, Colossus, Thunderer, Trafalgar*. As such it was daily a passing parade of history and very much in the tradition of railways from their earliest days. There was also local pride in having Royal Scot *Sherwood Forester* at Nottingham and, of course, the original motivation for bringing 45509 to Derby to be named *The Derbyshire Yeomanry*. When regiments returned from deployment overseas it was not unusual for the appropriately named locomotive to be cleaned and allocated to working the train.

Of note around this time was the mixture of liveries of passenger rolling stock. As a corporate policy, carmine and cream had been overtaken by maroon although the Southern Region was allowed to continue with green. The Western Region had been authorised to use (or re-introduced following an unfortunate interlude) chocolate and cream. Dependent upon personal or commercial perspective it either added to the visual attraction or maddeningly disturbed an intention to create uniform sets of coaches. Also by this time the BR Mark 1 coaches had formed many of the timetabled trains – the build programme for these new vehicles having borne the brunt of the cut backs to public expenditure in 1958 – leaving still a very fine array of older vehicles to appear as and when demand increased. To travel in a former twelve wheel dining car, or in the comfort of designs of Gresley, Stanier and Hawksworth was part of each summer. The BR Regional responsibilities for coaching stock sets became more apparent when their individual livery was in use. The Northbound *Devonian* was a chocolate and cream set on days one, three and five and maroon on days two, four and six.

With regard to the summer timetable there was just one item of significance apart from the introduction in early July of the *Midland Pullman*. The by then well-known Sunday diversion of a daytime Manchester-

London train via Stoke and the Midland main line entered a new and seemingly more efficient phase. The train was routed from North Staffordshire Junction into Derby where it reversed, changed locomotives and crew, thus saving for the management a Derby Pilotman and a lodging turn for the Longsight crew and giving an out and back working for a Kentish Town crew and locomotive. To make railway and travelling life around Manchester even more difficult, the Manchester-London diversions which had used London Road station were being themselves further altered to start from Manchester Victoria.

The popular Sutton Coldfield-Stirling car-sleeper train season began with one of the Aston (now 3D) Jubilees (45647) consistently working the first weeks of the service. As usual it was the return working from Scotland via Leeds that generally created the circumstances for something unusual. On 10 June a B16 (61410) brought the heavily delayed train into Derby where it was relieved by a Nottingham Jubilee (45641). On 5 July a Clan (72009) worked through to Aston and returned that night. The 19th August produced by far the surprise of the year when Holbeck's A3 60077 was allowed to work all the way through and returned on the Sunday night with the train (60077 had made an earlier foray to the Midlands on 16 July when it was allowed to work a Newcastle-Bristol passenger train from Sheffield as far as Burton).

Summer weekends again saw extensive use of 9F 2-10-0s on passenger trains, particularly on Saturdays but also on Sundays when the locomotives were returned often with empty coaching stock or relief trains. The locomotives seen on Sundays by myself tended to be drawn from Wellingborough, Leicester and sometimes Saltley; these depots plus Toton and Westhouses (near Chesterfield) had a total allocation of seventy-eight of these machines so it can be concluded that seeing ten or a dozen out on a Saturday was well within the resource capability. Mention of the 9Fs allows me to introduce the human element to the events of the summer. On this particular Sunday morning a Derby 4 Shed crew of a Passed Fireman rostered as a Driver and a Fireman Geoff Morris were to relieve the crew of a passenger train from the North and heading for St Pancras. Upon arrival the locomotive was a 9F of the Crosti boilered type and no doubt being worked back towards its home territory of Wellingborough to Brent/Cricklewood. The majority of the locomotive crews could manage to look respectable even after several hours on the footplate and would try to find time for a quick wash from a bucket prior to stepping off. Not this incoming crew; both looked as though they had pushed each other in and out

of a sooty chimney having a diameter just equivalent to their girth. No words of greeting, no advice, just 'Best of British' [luck]. The Derby crew quickly realised and saw the problem. On these ten locomotives exhausts were expelled via a longitudinal port on the right hand (Fireman's side) side of the locomotive, above the high running plate, but the restrictions of the loading gauge meant that the designers did not have the luxury afforded to locomotives in Dr Piero's native Italy where the exhaust would be thrown well clear of the top of the locomotive beyond the port. Add to that any wind beating down the exhaust, poor quality coal and a poorly steaming locomotive and you have a 'Best of British' luck type event. On its journey from Sheffield the locomotive would have worked or at least had the blower on through several tunnels and all of these factors accounted for a cab full of soot, a filthy, unhealthy working environment … and a service to London to be run. At the Loughborough stop the Driver said 'look after it, I'm going to request a replacement locomotive from Leicester'. Running in to Leicester and passed the depot several 4-6-0s facing south were in steam so no problem then. The platform Inspector was aware of the request and said 'your engine is just coming down'. A 4F 0-6-0 shuffled by; that obviously was not the one produced by Leicester depot so 'where is ours?' 'That's it', said the Inspector. The state of the 9F was such that the 4F was given the task and much though I would like to record an outstanding run, that was not the factual case and, understandably, so much time was dropped over the 27 miles to Kettering that for the sake of following, delayed traffic if nothing else, Control arranged a further exchange of locomotives at Kettering. Where they found it or how it was at Kettering are mysteries, but a Black 5 in good nick was manna from Heaven. Coming back to Derby was an altogether better experience; Jubilee 45610 ex-works and in pristine condition and an exhaust steam injector that could be finely set and (unusually) confidently left to do its job and thus save water and the use of the live steam injector. In fact the brake was applied to observe the 80mph restriction at Bedford North.

The second 9F story also involved Fireman Morris with his then regular Driver Reg Beardsley, a man who was amongst the few who could consume a cup of tea whilst continuing to smoke a cigarette. On this particular Saturday afternoon the pair had relieved a crew at Birmingham New Street and were looking forward to a good run home to Derby with booked stops at Tamworth and Burton-on-Trent. Given a clear run through Water Orton Reg observed the permanent speed restriction and then accelerated hard all the way

Apart from the station itself, Derby was blessed with two excellent viewing positions. In addition to Five Arches bridge was London Road bridge, which overlooked the lines to Birmingham, London, the Carriage and Wagon Works and the extensive yard of the motive power depot. The locomotives in the yard always included plenty of those allocated locally, but in addition also offered others arriving for periodic works attention or awaiting return following attention.

In the foreground is an area which was once the preserve of locomotives of the North Staffordshire Railway coming in from Crewe/Stoke-on-Trent, but with the advent of diesel multiple units it looks as though the Civil Engineer had spotted an opportunity. Immediately beyond is part of a long line of locomotives (1 to r a 3F, a Compound, a 3F tank fitted with condensing apparatus and a 4F), which were not actually in the shed yard: they were in store awaiting a decision as to their fate. Beyond that line up are the main running tracks for trains to/from Trent before the environs of the yard were found. Identifiable are the following Classes; 3F tanks, 4P tanks of two different designs, an 8F, Jubilees, 9Fs, Black 5s and Ivatt 2.

At the time of the photograph – late 1950s – Derby (17A) had an allocation of some 130 steam locomotives and at any time was a sight to behold. To assist staff, different areas of the yard were designated by code letters and numbers; the area around the outdoor turntable being 'X'.

On still days a pall of hazy, black smoke above the yard could be seen for miles, and at midnight on New Year's Eve the sound of multiple whistles could carry a similar distance. (*Colour-rail, BRM1126*)

The gradient of the first 6 miles South from Sheffield was at 1 in 100 against the locomotive(s) and footplate crew(s) and thereby produced for photographers some wonderful opportunities of exhaust effects; the fact that much of that section runs along an axis that provided good morning and evening light angles was a bonus. Here, well before the class 7 power on Sheffield–St. Pancras expresses a Nottingham 2P and a Jubilee (thought to be 45648 Wemyss) lift one such train up the grade. 11 May 1959. (*David Marriott, 223e*)

Mill Hill station 9½ miles from St. Pancras, has all the appearance of a typical Midland Railway layout. Royal Scot 46133 (*The Green Howards*) is on the down fast with an express. (*John Carter, MID 28*)

In May 1957 diesel electric 10203 was employed on special trains from London Euston to Birmingham (via Nuneaton) in connection with the annually held British Industries Fair, held at Fort Dunlop near Castle Bromwich. Here it is at Water Orton. (*Colour-rail, 2152*)

The middle of the day out and home St. Pancras–Leicester/Nottingham runs of the *Midland Pullman* attracted little custom, but in its Nanking Blue livery certainly added colour to more mundane surroundings. Here the return service takes the station avoiding line at Trent and with clear signals will soon be accelerating South. (*Colour-rail, 211819*)

Oh dear Holbeck! How could one of your Britannia's come to look like this? *Moray Firth* (70053) was one of two Scottish based Britannias re-allocated in 1958 to enable two of the Holbeck Royal Scots (46103/33) to be moved South to Kentish Town, and it does not seem to have received much 'tlc' since. On 9 July 1960 the locomotive was assigned to work The Thames-Clyde Express and was photographed between Dore and Totley station, the South Junction and the entrance to Bradway Tunnel. (*David Marriott*)

Freight trains originating in the Sheffield area – or through trains calling to detach/attach vehicles – also used the route between Sheffield and Dore and Totley. Here, on 15 August 1960, Grimesthorpe allocated Crab 42797 puts on a splendid show just beyond Heeley station, 1½ into the climb. (*David Marriott*)

A picture that for the author sums up what was the best of 1961. At that time Saltley had some class 7 power and turned out most of them in fine style. On 4 July 1961 Royal Scot 46157 (*The Royal Artilleryman*) has the 12.37 Newcastle - Bristol passing Heeley Goods, and I bet the photographer was relieved that his opportunity was not blocked by the passage of the train signalled in the opposite direction. (*David Marriott*)

A Northampton Castle - Bedford train passing the Midland style signalbox at Ravenstone Wood Junction (with the Towcester/Stratford-on-Avon line on the left of the picture). Despite various attempts with diesel units steam maintained a presence on these services until closure beckoned. (*John Carter*)

In addition to the Northampton branch, the Midland also provided a service from Bedford to Hitchin. Here, between Shefford and Southill, 41271 has the pleasant duty of pulling/pushing one carriage through equally pleasant surroundings. It just could not continue. (*John Carter*)

Based upon an 1875 Johnson design 2F 58148 was a 1917 rebuild with a Belpaire (as opposed to round top) firebox. It was one of several that saw out its days at Coalville and used in particular on the Leicester West Bridge line, including the severely restricted clearance in Glenfield tunnel. (*John Carter*)

The run up to Christmas brought with it a need for additional trains to convey parcels traffic. One such train was operated between York and Derby using motive power from the former and started in mid-November. Motive power used included V2s (as seen here on 16 November 1963) and on occasions A1s and A3s. The locomotive was turned at Derby and worked a similar train back to York in the evening. In the picture the train has just passed under Woodseats bridge. (*David Marriott, 3076e*)

Of the ten members of the build of Type 4 2,300hp diesel electric locomotives in 1959/60, two (D4 and D8) survived into preservation. Here *Great Gable* has received at the Midland Railway Centre in Derbyshire a fresh coat of paint. The head code discs as displayed would have indicated a Royal train. (*John Palmer*)

The production build of D11-D193 included a batch for allocation to the North Eastern Region. D182 was one of the NER batch and later was saved from scrapping following a period of use by the Research Department of British Railways Board. It was photographed at the Midland Railway Centre and has the small yellow warning panel and displays a headcode indicating an express passenger train destined for the London Midland Region. (*John Palmer*)

Lengthy trains of empty coaching stock were not uncommon on summer Sundays and here, just south of Duffield, crosti 9F 92029 has one such train. (*Rail-online*)

to Kingsbury and then maintained a high speed until braking for Tamworth. At Tamworth a youngish fellow came along the platform and clearly wanted to engage Reg in conversation: 'I've been timing trains along this section for years and have never ever known acceleration like that between Water Orton and Kingsbury, I want to know how you did it?' 'We always do it like that' said Reg 'and if you buy me a packet of cigarettes you can come with us to Burton and we'll show you how we do it!' The deal was struck and the capabilities of a 9F were ably demonstrated in the achievement of a speed to allow water to be lifted from the troughs at Wigginton and a very prompt arrival at Burton. As an aside, I just wonder if the timing of the need for extra motive power over the Midland main line from Manchester to London had been 1960 rather than 1958, whether utilising, say, a batch of six 9Fs between Derby and Manchester may have become an option (as for the Somerset and Dorset).

My records for the summer of 1960 are good, although given the range of what was on offer locally myself and friends did not feel the need to travel as widely as in 1959 ... who would want to go to Crewe or Tamworth to see D1-D10 and D210-D235?

There is a danger of records becoming mere catalogues of numbers so I have selected a few days around the August Bank Holiday as the main feature and a specific reference to a (then) truly outstanding occurrence on Saturday, 9 July.

During the course of a pleasant carefree afternoon, the gallery of perhaps fifteen had enjoyed watching the passage of the steam passenger trains in each direction. From our vantage point at Breadsall Crossing, 3 miles north of Derby, we had a clear view for at least one quarter of a mile of trains coming towards Derby, but only perhaps half of that for the other direction. The previous hours had included two 9Fs from the North (Scarborough), one from Derby plus a common Britannia so when another BR Standard with smoke deflectors came into view from Derby no-one showed much interest ... until it passed us. We could not believe it and the celebration was immediate and loud ... 72005 *Clan Macgregor* of Carlisle Kingmoor. Unknown to us the locomotive had worked south overnight 7/8 July with the Stirling-Sutton Coldfield train and rather than being allowed to stand idle awaiting the return on the night of the 10th, it had relieved at Birmingham the locomotive on the 8.45pm Bradford to Bristol and was being returned north instead on the 7.45am Paignton to Newcastle Saturdays only train. Those observing at Temple Meads station managed to miss it as it picked up its train at St Philip's Marsh and proceeded via Filton Junction to Yate. Clan Class locomotives through Derby were rare but not unknown; 72005 had worked into Derby (ex-works Crewe) when deputising for a failed locomotive on a Saturday Llandudno-Derby train in 1956 and all the others in the 72005-9 block (all Carlisle) put in an appearance sooner or later. I have never met anyone who saw at Derby a Scottish Region allocated Clan from the 72000-4 block, although 72001 worked through on 12 May 1960.

As for the lead up to the August Bank Holiday weekend, a typical day would be from around 8.45am to 7pm with a short break for lunch and tea immediately following the passing of *The Devonian* in each direction. Around eighty-five trains would be seen daily often

starting with a brand new four car or two, four car diesel multiple units going on a test run. Such was the case on 29 July with two units working in multiple prior to heading to Stratford (East London) on loan for a short term use whilst electrification works on part of the Great Eastern lines required diesel unit operation. On that day and also subsequent weekdays the incidence of double heading was limited to five trains (all cross country and always including the Cardiff-Newcastle and v.v.) and worked by combinations of a Gloucester Standard Class 4 plus Jubilee, a B1 plus Standard Class 5, a B1 plus Jubilee and a Black 5 plus Jubilee. For cross country it was another year so like the previous ten. On 29 July just three diesels (10202, D5702 twice and D5706), one Britannia, sixteen Jubilees, four Royal Scots, one Patriot and four B1s. The 30th was a Saturday and on a strangely shortened day for me, appeared four double headers (the usual trains plus a pair of B1s), all three of the Barrow

This is the (extension to) west end of Platform 1 at Derby Midland, a popular spot in the 1950s/60s for watching trains and keeping an eye on movements of locomotives in the yard of the engine shed. The daunting prospect facing anyone such as a young Geoff Morris wishing to access the lines of locomotives on the shed was represented by the network of tracks to the West (towards Birmingham) and to the East (towards Trent and Nottingham). From the latter direction Fairburn tank 42228 is arriving with the 5pm Nottingham-Derby to form the 5.50 pm to Darley Dale. Rampant trespass around the shed suggests this is August Bank Holiday Saturday, 1960. (*Rail-online*)

Road Patriots, the same three diesels as the previous day, fourteen Jubilees, two Royal Scots, one Britannia and one K3 were amongst the power on sixty-seven trains seen. At that time there was an occasional surprise of a Bath or even Southern Region allocated Standard Class 5 4-6-0 working through to Sheffield, but not on that day. Over a period of six days and seeing hundreds of trains and locomotives the number of surprises in terms of types of locomotive seen was nil and the proportion of 'foreign' locomotives (that is from depots not usually providing power for trains along the route) was no higher than 3 per cent. The Britannias seen tended to stick to the same daily diagram and perhaps reflecting a shortage at Trafford Park 70043 appeared on two consecutive days as being on loan from nearby Longsight. August Bank Holiday Saturday at St Pancras was interesting in that three Patriots in original form (45508/9/11) arrived on relief trains. This threesome included the much derided 45509, *The Derbyshire Yeomanry* which had strayed or been allowed to stray from Newton Heath and was soon on its way back in that direction.

The final Saturday in August saw Derby Works swamped by enthusiasts who were far more interested in the locomotives than the annual horticultural show that the event was really about. The year 1960 was unusual in that there was nothing to prevent hundreds of youths and families under varying degrees of control from having access to the adjacent motive power depot. Locomotives in steam, every whistle blown, locomotives moved without authorisation, souvenirs taken … it was simply wonderful.

The savings accrued through a reduction in the amount of double heading (for footplatemen a return Derby to London mileage payment was handsome) had been noted and for the winter timetable the timings of most London line expresses were eased by up to five minutes for XL and Special Limit trains, thus enabling two extra carriages to be conveyed by Class 6 and Class 7 power with trains of 350 and 405 tons tare respectively. The need for heavier loads over the Derby to Manchester section saw an increase of seven minutes Northbound and nine Southbound. The accountants were winning.

One other point of interest was the introduction of a through carriage from/to Halifax on a day-time Leeds to St Pancras service, returning in the evening. This was an ill-advised reaction to the loss of express services on the former Great Central line to Marylebone.

The commencement of electric locomotive haulage between Manchester and Crewe from the start of the winter timetable resulted in the re-allocation of Class 7 steam power away from Longsight depot and for a while the diverted trains to St Pancras ran with Class 6 and more frequently the English Electric type 4 2,000hp diesels.

On the freight side a new train of interest had been started to convey new Vauxhall cars from Wilshampstead to Bonnybridge, Scotland (near Falkirk) from which point distributorships took delivery. These trains utilised twenty-one former carriage underframes/running gear and with a length of nearly one quarter mile made for an unusual sight when on curves or reverse curves. The trains normally used the Erewash Valley route between Trent and Clay Cross and for working them Cricklewood was allocated a low number of 9Fs.

Between October and December six of Trafford Park's Britannias were transferred away (70031 to Longsight, 70004/17/42 to Willesden and 70014/5 to Newton Heath), leaving three and they were joined there over the same period by five Royal Scots (46106/22/41/43/58), four of which were new to the Midland line. It was, though, another Scot (46152) that raised eyebrows and very nearly an overbridge near Whaley Bridge when it was destined for Shallcross Sidings.

During the year Bow Works was closed and residual work transferred to Derby. One of the final involvements for staff based at Bow had been the development of the BR Automatic Warning System; the Works having previously produced the similar Hudd system for use along the London Tilbury and Southend section of the LMS.

For observers along the routes of interest it had been another wonderful year. Change was closer than seemed apparent, but the advent of diesels had brought with it far more teething problems than anticipated and both availability and reliability were much less than required. The faults were generally not with the major components, rather a whole raft of interface and steel wheel on steel rail matters, plus seemingly anything to do with steam heating boilers. At the end of the year 842 main line diesels had been delivered (409 in the year) and during the year 1,209 steam locomotives had been withdrawn, including Millhouses Jubilee 45609 (the first of the class apart from 45637 which had been destroyed in the Harrow and Wealdstone disaster). The final steam locomotive to be built by British Railways – 92220 *Evening Star* – had entered service in March from Swindon Works.

Chapter Eight

1961: The Capital Investment Starts to Pay Off

At the start of the New Year, production of the BR/Sulzer type 4 diesel locomotives was continuing at the locomotive works of both BR Derby and BR Crewe. Of the locomotives accepted for service Derby 17A already had an allocation of nineteen and received further locomotives from Crewe after they had spent a very short time on proving runs from Crewe North 5A.

There was a change to the build programmes and running number sequence of production. That change was as a result of a decision that Crewe would complete the locomotives to be equipped with Crompton Parkinson electrical equipment and that Derby built locomotives would incorporate Brush electrical equipment. As a consequence production at Derby, after completion of D49, would re-start at D138 and continue to D165 inclusive, followed by D166 to D193. At Crewe the sequence would be D68 to D137 followed by D50 to D67. D11 to D165 were destined for the Midland lines, including cross country whilst D166 to D193 were to be dedicated to routes within the North Eastern Region extending into the Eastern Region.

The conclusions from this included that the BR/Sulzer type 4s (D11-D165) would replace steam locomotives initially on all express passenger trains along our routes of interest and that such a concentration of a single type would enable training, maintenance, timetabling, diagramming and inventory management to be planned and implemented far more easily than with a mix of traction types. For the time being the Western Division of the London Midland Region would retain D1-D10 to ease the transition from steam to diesel/electric traction, but in due course they would revert to the Midland Division.

The development of the class (starting with D1 to D10) had been protracted and at the design stage the Civil Engineer had expressed concern over the projected weight (136 tons) which if spread equally over just six axles could have serious repercussions for the incidence of rail breakages. Hence the 1-Co-Co-1 configuration with the 1 at each end being non-

powered and allowing the average weight per axle to be reduced and meet the then desired ratio of axle weight to wheel diameter. The length of the wheel bases was also longer than would generally be preferable for operating freight trains as well as passengers. The BR/Sulzer type 4 required seventeen chain curves whilst the later Brush built type 4s (Co-Co), weighing 114 tons required just ten. All these considerations having been satisfied the task of production continued apace, with up to six new locomotives of the type emerging from Crewe every four weeks. In June D34 became the 1,000th member of the BR main line fleet of diesel locomotives.

Of our routes of interest that between Manchester and St Pancras became the first to feel the influence of the change. Whilst work progressed with training of footplatemen in the three variants they may be called upon to operate (D1 to D10: D11 to D49 and D138 to D165: D68-D137 and D50 to D67) and maintenance plus fuel and inspection facilities were installed at particular depots/stabling points the locomotives were operated from and returned to Derby. The initial (February) diagrams were:

Diagram: Workings (passenger except as shown)

A	2.02 a.m.	Derby–Manchester parcels
	7.20 a.m.	Manchester–St Pancras
	2.25 p.m.	St Pancras–Manchester
	7.45 p.m.	Manchester–Derby
B	8.12 a.m.	Derby–Manchester
	10.25 a.m.	Manchester–St Pancras
	4.25 p.m.	St Pancras–Manchester
	12.01 a.m.	Manchester–Derby newspapers and passenger
C	3.57 a.m.	Derby–Nottingham parcels
	8.15 a.m.	Nottingham–St Pancras The *Robin Hood*
	5.30 p.m.	St Pancras–Nottingham The *Robin Hood*
	10.50 p.m.	Nottingham–Derby

Note: A and B, 500 miles

Additionally there was a two day cyclic diagram involving the:

11.17 p.m.	Derby–St Pancras parcels
7.55 a.m.	St Pancras–Manchester *The Palatine*
5.30 p.m.	Manchester–St Pancras
10.25 a.m.	St Pancras–Manchester (to Derby)

Training diagrams included the 8.41am, 9.19am and 3.31pm Leeds-St Pancras passenger trains with the 9.25pm return passenger to Leeds; also the 8.24am Bedford-Wellingborough parcels with a return working at 1.25pm.

At the end of March D11/2/4-6 were based at Leeds (Neville Hill depot rather than Holbeck) and D17-21/68-91 working from Derby with one on loan to Darnall (Sheffield) for training.

By the end of April the number of weekday diesel turns had increased to twenty-three and incorporated certain services between St Pancras and Manchester, Nottingham and St Pancras, Leeds and Sheffield to St Pancras (including the 7am up fast from Sheffield which was the first involvement for Millhouses based footplatemen). The good performance of the diesels during spring resulted in a desire to revise earlier plans; it was decided that rather than dieselise London to the North fast fitted freight services before the passenger trains on the Leeds/York to Bristol route, that sequence of planned events would be reversed. Desirable though it may have been for the London Midland Region it was unattainable as the footplatemen at York, Heaton and Gateshead (both Newcastle) were being trained on Deltics and English Electric type 4 diesels. This, though, enabled a fitted (with continuous vacuum brakes) freight service from London (Somers Town) to Masborough (Rotherham) and thence through with traffic for Scotland to Glasgow, returning the following night with the 5.42pm Glasgow (Buchanan Street) to Somers Town fitted freight. Men at Corkerhill depot Glasgow were trained for this and other new Scottish-Anglo services referred to later. Pending routes clearances for the Leeds to Glasgow and Edinburgh sections, crew training was further extended and diesels were introduced into day trains (only) from 3 July.

A similar management process for training was applied to the cross country route, starting in March. D19/75/86 were employed from and back to Derby on the 8.05am Birmingham to York passenger returning with the 12.43pm ex Newcastle and D21 was sent to Saltley (Birmingham) for training purposes. On 10 April D93 commenced a programme of training for footplatemen based at Bristol Barrow Road depot. The daily workings were:

8.15 a.m.	Bristol–Gloucester empty coaching stock and return
4.20 p.m.	Bristol–Gloucester passenger
5.47 p.m.	Gloucester–Bristol passenger

From the commencement of the summer timetable the use of diesels was extended to include the:-

7.05 p.m.	Newcastle–Bristol mail and passenger (ex-Sheffield)
7.40 a.m.	Bristol–Bradford passenger
12.48 p.m.	York–Bristol passenger
8.15 p.m.	Bristol–Derby parcels

Further developments were planned and introduced from 3 July by which time six of the class were allocated to Bristol St Philip's Marsh depot. As had been applied to the London lines, the diesels as available were concentrated upon regular, time-tabled passenger trains, particularly *The Devonian* in each direction between Bristol and Leeds, the 12.48pm York-Bristol, the 8.40am, 10.30am and 7.25pm ex-Bristol to Sheffield (8.40am only) and Newcastle. The potential benefits from dieselisation along the cross country route were huge and were the subject of discussions involving all four Regions involved. Through workings between Bristol and Newcastle, there would be no need for a change of locomotive at Sheffield and/or York, no need for pilot locomotives and out and home 600 miles a day.

In September trials were held on the Lickey incline between Bromsgrove and Blackwell; this having been an operating constriction for over 115 years. Locomotive D40 with fifteen empty coaches plus a dynamometer carriage made a series of runs; from a standing start south of Bromsgrove station, from a start at that station, a 'flying' ascent from a point some way south of Bromsgrove and from a series of re-starts whilst on the incline. On the following day a similar series of trial runs happened though for those freight stock was used. Throughout these trials the trains were closely followed by 9F 92234. The tests proved the capability of the type 4 diesels and added further evidence for the consideration of future timetables and the need for banking assistance.

With the commencement of the winter timetable the use of type 4s was further extended along the cross country route and involved some interesting cyclic diagrams (passenger except where shown):

10.30 a.m.	Bristol–Newcastle throughout
8.15 a.m.	Newcastle–Cardiff, thence local to Bristol
★	
6.47 a.m.	Bristol–Gloucester thence on 8.30 a.m. ex-Cardiff to Newcastle throughout
	Newcastle–Bristol throughout. Mail and passenger
7.5 p.m.	
★	Bristol–Newcastle throughout. Mail and passenger
7.25 p.m.	Heaton (Newcastle)–Dringhouses (York) perishables
6.25 a.m.	York–Bristol throughout
12.52 p.m.	
★	Birmingham–York perishables
11.38 p.m.	York–Newcastle
6.55 a.m.	Newcastle–Bristol throughout
12.43 p.m.	
★	Birmingham–Newcastle throughout
8.5 a.m.	Newcastle–Birmingham throughout
3.30 p.m.	

In all there were twenty-seven diagrams involved; nineteen for the North Eastern Region based locomotives and eight for the Western Region. By early November utilisation was extended to fitted freight work including two each Washwood Heath (Birmingham) to Westerleigh (Bristol), to Dringhouses (York) and Leeds/Stourton to Water Orton (Birmingham area) trains.

Towards the end of the calendar year, most timetabled passenger trains along the cross country route were diesel hauled, although the following remained strong candidates for steam:

7.35 a.m.	Nottingham–Bristol
10.25 a.m.	Sheffield–Bristol
12.43 p.m.	Newcastle–Bristol
2.15 p.m.	Bristol–York
5.15 p.m.	Bristol–York
10.15 a.m.	Manchester–Bournemouth West ex Birmingham to Bath (Green Park) The *Pines Express*
9.45 a.m.	Bournemouth West–Manchester (ex Bath) The *Pines Express*

Meanwhile on the Midland lines to St Pancras the locomotive section of the new Cricklewood maintenance depot became available in early autumn and the 4s helped out by hauling carriages as theoretical St Pancras-Bedford peak hours diesel multiple unit turns. In October utilisation was extended to include Somers Town to Ardwick (Manchester) fitted freight trains. The only significant change from the introduction of the winter timetable was the use of a Derby based locomotive on *The Waverley* (9.15am from St Pancras) to Leeds and continuing north with the following *Thames-Clyde Express* from Leeds to Glasgow. At that date three diesel turns were in place on the Anglo-Scottish routes north of Leeds.

The use of cyclic diagrams was extended and it was not unusual for a locomotive to be away from its home depot for several days. For example:

Day	Location	Arrival	Departure	Notes
1	Holbeck depot	–	10.27 a.m.	Light engine
	Leeds		11.00 a.m.	Passenger
	London St P.	3.43 p.m.	–	
	London St P.	–	6.30 p.m.	Passenger
	Derby	9.00 p.m.	–	
	Derby	–	11.17 p.m.	Parcels
2	London St P.	4.12 a.m.	–	–
	London St P.	–	10.45 a.m.	Passenger
	Manchester	3.30 p.m.	–	
	Manchester	–	5.55 p.m.	Passenger
	London St P.	11.20 p.m.	–	

3	London St P.	–	7.55 a.m.	Passenger
	Manchester	11.54 a.m.	–	
	Manchester	–	4.30 p.m.	Passenger
	London St P.	8.41 p.m.	–	
	London St P.	–	11.50 p.m.	Parcels via Derby
4	Leeds	5.59 a.m.	–	
	Leeds	–	6.24 a.m.	Light engine
	Holbeck depot	6.40 a.m.	–	

Re-fuelling/coolant/water and daily exams at
Cambridge Street, Manchester and Derby

At the end of the cycle the locomotive could repeat it or take up another diagram. It was early days; the above does not represent particularly high utilisation and, for example, the Eastern Region was squeezing far more miles out of their English Electric type 4s.

In mid-year 1961 two-thirds of the four and a half million passenger train miles run weekly by BR were covered by diesel or electric traction, an increase of 10 per cent over the equivalent time in 1960. On comparable duties (express passenger trains) steam locomotives were averaging 170 miles per calendar day, with an average casualty rate of one every 17,000 miles,

diesels were managing an average of 300 miles with a casualty rate of between one every 12,000 miles and one every 22,000 miles, depending upon Region. If failures resulting from train heating deficiencies were excluded the Regional averages for diesels increased to 15,000 and 26,500 respectively. It started to become clear that whilst the main components and electrical gear of diesel electric locomotives could be relied upon, the 'Achilles heel' was the seemingly simple requirement to generate steam with which to heat carriages.

Before moving on, the changing situations with steam motive power needs to be explained.

Depot	Class 6 Jubilee + Patriot			Class 7 Patriot			Class 7 Royal Scot			Class 7 Britannia		
	1961			*1961*			*1961*			*1961*		
	Start	Mid	End	Start	Mid	End	Start	Mid	End	Start	Mid	End
Holbeck	18	18	17	-	-	-	5	5	-	3	3	3
Millhouses	12	12	12	2	1	1	5	5	5	-	-	-
Kentish Town	6	4	3	1	1	-	9	5	-	-	-	-
Trafford Park	-	-	-	-	1	-	5	3	3	3	-	-
Barrow Road	12	12	6	-	-	-	-	-	-	-	-	-
Derby	9	7	2	-	-	-	-	4	-	-	-	-
Saltley	-	2	-	-	2	2	-	7	10	-	-	-
Burton	-	-	20	-	-	-	-	-	-	-	-	-
Nottingham	4	4	1	1	1	1	1	1	2	-	-	-
Leicester	6	1	-	-	-	-	-	-	-	-	-	-

Several notes of clarification apply:

• The total number of Class 7 locomotives available along the two routes of interest at mid-1961 was very similar to mid-1960, dependent upon actual date.
• Holbeck also had a total allocation of nine A3s, but at year end was one (60038). Holbeck's five Royal Scots were re-allocated to Low Moor (56F) and Jubilee 45619 was condemned.
• Millhouses depot was closed as at 31 December 1961 and its allocation transferred to Canklow (41D) (Part of the extensive Sheffield rationalisation) and mostly placed into store.

• Kentish Town was heavily affected by the introduction of the type 4 diesels.
• Trafford Park as for Kentish Town.
• Barrow Road had six of its nine Jubilee's re-allocated (at the start of the winter 1961/2 timetable) to Shrewsbury (89A). Left with 45682/5/90 (plus 45504/6/19).
• For part of the summer Derby received its first allocation of Royal Scots 46100/6/18/37 (Note: although 46120 had been allocated in 1949 and 1955 it was for testing and trials only). Affected as for Kentish Town.

- Saltley was a major beneficiary of the re-organisation and utilised the Class 7s on passenger work particularly on summer weekends, as stand-by locomotives to cover for type 4 diesel failures and on other duties as required including fitted freights.
- Saltley's Royal Scots were 46103/6/18/22/3/37/41/57/60/2 and Patriots 45532/40.
- Burton received multiple Jubilees (and would continue to accumulate members of that class up to a total of twenty-four) in November.
- Royal Scots that were newcomers to the routes were 46106/18/22/37/41/3/53/8. Also 45540 (Patriot).
- Newton Heath (26A) was a major beneficiary of locomotives re-allocated from Midland lines depots.

To round off the review of motive power the bulk of the Metrovick Class diesels remained 'laid up' until late summer when after agreement between BR and the manufacturer of the locomotives, each one was put through works and upon completion all twenty were re-allocated to Barrow (12C).

Public timetables continued to be published for the winter (from mid-September) and summer (from mid-June) periods. One need was for the timetable planners to be advised whether or not they should allow for the continued use of steam traction or to base timings upon the availability of diesel locomotives. The difference between the two could be considerable. As an example a steam hauled passenger train between Sheffield and Derby with a call at Chesterfield would be allowed a time of fifty-five minutes with the challenging climb to the far end of Bradway Tunnel (6 miles at 1 in 100) requiring anything up to a quarter of one hour, followed by a dash down to Chesterfield, a further less demanding climb to Clay Cross and an easy run to Derby. BR/Sulzer type 4 diesel would regularly complete this 36 mile section in forty minutes, including a pause of two minutes at Chesterfield. Trains running early are just as much a potential problem as trains running late; conflicting movements over junctions, lengthy waiting times in platforms and frustrated passengers on trains awaiting advertised departure times being examples. Also to be included in the equation were the needs for advertised connections to be upheld, for mail to be conveyed and exchanged between connecting trains, the desire of one or more railway Regions to integrate services with others solely in their Region (the Newcastle to Cardiff service passed through four Regions), and for the ability of Drivers and Second Men/Firemen to have been trained for managing diesel traction types of various types.

It was a recipe for conservatism in approach and also a recipe for misunderstandings by political masters who saw seeming inefficiency rather than the complexity of the challenge. Although there was a clear case for revising some of the passenger timetables both the cross country and Midland lines to St Pancras would not see a radical change before September 1962. In September 1962 demands upon the Manchester Central to St Pancras route would increase as electrification work along the route to London (Euston) extended south along the Trent Valley. For the cross country route and the Anglo-Scottish trains via the Midland route the various Regions would work together to progressively increase the utilisation of the type 4 diesels and put into place a maintenance regime with suitable facilities.

Where diesels were operated and they performed reliably to their capabilities, timekeeping in the winter/spring of 1960/61 was better than in previous comparable periods. Against most predictions, the power generation units did not give rise to engineering concerns; the most common cause of failure was a need to replace split water tanks (for steam heating of carriages) and the improve the day-to-day reliability of the boilers themselves.

Bank Holiday traffic, relief trains, sporting and other excursion traffic together with the summer season peak continued much as before except that diesel multiple units were used on more occasions and along our lines of route a cascade of motive power resulted in less double heading and less use of 9F locomotives (see later in this Chapter).

The winter 1961/62 timetable revisions included a saving of ten minutes on the 4.25pm up from Manchester to St Pancras to give a journey time of three hours and fifty-five minutes. Elsewhere along the line the accelerations which were introduced in 1959 had been replaced with a return to just two mile a minute non-stop runs between London and Leicester and none in the up direction, although the 10.25am ex-Manchester was allowed just sixty-seven minutes start to stop between Leicester and Luton (69 miles). St Pancras to Nottingham via Manton/Edwalton had returned to 128 minutes and there were no mile a minute averages between London and Kettering. It is probable that the adjustment to the timings for the 4.25pm from Manchester came about from pressure from the business community, as on the alternative route via Crewe to Euston the average time during the day was four hours nineteen minutes with only *The Comet* achieving three hours fifty-five minutes. The electrification work continued until 1966 before the north-west could feel the full benefit of the investment. The middle of the day diversions of the 12.10pm Manchester Piccadilly to London St Pancras

Work in connection with the electrification of the Manchester (London Road/Piccadilly) to London (Euston) route resulted in the diversion of certain trains via Stoke on Trent, the Derby area and thence the Midland main line to St Pancras. One such train, the 1.55pm from St Pancras was the preserve of English Electric type 4 diesels and here D221 (*Ivernia*) has taken its usual route from Spondon Junction and is running in to Derby station over Five Arches bridge. From Derby the train will head for North Staffordshire Junction and thence to Stoke on Trent/Manchester. 20 July 1962. (*Kidderminster Railway Museum 090921, Courtesy P. J. Lynch*)

and 1.55pm return via Stoke and Leicester continued; both being routed via Derby and the former no longer reversing and changing locomotives.

From 2nd October 1961 the *Midland Pullman* recommenced a middle of the day fill in return trip, in this case to Nottingham. At that time of the day there was little demand for such a premium service, but the London to Leicester (and v.v.) start to stop times of eighty-five minutes (down)/eighty-seven minutes (up) gave impressive average speeds of 70mph/68.4 mph respectively.

The year 1961 saw two planned attempts along the London lines to introduce diesels onto more passenger train services than reliability and availability could support in practice and throughout the year, the service both on these routes and on cross country produced a rich mix of steam and diesel traction.

Passenger train workings have tended to dominate the annual Chapters and the following attempts to redress the balance. This will be achieved by referenced examples of how the corporate needs for rationalisation,

understanding and planning for future requirements of major customers, and attempts to secure and retain new traffic flows were being met. Within our area and routes of interest the examples selected are rationalisation around Sheffield, the need for planning with the National Coal Board and the Central Electricity Generating Board and new traffic flows being oil and those which were either perishable or sensitive to time/cost constraints.

As a centre for the iron and steel industry the Rotherham/Sheffield area had attracted railways from its and their formative days. The Midland and the Great Central railways were the dominant Companies and their controlling influence extended to involve Kilnhurst and Parkgate & Rawmarsh. Raw materials flowed in by the thousands of tons – coal, coking coal, iron ore and limestone – and all sourced along the routes of the Midland and Great Central. Once the production process was complete the finished and semi-finished products could be taken out to Lancashire and to the West Midlands in particular (strip, sections, plate, ingots, blooms and slabs).

With the arrival of Class 7 power in quantity, the double heading of *The Thames-Clyde Express* between Leicester and Sheffield became a thing of the past. Here, at Coates Park Patriot 45536 (*Private W. Wood VC* – please refer to the 1960 Chapter to learn who he was) is in sole charge. (Science Museum/National Railway Museum)

By the mid-1950s and in the nationalised railways era, there was huge scope for rationalisation and for investment in new facilities. The Sheffield Division of British Railways was identified in the Modernisation Plan as being of particular attraction and Regional boundary change in 1958 created an opportunity for the Eastern Region to refine and present proposals. The proposals included the total or partial closure of eighteen BR yards and their replacement with two new mechanised installations; a large mechanical goods depot would replace those at four outdated locations and 180 diesel locomotives would replace 400 steam locomotives and the need for six motive power depots. The detailed proposals were accepted by the Ministry of Transport. D55XX diesels built by Brush Traction were installed at Darnall and these type 2s were quickly in evidence as far as Somers Town on vacuum fitted freight trains and on excursion passenger traffic. As part of the rationalisation Millhouses motive power depot was closed with effect from 1 January 1962 and its allocation of thirty-one (apart from four Standard Class

2 2-6-0 tender locomotives) was transferred to Canklow, near Rotherham. In practice fourteen of the steam locomotives were placed into store at the two depots at Staveley; nine Jubilees, four Royal Scots and one Patriot. That left three Jubilees (*Bombay, Nelson* briefly, and *Hogue*) and one Royal Scot (*The Northamptonshire Regiment*) and three BR Standard Class 5 4-6-0s as 'cover' at Canklow.

To service the need of the Sheffield Division's freight traffic some 9,000 wagons were required daily, many being of a specialist type for the conveyance of particular commodities. A few miles further south in the coalfields of the Erewash Valley that quantity of wagon requirements was well exceeded and, unfortunately, their use as immobile storage bunkers at many collieries contributed to a continuing inefficient method of operation.

Over a period of five years from the end of 1956 the total production of coal nationally had fallen from 227 million tons to around 190 million tons and also during that period the total tonnage forwarded by rail had fallen to 133 million tons (in 1961) whilst the tonnage by road had increased to 39 million tons (the balance being by private railways, canals and coastal shipping). The proportion of the total production used for electricity generation had increased from 46 million/217 million tons in 1956 to 55 million/192 million tons in 1961 whilst that for all other main consumers (town gas, iron, steel and coke ovens, other industrial and household) had fallen. The expectation of the National Coal Board was that total annual production would rise by 1966 to 200 million tons and remain at that level. Here was a bulk traffic ideally suited to movement by rail, but one which was characterised by poor terminal conditions and very low utilisation of the huge fleet of railway wagons. The stark need was for the National Coal Board, Central Electricity Generating Board and British Railways Board to work together to shape the future logistical arrangements. In the short term little

would change in terms of proportion of coal used as a source of power generation, but a new source was developing fast and also provided an opportunity for rail; the transport of refined petroleum products.

Demand for petroleum products was increasing for both the industrial and domestic sectors. Private car ownership was burgeoning, road hauliers required bunkering facilities, new age factories wanted more efficient heat generation facilities and the railways themselves had over a thousand main line diesel locomotives requiring refuelling on a regular basis. The principal companies then involved with refining and distribution of refined products to major storage centres – Esso Petroleum Co Ltd and Shell Mex Ltd (including British Petroleum) – recognised the need to manage their own assets, including fleets of two axle wagons. As a national strategic policy the transportation of oil from refineries in mainland UK would be by underground

The changing demand for fuel types resulted in the major oil companies leasing fleets of two axle tank wagons for the conveyance in bulk (as block trains) of petroleum products from Fawley (Southampton Water) and Avonmouth the Bromford Bridge (Birmingham). Bristol Barrow Road depot received an allocation of 9F 2-10-0s to handle this traffic (and also other heavy trains out of Avonmouth for Cadbury at Bournville) and have one of that allocation (92007) is on the Lickey incline. The second and third vehicles are barrier wagons to reduce the probability of sparks from the locomotive's exhaust or brakeblocks reaching the oil tank wagons. The first vehicle is a brakevan to assist the speed of 'turn round' of the train at Bromford Bridge and again at the loading point; the far end of the train would be similarly marshalled. (*Kidderminster Railway Museum 024610, Courtesy J. Tarrant*)

pipeline as well as by rail and coastal shipping. The method of rail transport was by block trains. These were trains formed purely of vacuum braked private owner wagons with non-oil product carrying barrier wagons to minimise the risk of sparks from the steam locomotive hauling the trains falling onto the oil tank wagons. The oil companies leased the fleets of wagons including a maintenance agreement and then entered into an agreement with British Railways Board for the timetabled haulage of their trains.

One such flow of oil product traffic was between Avonmouth and Bromford Bridge (near Washwood Heath, Birmingham) and involved loaded trains from the former at 11am (Saturdays excepted) and 11.30pm (Fridays and Saturdays excepted) with returns at 10.40 am and 8.05pm. Later a daily service (Saturdays excepted) was added between Fawley (Southampton Water) to Bromford Bridge and then re-routed via Basingstoke and Oxford rather than via Bristol.

To work these trains Bristol Barrow Road received an allocation of 9F 2-10-0 locomotives. Two arrived in September 1960 and were followed by three more to give an allocation of five (at 31 December 1960). The spectacle of a 9F hauled oil train being banked up the Lickey incline by another 9F plus on occasions, by a pannier tank was memorable and equalled (minus the pannier tank) only on the Tyne Dock – Consett section. After the re-routing of the Fawley refinery trains motive power seemed to be shared between the Southern Region (Eastleigh receiving 9Fs for this work) and Saltley which turned out their class 7 4-6-0s on occasions in 1961. (The 82E 9Fs were also employed on heavy trains out of Avonmouth with cocoa beans imported from West Africa and destined for Cadbury's at Bournville.)

Elsewhere on the system the network of vacuum brake fitted freight trains continued to be extended and allied to the use of diesel locomotives enabled new out and home train crew workings without the need for changes of crew en-route at Regional boundaries e.g. Eastern Region type 2 diesels from the Sheffield area to London. One new traffic flow which attracted attention because of its potential motive power was the 9.20pm Edinburgh Lothian Road to Stoke Gifford (Bristol area) one of four such new services linking Scotland with the Western Region, but the only one routed via Carlisle, Leeds and Birmingham. This was a mid-morning Derby turn between Derby and Gloucester, giving a round trip of 186 miles and with the return half for the crew as passengers on a Bristol-York train; as such it was a popular duty. Rather like the Stirling-Sutton Coldfield car-sleeper train, it was a service upon

which a Carlisle allocated locomotive could be allowed to slip south and then south-west. Probably reflecting the contents of the wagons the train was later afforded a better path and was timed to arrive at Stoke Gifford at 3.38pm rather than 6.55pm.

Other new traffic flows along part of our routes of interest arose from the diversion of trains away from their usual route via Crewe whilst installations for electrification work were put into place. One such train was a Camden (North London) to Carlisle and brought a Nuneaton based locomotive to Burton and thence via Derby to Chesterfield/Rotherham/ Leeds. Although the Northbound run was during the early hours of the morning, the return working for the locomotive brought it through Derby in mid-afternoon. For this Nuneaton initially provided a Stanier 2-6-0 (Class 5), but upon later receipt (from Rugby) of a small allocation of Patriot 4-6-0s examples of that type were also used (45533/7/41/8). Other freight trains between Manchester/Stockport and London were routed in each direction via the Churnet Valley line then Tutbury, Burton and Nuneaton, usually with motive power from Longsight. Footplatemen from Nuneaton worked these latter trains between their home station and the Manchester area. A regular practice was to take water at Tutbury; a convoluted process involving detachment of the locomotive, closure of the level crossing gates, moving the locomotive forward to the watering point and then repeat in reverse, brake test and set off again. For the middle of the day working arrival in Manchester would be at a time when, with no balancing working, the men would return on a parcels/stock train via Crewe which was not booked to call at Nuneaton. A reduction in speed was arranged with the Driver of the train allowing the Nuneaton men to literally jump from the brakevan.

On the Midland main line the *Condor* service now saw a range of diesel and steam motive power; types 2 and 4 of the former and Black 5s, Jubilees and 9Fs. At the end of August trials commenced with a braking tender vehicle plus type 4 D77 and a coal train. The brake tender was to be placed either in front of, or directly behind, the diesel and its sole purpose was to apply additional brake force to that available from the locomotive and brake van.

Beyond the fitted (to some extent) freights was a vast raft of other services. Dependent upon the place of observation the exact routing of these trains and their places of origin and destination could be unidentifiable. The Midland Railway's network of junctions in Nottinghamshire and Derbyshire and local operating requirements could on many occasions confound logic.

One related anecdote (from a former signalman) was of the local daily trip working from Derby which went as far as Trent and then having used the North Curve, the station and the curve back to Sheet Stores Junction the train was starting out on its return to Derby. The story goes that the signalman at Sawley Junction would advise the next signalman (at Trent) of the approach of the train, the signalman at Trent would advise the next signalman (at Sheet Stores Junction) of the approach of the train and the signalman at Sheet Stores Junction would advise the next signalman (at Sawley Junction) of the approach of the train. So the signalman at Sawley Junction was being offered the same train coming back even though it had yet to pass him going in the opposite direction (see map!).

A surprise at the end of the calendar year was the rostering of a York V2 2-6-2 to the following freight trains:

12.45 a.m. (Mondays excepted) to Burton
1.15 a.m. (Sundays only) to Burton
6.50 p.m. (Mondays only) to Washwood Heath

The locomotive off the 1.15am had a return working, but for the others the locomotive was sent forward to Toton and was returned north as suitable traffic arose.

From the perspective of an observer 1961 was another year full of interest. At the beginning of the year British Railways, London Midland Region, introduced a new system of headcoding for the identification of individual trains. This relied upon a four character train classification number (e.g. express or local passenger train) destination letter and specific train numerics (e.g. 35). The bulk of our routes of interest lay within the London Midland Region and the letters as applicable were:

C   terminating area St. Pancras
D   Nottingham
F   Leicester
G   Birmingham
H   Manchester South and Stoke
K   Liverpool
P   Derby
T   Excursion and special trains local to London Midland Region and also for trip freight train
Z   Excursion and special trains local to LMR

For inter-Region trains:

E   to Eastern Region
M   to London Midland Region
N   to North Eastern Region
O   to Southern Region
S   to Scottish Region
V   to Western Region
X   inter-Region excursion or special train

In summary only, the train classification numbering system was:

1   Express passenger or newspaper, breakdown train
2   Ordinary passenger train
3   Parcels, fish, fruit, horses, livestock, meat, milk, pigeon or perishable train conforming to coaching stock requirements.
     Empty coaching stock.
     Express freight with continuous brake operable on not less than half the vehicles.
4   ⎱ Express freight with various proportions of total
5   ⎰ vehicles with operable continuous brake.
6
7   Express freight not fitted with continuous brake.
8   Through freight or ballast train.
9   Mineral, empty or branch freight train.
0   Light engine(s) with up to two brake vans.

The final two numerics confused us for a while, but then we discovered that anything shown between 50 and 98 indicated a route rather than a specific train. So IN37 was *The Devonian* bound for the North Eastern Region, ID15 was the down *Robin Hood*, 2H53 was any Derby to Manchester slow and 4M49 seemed to be the Edinburgh to Stoke Gifford fitted freight. Scanning the Special Traffic Notices (Barnt Green to Chesterfield) which arrived at the local signal box on Thursday afternoons became one of the events of the week … we were looking for anything headed IX _ _ or IZ _ _ or 3Z _ _ (for pigeon specials).

The first part of this Chapter summarised how the transition from steam to diesel was effected and how it impacted upon the fleets of steam express passenger locomotives. Part of the fascination of the first half of the year was in the fact that on many timetabled passenger trains either steam or diesel could appear, whilst most excursion and relief passenger trains would be steam hauled. There was a 'turnover' in terms of the Class 7 locomotives plying their trade and eight Royal Scots and the one Patriot now new to the routes, including 46106 with non-standard (for the class) smoke deflectors and for part of the summer both Derby and Saltley turned out home based Royal Scots, most of which were in good external condition and some – 46137 of Derby in particular – in exceptional condition. The star turn was reckoned to be 46143 although I never had a run behind it. However, classmate 46103 provided me with my best ever run from St Pancras to Leicester, non-stop on a Saturday relief.

Whilst high speed runs with Royal Scots and Britannia's plus 9Fs on summer weekends were highlights, the era also benefitted from the use of 4F 0-6-0s on certain Saturdays only trains during the summer. Leicester and Derby folk were a long way from any seaside resorts and in recognising this the Midland (plus Midland and Great Northern) followed by the LMS and then BR offered through trains to Yarmouth/ Hunstanton/Cromer/Lowestoft/Sheringham/ Gorleston whilst the Great Northern followed by the LNER and then BR offered trains to Mablethorpe/Skegness/ Cleethorpes, from Friargate station in Derby and Belgrave Road station in Leicester. Derby Friargate also offered a Friday night only through train to Ramsgate and following the withdrawal of many services via the Somerset and Dorset route, a Saturdays only train from Bournemouth (West). Leicester London Road also offered a train to Paignton.

Typically the 4Fs could be found on any of the following Midland services (plus their return workings) at least as far as Peterborough:

The date of this photograph is not known, but it may have been at one of the times when poor availability of diesel multiple units in the Nottingham/Leicester/Birmingham/Derby area resulted in short term substitute, locomotive hauled services. Locally allocated 4F 44556 is doubtless giving its footplate crew something to remember it by and providing linesiders with the Derby roar; otherwise likened to squeezing gritty wool out of a small hole in a large tank! Woolley's Bridge near Burton. (*Phil Waterfield*)

7.00 a.m.	(4 August–28 August) Leicester–Yarmouth (Vauxhall)
7.27 a.m.	(28 July, 4 August, 11 August only) Leicester–Hunstanton
8.30 a.m.	(30 June–1 September) Leicester–Sheringham
9.12 a.m.	Leicester–Yarmouth (Vauxhall)
8.15 a.m.	(23 June–1 September) Derby–Yarmouth (Vauxhall)
9.28 a.m.	(14 July–1 September) Derby–Cromer/Sheringham
10.05 a.m.	(23 June–1 September) Derby/Nottingham–Yarmouth (Vauxhall)
11.00 a.m.	(23 June–1 September) Leicester/Nottingham/Derby–Lowestoft/Gorleston-on-Sea
10.00 a.m.	(30 June–1 September) Kings Norton–Yarmouth (Vauxhall).

There is a danger in associating the arrival of the type 4 diesels with a dramatic and immediate downturn in steam performance and condition. It was not like that and assisted by the conservative approach taken to timetabling the two forms of traction worked turn and turn about. An attempt in April to increase the proportion of type 2 diesels on the Midland lines to St Pancras proved to be unsustainable and Jubilees plus the occasional Britannia supplemented the Royal Scots on the longer distance work whilst the Leicester turns remained or reverted to Class 5 haulage. The *Robin Hood* reverted to steam for nearly every day over a five week period as clearly, particular diesel diagrams were sacrificed. Holbeck even saw its Royal Scot 46113 allowed to go as far as Bristol (on 17 April).

For additional trains, reliefs and excursions little seemed to change except for more extensive use of diesel multiple units; for example, five of the seven excursions to the Uttoxeter-Buxton line on 13 May were formed by such units.

Each summer from the 1950s until the early 1960s, some of the Divisions of the London Midland Region arranged and marketed excursion trains aimed at the family wanting a day out during the annual holiday week or fortnight. The idea of the *City of Birmingham/Leicester Holiday Express* was to offer on each day of the week a different destination, with a departure around breakfast time and a return by mid-evening; maybe Southport, Blackpool, Belle Vue or somewhere beyond the Regional boundary. Here Saltley's well turned out Black 5 44942 is heading for home at Horninglow, Burton upon Trent, having been somewhere within the LM Region (denoted by the Z). Note the Cafeteria Car in the train. (*Phil Waterfield*)

Horninglow Gates and a train heading for the Eastern Region – probably one of the Skegness, Mablethorpe or Bridlington – with Black 5 44813 complete with trademark Saltley glossed smokebox is making haste. The train will be routed via Dove Junction to Egginton Junction thence via Derby Friargate to Colwick where an Eastern Region locomotive and crew will take over. In the background is the spire of Trinity Church, Burton, a victim of the bulldozer-fest of the early 1960s. (*Phil Waterfield*)

Leicester City Football Club had a run of success in the FA Cup defeating Oxford United and Bristol City at home in Rounds three and four respectively. Round five saw them drawn away to nearby Birmingham City with trains for supporters (reflecting the appeal of a true county team) originating from Kettering (45615) and Loughborough (45620) as well as from Leicester itself (42875 of Carlisle spare on the day and 45636). That match ended in a draw and a replay the following Wednesday. Leicester City then seemed attracted to drawn matches (home to Barnsley which brought in Brush type 2s D5680 and D5683) and two in the semi-final against Sheffield United (at Leeds and then Nottingham) before a victory at Birmingham on 27 March, for which locally allocated motive power was used. For the Final itself on 6 May both the Midland and Great Central routes were used; Jubilees, Black 5s and Standard Class 5s along the former and Royal Scots specially cleaned (46133/40/60) plus one Patriot

(45532 not needing any special cleaning) and one V2 (60890) on the latter, with Trafford Park's Patriot 45540 as stand-by locomotive. Sadly Leicester was unsuccessful in a match again characterised by a cruel twist of fate in the form of a broken leg.

The Sutton Coldfield-Stirling car-sleeper train season started earlier in the year than had applied in 1960, running north on Sundays and Thursdays only from 2 April to 23 May and then additionally on Tuesdays from 23 May to 12 September. The trains were extended to Inverness between 12 June and 9 September. Early season motive power was again the responsibility of Aston depot which turned out Jubilees either 45586 or 45647. However, once the season proper started and the number of loaded vans increased the requirement was for a Class 7 and Crewe North Royal Scots were utilised as part of a triangular diagram also involving Crewe-Birmingham and Carlisle-Crewe legs. Whilst that solved the

Northbound allocation it left the Southbound journey often needing power south of Leeds. Holbeck turned out Royal Scot 46145 (15 June) and Britannias 70053 and 70044 (6 July and 11 July respectively), but the events of note were on 25 and 27 June and 2 July. A3 pacifics were not allowed along the Wichnor Junction-Sutton Coldfield line, but apparently could be allowed to Birmingham New Street via Tamworth. So when A3 60088 appeared at Derby on 25 June it took the entire train on to New Street where the train was reversed and taken to Sutton Coldfield via Duddeston and the A3 locomotive went to Saltley; an exercise that was repeated with the same locomotive on 2 July. On 27 June A3 60038 was taken off at Derby and languished there for two days. Someone, somewhere took an interest and the workings for the rest of the season became an out and home Holbeck Class 7 (not A3s) working to Aston. However, right at the end of the season Aston turned out one of its recently acquired (ex-Western Region) Britannias (70025) for one trip.

Other items of interest during the year included:

- From 2 January 1961 there was an improved Birmingham-Nuneaton-Leicester service with diesel multiple units
- The accountants declaring that prior to withdrawal elderly Class 2 4-4-0s (40502/40632 of Nottingham) should run up to a mileage when a Works visit should normally be requested.
- The regular through working of an Eastern Region B1 from Cleethorpes to Birmingham ceased when the service was cut back to terminate at Nottingham.
- Bank Holiday and seasonal passenger trains not utilising 2-6-0 and 2-10-0 locomotives to the same high levels as in recent previous seasons.
- The variety of coaching stock in use on summer weekends showed little change over recent previous years.
- Diesel multiple unit trains saw more use on excursion trains.
- The start of the winter cold weather in November caused immediate failures of diesels due to train heating problems. Nottingham-St Pancras services reverted to Jubilee haulage.
- The Bedford to Hitchin and Northampton trains saw a further and final reversion to steam from December. One two-car diesel multiple unit was sent temporarily to Leicester, but not returned. 40026, 41224/5, 84005.
- In December a planned short-term withdrawal of a sub-fleet of 17 Cravens built two-car multiple units took place to enable an endemic axle defect to be corrected.

- Around Christmas the Miller's Dale-Buxton motor service was reinstated temporarily using 41286/41209.
- During the course of the calendar year the number of BR/Sulzer type 4s at Derby increased from 19 to 65.

Closures:

- Ashchurch to Upton-on-Severn 14 August 1961
- Stretton for Ashover (to passengers) 11 September 1961
- Bedford to Hitchin 30 December 1961
- Rugby (Wharf) to Leicester (Midland) 30 December 1961.

Whilst much of this book is about power, that word has generally referred to motive power. To set the scene for events in the final two years of the review it is appropriate here to refer to another form of power; political power. The Conservative Party had been in government continuously since 1951 and under the banner of Prime Minister Harold Macmillan's phrase 'You've never had it so good' had been returned to power in 1959 along with a healthy majority. The catchphrase had referred to full employment rather than the state of the national finances where pressure on the public purse was a constant. Quite apart from the huge investment made under the Modernisation Plan in and from 1955 and the lengthy period before any meaningful return could be anticipated, the day to day operations of the railways were also heavily in the red. There was a need for a review of all aspects of the nation's future requirements from railways and how the shape of the railways may need to be adapted to meet those requirements at a socially acceptable cost where actual costs could not be met from revenue.

In the government's White Paper published on 20 December 1960 the main proposals were that the:

- British Transport Commission would be abolished.
- BTC would be replaced by separate Boards for railways, canals, docks and London Transport.
- Railway Regions would be run as autonomous bodies controlling their own levels of charges and having commercial independence. They would also have responsibility for railway docks and steamer services.
- Railways accumulated debt of £1,600 million would be subject to £400 million being written off, £800 million attracting no interest charges leaving £400 as debt attracting interest.
- Overall control of the railways would be vested in the Ministry of Transport.

On 1 June 1961 Dr Richard Beeching assumed office as successor to Sir Brian Robertson (who had retired) in the role as Chairman of the British Transport Commission. Dr Beeching joined from his role as Technical Director at Imperial Chemical Industries who agreed to a leave of absence for up to five years. As part of the arrangement Dr Beeching would receive the same yearly salary as he was earning at ICI. Dr Beeching had come to know the Minister for Transport (Ernest Marples) through his work on a Committee set up by the latter to advise upon the financial state of the BTC (The Stedeford Committee). Arising from the work of that Committee much statistical information was available, but Dr Beeching wanted far more and to a depth not previously explored.

As part of his task Dr Beeching set out plans to collect data and to then convert that data into management information upon which proposals could be more firmly based. To assist him he would bring in specialists from private industry. The studies to be undertaken over a period of months would be:

1. A detailed further examination of the costs of handling existing traffics by existing methods.
2. To determine the forms of traffic which the railways then handled, or could handle, better and more cheaply than did other modes of transport.
3. To identify traffic flows by rail and other transport throughout the country as a whole, to discover what volume of traffic favourable to rail is available and how it moves.
4. To identify how the railways method of freight handling could best be modified to attract remunerative traffic.
5. To identify the volume of traffic likely to be attracted by various possible modifications of the system and the potential profitability of any such business so obtained.

By the end of the calendar year 1961 the government tabled a Transport Bill. This placed ultimate power over all nationalised transport into the hands of the Minister for Transport. The Bill proposed that the railways and canals would cease to be common carriers (i.e. obliged to carry whatever was presented to them) and be entirely free to fix their charges, except for passenger fares in the London area.

Dr Beeching became the designated Chairman of the British Railways Board which would have up to two Vice-Chairmen and between ten and sixteen members who need not be railwaymen (or presumably women). Power had been shifted to where the ensuing political and public debate could best be controlled. The publication in 1963 of the results of all the studies undertaken and proposed way forward would certainly lead to widespread debate and far-reaching changes.

Chapter Nine

1962: The Politics of Change and Steam in Decline

The route by which Dr Richard Beeching became Chairman of the British Railways Board is an interesting one.

During the Second World War Beeching worked on the design of armaments under that Department's Superintendent and Chief Engineer Sir Frank Smith. After the war Smith returned to ICI Ltd as Technical Director and his previous role was taken on by Sir Steuart Mitchell. Mitchell promoted Beeching to become Deputy Chief Engineer. However, in 1948 (at the age of 35) Beeching joined ICI Ltd as Personal Technical Assistant to Sir Frank Smith, a position he held for eighteen months before being appointed to the Board of the Fibres Division. In 1957 and on the recommendation of Sir Frank Smith, Beeching became Chairman of ICI's Metals Division and shortly afterwards became Technical Director on the ICI Ltd Board of Directors. Sir Frank Smith retired in 1959 and was asked by the Minister for Transport – Ernest Marples – to become a member of a special advisory group he was establishing to examine the finances of the British Transport Commission, to recommend what part the railways should play in the future economic life of the country and how they should be administered. That group became known as The Stedeford Committee and was appointed in April 1960 to conduct its work under Sir Ivan Stedeford, Chairman and Managing Director of Tube Investments Ltd. Sir Frank Smith declined the opportunity, but recommended Beeching. The Minister having accepted the recommendation Beeching worked alongside Mr C.F. Kearton, Joint Managing Director of Courtaulds Ltd, Harry Benson, Chartered Accountant and Partner at Cooper Brothers and Sir Ivan Stedeford.

The group worked quickly, completing their task in six months. Not a lot emerged into the public domain, but in hindsight it is clear that there was a divergence of views regarding the way forward for the railways and that the views expressed by Dr Beeching found favour with the Minister for Transport. No report from The Stedeford Committee in isolation appeared but the White Paper of December 1960 laid out how change would be enabled and how the deteriorating finances (operating deficit and charges on the capital account) would need to be tackled.

Beeching replaced Sir Brian Robertson as Chairman of the Commission and in March 1961 Ernest Marples announced in the House of Commons that on a five year secondment from ICI Ltd Beeching would be the Chairman of the British Railways Board when that Board was formed. Dr Beeching would have Sir Steuart Mitchell as his Deputy.

The political timetable allowed for the White Paper to progress to being a Bill and following passage through the legislative process would emerge as The Transport Act 1962. Dr Beeching had set to work to generate initial data via traffic studies (April 1961) and once that data had been assimilated with five further studies commenced, received and reflected upon he had a basis for developing far reaching proposals (which will be covered in the Chapter for 1963).

From purely an observational standpoint during the 1958-60 inclusive period it could be gathered that a move towards geographical area or Regional boundary control was favoured by the then Commission, and no doubt by some in the Conservative Party. I have in mind the decision of the Western Region to pursue a traction policy for main line diesel locomotives (hydraulic) at odds with other Regions, the painting of express passenger coaching stock in the chocolate and cream livery of the former Great Western Railway, allowing the Southern Region to retain their green (Southern Railway) and the re-painting of certain main line steam passenger locomotives of the London Midland Region into the maroon livery of the former London Midland and Scottish Railway. Whilst two of these policies could be put down to the Commission's wish to maintain *esprit de corps* the traction policy has always seemed an odd one. Corporatism rather than regionalism began to win the political will.

What was abundantly clear was a need for change. A review of business statistics reveals:

- Receipts £ million

	1960	1961	1962(1)
Passenger	160	157	151
Freight	315	306	292(2)

Note 1: No allowance made for increases in tariffs. Each figure is the actual for the year.

Note 2: Mineral traffic for the iron and steel industry affected by downturn in economic activity in Northern Britain.

- Working deficit for 1962. Total £159m (1961 £87m, 1960 £68m).
- Comparison of tonnage of freight moved by road between spring 1958 compared with spring 1962 (+26%) and decrease by rail over same period (-12%). Overall increase in tonnage moved +13% (rounded).

- Growth in private ownership of cars (millions)

1957	1960	1962	1963 (estimated)
4.2	5.5	6.6	6.8

The railways were changing:

- manpower reduced by 26,602 (in 1961)
- mainline diesels delivered total 1,673 and yet to be built (2,648)
- withdrawals: steam locomotives (2,924) carriages (4,927) wagons (102,199)
- proportion of train miles operated by diesel and electric traction (coaching 81%, freight 26%)
- freight trains fully or partially vacuum brake fitted. 2,310/daily or 47% total
- network miles equipped with automatic warning system, 1,232
- investment expenditure 1962 of £93m.

The progress made with the introduction of BR/Sulzer type 4 diesels along our two routes of particular interest enabled more through workings between the Western and North Eastern Regions. Such workings (between Bristol/Gloucester and York/Newcastle) eliminated the need for a change of locomotive(s) at the former boundary point of Sheffield and sometimes again at York. The use of diesel traction also eliminated the need for double heading, at least from a power availability perspective.

At the end of 1961 Millhouses motive power depot was closed by the Eastern Region, its allocation of passenger steam locomotives was transferred to Canklow (near Rotherham) and half of that former Millhouses allocation was placed into store, serviceable as required, at depots at Staveley (near Chesterfield); seven Jubilees three Royal Scots and one Patriot at the former Midland depot and two Jubilees plus one Royal Scot at the former Great Central depot. (Ten BIs were also stored at the latter). The first call for steam locomotives actually based at Canklow would be for timetabled services to London (for which there continued to be a need) and for additional trains such as excursions, reliefs and for seasonal/Bank Holidays. A consequence of these decisions was that a non-availability of diesel traction for cross country services from Newcastle/York meant substitution by steam power which would work beyond Sheffield to either Derby or Birmingham. Whilst this could affect any principal service it was two day-time trains which set the jungle telegraph into operation; Newcastle departures at 12.43pm and 3.30pm to Bristol and Birmingham respectively. The former of the two services would usually change locomotives at Derby (either with steam, or a diesel within a cyclic diagram), the latter would usually work through and possibly be returned with the 8.05am the following morning. January brought a rich bounty in the form of two A3s (60058/88), one A2 (60526), five V2s (60828/33/91/9/911) and one Britannia way from home (70005). February saw a continuation though it seemed that York became the usual boundary post for Newcastle based locomotives; ten V2s (60847/77/97/911/61/3, some more than once) plus another incursion by A3 60077 (then based at Ardsley). The return working by the A3 was interesting in that it fell on a Sunday when the usual route via Water Orton and Tamworth was closed due to engineering work. So the A3 made a trip via Sutton Coldfield and Lichfield to regain the usual route at Wichnor Junction and thereby complete a section from which the Class was banned. V2s were authorised to work through to Birmingham via either route.

The rare having become the half expected – plus the fact that most of the sightings in February were during half-term week – specific noting lapsed until Easter. That year Easter was late in the calendar and favourable weather allowed lengthy periods of observation; including the remarkable sights on several consecutive days of an A2 (60516) and, way off its usual territory, one of the two rarest of all Royal Scots, Polmadie's 46121. It did exist after all and must have surprised and delighted many as it worked through to Bristol on 24 April (12.48pm York to Bristol). That Easter weekend was interesting in that more Carlisle based steam locomotives were in evidence along the routes whilst one friend returned from a trip to Scotland to say he had seen half a dozen Holbeck Jubilees well north of the border. Although Royal Scots 46102/21 were the subject of folklore in the Midlands I suspect that over the years they were seen there more than 46104/5 and 7. Diesel traction was disturbing long held traditional routings and Easter also provided an opportunity to gauge the extent of the change. On the Saturday most of the timetabled passenger trains were diesel hauled, but still saw the use of twenty-two steam locomotives of

seven different Classes; Jubilees (nine) Black 5s (three) B1s (four) Royal Scots (two) Patriot (one) Standard Class 5 (two) A2 (one).

The use of steam power from the North Eastern Region through to Birmingham on timetabled trains continued though reduced as the requirement for steam heating of carriages ceased for the railway summer. The story beyond Birmingham to Bristol was similar in that after March diesel power predominated for timetabled trains and with effect from 12 March 1962 the banking of type 4 hauled trains (up to twelve carriages) up the Lickey incline ceased. During the second half of the winter, Barrow Road's ten 4-6-0s of three types had been used intensively and with typically heavy trains the lack of assistance from pilot locomotives (Gloucester to Sheffield, Sheffield to York for example) took its toll in timekeeping of through inter-Regional expresses.

The early months of the year had provided plenty of challenges also along the Midland lines to St Pancras. Kentish Town Trafford Park, Holbeck, Derby and Nottingham had a stock of Class 6 and 7 steam power

A new Hymek diesel hydraulic not yet painted in a top coat of two-tone green and destined when 'accepted' for the Western Region has arrived on a proving run over the Peak line from Gorton, has been run round its train and is awaiting departure from Derby. The shadows suggest this is quite early morning, much earlier than was usual for such trains. D7046. 23 July 1962. (*Kidderminster Railway Museum 088693, Courtesy P. J. Lynch*)

Evening, 7 September 1962, at Five Arches bridge, Derby. 4F 44419 and 3F 43637 (the latter probably having brought in a train from Shirland Colliery between Ambergate and Clay Cross) are backing down towards the motive power depot whilst North end station pilot 46440 (now preserved) is busy with a Stores van and a carriage. (*Kidderminster Railway Museum 088683, Courtesy P. J. Lynch*)

A Bedford allocated Jinty has probably arrived for attention at the Works or maybe has just been out-shopped and is running-in; whatever, Derby shed is using it as a station pilot. A varied selection of stock is being shunted and it is possible that the Royal Mail vehicle (second behind the engine) is destined to be attached to the Bradford-Bristol passenger train later that evening. 24 May 1962. (*Kidderminster Railway Museum 089231, Courtesy P. J. Lynch*)

In October 1962 the Locomotive Club of Great Britain organised a railtour titled 'The Midland Limited'. The tour featured haulage by J11 64354 between Nottingham Victoria and Burton upon Trent (via Derby Friargate), 3F 43658 between Burton and Derby (via Trent) and Patriot 45543 *Home Guard* between Derby and St Pancras. For the J11 (seen here at Egginton Junction) and the Patriot this was in their final weeks of service and the 3F would not survive much longer. (*Phil Waterfield*)

'The Midland Limited' railtour on 14 October 1962 is seen again, and after passing from its Great Northern origin route onto North Staffordshire territory, it is now firmly in a Midland area with 3F 43658 taking it forward to Derby. Patriot 45543 would then take it to Northampton via Market Harborough where – because of concerns over the state of the track to Bedford – it would be relieved by Black 5 45392. What a wonderful day out and a B16 in the morning from Marylebone as a bonus. (*Phil Waterfield*)

Normally by then (30 March 1962) a BR Sulzer type 4 duty the 12.43 Newcastle-Bristol has received a fresh engine from Derby in the form of Nottingham allocated Royal Scot itself, 46100 (now preserved). Not seeming to be in the best of health, the varying and often unpredictable demands for motive power at that time meant that home depot servicing arrangements became difficult, at best. Having spent time at a Butlins Holiday Camp and passing through the hands of private owners who could have done better the locomotive is (as at the time of writing) about to re-enter service in the BR green livery not evident at all in this illustration. (*Kidderminster Railway Museum 088471, Courtesy P. J. Lynch*)

to provide cover for notionally diesel hauled passenger trains and for additional services as required. In addition Burton had a substantial stock of Jubilees which could – and were on occasions – drafted in to support.

The need to retain sufficient steam power in reserve was a problem for most of the railway Regions. At the start of 1962 only 582 passenger tender locomotives remained nationally (plus 3,000 mixed traffic types) and elsewhere on the London Midland Region six Class 8 pacific locomotives were taken out of store to supplement available total power resources.

Not only front line express passenger services were exposed. It was necessary in late February/early March for some Luton/Harpenden to Moorgate services to revert to steam haulage; the reason being the familiar problems with diesel train heating boilers. The situation was eased not only by the season, but by the arrival at Cricklewood depot from May of the first of a batch of up to thirty-seven type 2 diesels built by Birmingham Railway Carriage and Wagon Ltd (D5379-D5415). On the services between Birmingham/Nottingham/ Leicester/Derby/Lincoln/Crewe that had been operating diesel multiple units, problems endemic and epidemic

were experienced. Vehicles/whole units awaiting rectification/modification/overhaul at Derby Carriage and Wagon Works were placed temporarily at Burton and Nottingham.

For this review of the first half of the year it is worthy of note that the batch of sixteen new BR/Sulzer type 4 diesels with Brush electrical equipment was progressively delivered. Following crew training these became available for route usage from Carlisle, Nottingham, Trafford Park, Leicester/Kettering, Saltley, Neville Hill/Holbeck, Sheffield Darnall, Bristol, Gateshead, Corkerhill (Glasgow), Derby and Cricklewood.

Passenger services between Bedford and Northampton were withdrawn with effect from 5 March 1962.

On the freight side of operations the original batch of ten BR/Sulzer type 4s (D1-D10) was transferred to Toton for freight workings between there and Castle Donington/Willington/ Drakelow power stations and to Wichnor Junction/Washwood Heath. The use of these 2,300hp rated units was partly to allow improved point to point timings over the two track sections of the Derby to Birmingham main line and also allow improved productivity from better (than steam) daily mileages, but despite being only three years old they proved to be less reliable than hoped and expected. Concentration of available units (plus D140/5/9/52/8) was placed onto the Washwood Heath out and back diagrams of which there were eight daily (Monday to Friday), saving nine sets of men and nine steam locomotives.

Finally, a new overnight fitted freight service was introduced between London (Victoria Docks) departing at 9.15pm and routed via Derby arrived at Liverpool (Brunswick) at 6.30 am. This was known as the Night Importer service and was probably as much about sending a message to the dockers of Liverpool as it was to transport perishable traffic.

At this middle part of the year it may be useful to have a summary of the trend affecting steam traction at principal depots and to show how that trend was then progressed. First, what happened to the Millhouses allocation of Class 6 and 7 power.

Class	Number	January 62	March 62	June 62	Notes
Patriot 7	45536	41E	-	41A	1, 2
Jubilee 6	45570	41E	-	41A	1, 2
	45576	-	-	41A	3, 2
	45590	41E	26B	-	1, 4
	45594	41H	-	41A	5, 2
	45602	41E	26A	-	1, 6
	45607	41E	26B	-	1, 4
	45627	41E	27A	-	1, 4, 7
	45654	41H	26B	-	5, 4
	45656	41E	26B	-	1, 4, 8
	45664	-	26B	-	9
	45683	-	-	41A	3, 2
	45725	41E	-	41A	1, 10
Royal Scot 7	46131	41E	6G	-	1, 11
	46147	-	1A	-	12
	46148	41E	1A	-	1, 13
	46151	41H	-	41A	5, 2
	46164	41E	-	41A	1, 2

Notes:
1. Placed into store at Staveley Midland.
2. Transferred to Darnall in June 1962, condemned at end of 1962.
3. In traffic throughout year, condemned at end of 1962.
4. Transferred to Agecroft.
5. Placed into store at Staveley Great Central.
6. Transferred to Newton Heath.
7. Transferred to Bank Hall.
8. Transferred to Darnall in December for condemnation.
9. In traffic until transferred to Agecroft.
10. Taken out of store in May for use at Whitsuntide weekend.
11. Transferred to Llandudno Junction.
12. In traffic until transfer to Willesden.
13. Transferred to Willesden.

Sundays at both of the Staveley BR depots were 'open house' and it was a pleasure to have a look around even though the future was bleak for most, if not all, of the 4-6-0 locomotives. There was interest a plenty in the locomotives that were employed in and around the extensive works of the Staveley Iron and Chemical Company; known as the Old Works and the Devonshire Works. In 1866 the Midland Railway had entered an agreement with the then works management to provide motive power to supplement that owned by Staveley and nearly a century later that agreement still stood. The locomotives supplied by BR were tank locomotives, 0-4-0s and 0-6-0s, the latter with half cabs only. The industrial locomotives provided a catalogue of the traditional builders of such; Avonside (three), Andrew Barclay (one), Manning Wardle (two), Black Hawthorn (one), Bagnall (three), Hawthorn Leslie (one) and Markham (five, including the oldest, *Staveley* built 1891 and *Gladys* of 1894). As with their mainline counterparts dieselisation threatened a continuation, with options limited to transfer elsewhere in the Company's activities (Northamptonshire) or withdrawal.

For the other principal depots of interest, the trends were as follows. For Derby, Kentish Town, Trafford Park and Holbeck I have included Class 5 power as that emerged as the preferred stand-by, go anywhere, burn anything and steam adequately for both passenger and freight services. Re-allocation of locomotives happened on a weekly basis and the periods selected are simply to align with timetable periodicities and the summer peak. Notes have been added where significant detail may be useful to certain readers.

Depot	At Start	Middle	At end	Note
Derby 17A	2 Jubilees 4 Black 5s 6 BR Std Cl 5s	17 Black 5s	8 Black 5s	1
Kentish Town 14B	4 Jubilees 8 Black 5s	1 Jubilee 4 Black 5s	No allocation of any locos	
Trafford Park 9E	3 Royal Scots 5 Black 5s	3 Royal Scots 3 Black 5s	3 Black 5s	2
Holbeck 55A	3 Britannias 1 A3 17 Jubilees 14 Black 5s 2 BR Std Cl 5s	3 Britannias 1 A3 15 Jubilees 14 Black 5s 3 BR Std Cl 5s 5 Royal Scots	1 A3 11 Jubilees 14 Black 5s	3
Nottingham 16A	3 Royal Scots	2 Royal Scots	-	4
Barrow Road 82E	3 Patriots 3 Jubilees 4 BR Std Cl 5s	3 Jubilees 6 BR Std Cl 5s	3 Jubilees 3 BR Std Cl 5s	5
Saltley 21A	10 Royal Scots 2 Patriots	10 Royal Scots 2 Patriots	-	

Notes:

1. Derby — Two Patriots (45532/40) allocated in April, then re-allocated in June to Carlisle Upperby via Saltley. Two Jubilees (45575/614) re-allocated in April to Burton. All BR Std Cl 5s to Rowsley.
2. Trafford Park — Three Royal Scots (46143/53/8) re-allocated in October to Annesley.
3. Holbeck — Five Royal Scots (46109/13/7/30/45) allocated in June from Low Moor, condemned in December. Three Britannias (70044/53/4) re-allocated in August to Crewe North.
4. Nottingham — One Patriot (45532) re-allocated in April to Derby. One Royal Scot (46157) re-allocated in June to Carlisle Upperby via Saltley. One Royal Scot (46112) re-allocated in October to Annesley. One Royal Scot (46100) condemned in November. Sold to W. Butlin & Sons Ltd.
5. Barrow Road — Three Patriots (45504/6/19) condemned in March.
6. Saltley — Six Royal Scots (46103/22/32/7/60/2) placed into store in June. Two Royal Scots (46106/18) returned in June from Leicester Central. All eight as above plus operational 46123/57 re-allocated in June to Carlisle Upperby. Two Patriots (45532/40) re-allocated in June to Carlisle Upperby.

As at the beginning of 1963 the sole remaining Class 7 power steam locomotive was the A3 (60038) at Holbeck. Kentish Town ceased as an operational steam depot and any incoming steam power would be serviced at Cricklewood. Barrow Road, with six Classes 5 and 6 locomotives would be exposed by any significant reduction in diesel availability/reliability or disruption of rosters due to adverse weather.

That summary provides a glimpse of the future, but for now we can review the summer and changes made to timetables.

Spring had included the welcome resumption of the overnight car-sleeper service between Sutton Coldfield and Stirling, extended in the peak of the season to/from Inverness. The gross weight of this popular service called for Class 7 steam power and as the season settled Carlisle locomotives (Royal Scots and the occasional Clan) were predominant, reflecting the locally increased allocation of that former type. Later in the season Britannias became more frequent; Aston having received a few examples from the Western Region and kept them in very respectable condition.

The lunchtime Manchester Piccadilly-St Pancras service via Stoke and Derby continued to be steam hauled and for many consecutive days (Mondays–Fridays) was hauled by further examples of former Western Region Britannias 70020 and 70019, *Mercury* and *Lightning* respectively. In its final few days of operation the 12.10 from Piccadilly featured pairs of Longsight Black 5s. The middle of the day working in the opposite direction was consistently an English Electric type 4 diesel.

There was, though, no hiding from the facts that by the summer steam was very much on the wane. Certainly it was still in irregular evidence with timetabled services particularly on cross country, but apart from weekend/seasonal reliefs and excursions the lines to St Pancras were dominated by types 4 and 2 diesels on both passenger and freight. Reflecting its still strong and varied selection of steam motive power types, Holbeck lifted spirits with forays by Jubilees (and those five returned Royal Scots), Trafford Park occasionally had access to Longsight Britannias, V2s and B1s from various depots continued to find employment on cross country (and in August two found a way to St Pancras). But the buzz had gone; instead of nearly forty Class 7s (and some new to us) of the previous two summer seasons we were by August down to penny numbers. The 9Fs stayed at home and in a summer characterised by poor weather so did many families, probably unwittingly supporting the statisticians who later successfully argued for a reduction from 1963 in the number of seasonal additional passenger trains operated and enabling the withdrawal of carriages and motive power.

Of note during that summer was the national adoption of the four character train classification system that had been in use for a year on the London Midland Region. That in itself must have made for an interesting afternoon and evening on 7 September when a derailment caused the diversion of the up *Northumbrian* (Newcastle to London Kings Cross) via Newark/Nottingham Midland (with 73053), D85 with the similarly affected *Scarborough Flyer* and in the reverse direction Britannias 70000/13 on London to Leeds/York relief services via Derby and the Cliffe (Southern Region) to Uddingston (Scottish Region) fully fitted cement train which had 9F 92141 in charge.

On the freight side of operations there were developments with trials with a diesel brake tender; a device which was a vehicle weighing 34/35 tons which had the sole purpose of providing additional brake force for diesel locomotives on loose coupled trains. In parallel the very long running trials with vacuum fitted coal trains continued with a pair of 9Fs being deployed between Cricklewood/Wellingborough and Toton. One new service that was very much fully fitted was between Thornaby and Severn Tunnel Junction and of some 1,300 tons. When steam hauled this train was required to wait at Blackwell (prior to the descent of the Lickey incline) whilst two additional locomotives (i.e. banking locomotives) were attached at the head of the train locomotive to provide additional brake force on the descent.

Turning now to timetables and timetabling considerations, in 1962 the electrification work on the routes south of Crewe from Liverpool and Manchester to London Euston had caused considerable allowances to be added in public timetables. The travelling public between terminal stations did not take kindly to being on trains hauled by diesel locomotives which were running to steam schedules and which tended to arrive and wait at intermediate junctions and stations. The first-class business traveller between London and Glasgow (and later to Manchester) had a new, alternative option in the form of five, daily British European Airways Vanguard flights with a duration of just 75–85 minutes. Time is money and when the travelling statistics for 1962 became available, the total number of first-class passenger journeys on the London Midland Region was 13 per cent down on the previous year. Along the route to/from Euston it would be a further three and a half years before the benefits of electrification to Manchester/Liverpool/Birmingham/Wolverhampton would become available and in the interim passengers would be faced with considerable disruption, initially as work at Euston station would necessitate the closure of several platforms. The unpalatable result of this was that from 10 September some Manchester services would be cancelled and some others diverted to start/terminate at Marylebone or St Pancras. Services cancelled included *The Comet* business train in each direction, the up *Lancastrian* and the latterly diverted (via Stoke and Derby) 12.10pm up and 1.55pm and 1am down. Those diverted were to be the sleeping car services from/to Manchester and Liverpool plus (later) two from Glasgow (all of which would operate from Marylebone) whilst the Barrow/Workington service would be routed from Nuneaton via Wigston and then up the Midland line to St Pancras.

Of the services that remained the 8am from Manchester Piccadilly with calls at Stockport, Wilmslow and Alderley Edge was due into Euston at 11.40am and provided a smoother riding alternative to the faster 7.45am from Central (*Midland Pullman*) calling only at Cheadle Heath and due St Pancras at 10.55am. The corresponding down morning train (a portion of *The Lancastrian*) did not fare so well, taking just seven minutes under four hours. In all the Midland line offered ten down and eleven up daytime services to/from Manchester (an increase of three/four respectively) at an average journey time of three hours and forty-eight minutes. The average timings were via the most direct route and included six trains which avoided Derby by taking the Spondon Junction to Derby North Junction route, the Chaddesden curve. Of particular note were the nine carriage 7.25am from St Pancras (with calls at Leicester and Cheadle Heath) and the 12.15pm from Manchester (with stops at Chinley, Derby and Leicester) which completed their journeys in three hours and thirty-five minutes; the former service being the substitute for the cancelled *Comet* from Euston which had latterly taken three hours and fifty-five minutes (public timetable) three hours and forty-five minutes (working timetable). Manchester did well. In the up direction the 4.25pm ran non-stop from Didsbury to Leicester and the new 5.25pm and 6.25pm had a stop inserted at Luton which was aimed at business travellers who previously would have alighted at Watford Junction.

Sheffield also benefitted in terms of journey times with the best up train timetabled to complete the journey in three hours and the down, via Trent and the Erewash Valley to Class Cross, in three minutes under three hours. There also seemed to have been some co-ordination between the planning authorities of the Eastern and London Midland Regions with the fastest trains from London King's Cross (via Retford) not directly duplicating/draining revenue from fast services from St Pancras and apart from the 7.03 am/7.20am up trains from Victoria and Midland respectively, similarly in the up direction. Sensibly the through carriage service from/ back to Halifax was discontinued. Leicester, Nottingham and Derby also benefitted both in terms of journey times and quantity of services (excluding *Midland Pullman*).

	Leicester	Nottingham	Derby
Fastest down service:			
old (minutes)	100	127	135
new (minutes)	90–91	117–118	128
Fastest up service:			
old (minutes)	98	127	135
new (minutes)	94	119	130
Number of down services:			
old	12	9	11
new	13	9	12
Number of up services:			
old	13	8	10
new	15	10	11

Dieselisation was also extended to the timetabled use over longer distances than previously for a four-car diesel multiple unit and a BRCW type 2 diesel plus carriages to work the 7.15am St Pancras to Leicester express and 10.00am return and 7.45pm Luton to Nottingham (SX) respectively.

The timetables finally reflected the (expected) wider spread use of type 4 diesels and encouraged the use of heavier trains; or, in other words, longer trains. However, the infrastructure and geometry of the Midland Railway offered stations with relatively short platforms – often on curves – which resulted in excessive overtime in stations whilst, for example, the train was drawn forward to allow access to parcels traffic. To address this problem it was necessary to re-form certain sets of coaching stock with the commercially undesirable result of a full brake vehicle being between passenger carriages. A welcome increase in daily mileages of some coaching stock sets accrued from Manchester and London home based sets working two day cycles with some 600 miles daily. One Leeds set also included a Bradford–Bristol return within its London route dominated pattern.

The capability of the diesels over short sections was such that particularly good times of eighteen minutes were included for six trains stopping at both Luton and Bedford. At that time the route still lacked any form of automatic warning system protection. During the currency of the summer timetable it was possible for the four-car, Leyland engine powered diesel multiple units diverted for use on the St Pancras to Bedford service to be released for use on their intended route out of Marylebone, being replaced by Rolls Royce powered sets latterly on the Barking line.

The cross country route also began to feel the benefits from dieselisation. Of note were the standard clock face departures from Bristol at XX.40, *The Devonian* running non-stop between Bristol and Birmingham, an additional service in each direction between Cardiff and Leeds, an extension of the accelerated (saving nearly one hour) Cardiff to Newcastle train from/ to Swansea and a new, three (diesel multiple unit) trains a day service from South Wales to Gloucester, Birmingham and Derby at 8.25am, 12.20pm and 5.20pm returning at 7.05am and 5.20pm plus 11.25am from Birmingham only. Also of note were the diversions from parts of their traditional routes of the *Pines Express* (Bournemouth West to Manchester Piccadilly) and *The Cornishman* (Penzance to Sheffield rather than Wolverhampton Low Level). The former service would be routed from Crewe via Birmingham Snow Hill, Oxford. Reading and Basingstoke, the latter taking the Midland line from Bristol through to Sheffield rather than the Cheltenham-Broadway-Stratford route to the West Midlands. The 8.40am Bristol to Sheffield passenger train continued to be consistently steam with power provided by Holbeck.

On through passenger trains along both routes of interest, the changing of locomotives at Derby was planned to soon become a thing of the past. Towards the end of the year – before the winter arrived in mid-November with a vengeance in the form of heavy snowfall, frost and freezing fog – much of the planning for dieselisation of both passenger and certain freight trains had come to fruition. Freight traffic classes included had been extended along the Midland line to London to include former Class E. Loads equivalent to those allowed for a steam 9F were included subject to there being a fitted head of at least 20 per cent of the total train weight. The new diesel brake tenders were also expected to allow greater use of diesels where brake force available needed to be enhanced.

One of the problems of seasonality was the overnight switching to the steam heat season. This tended to expose under-maintained boilers and led to varying levels of attempts to make such function. There had been a programme to replace tanks that split and the balance of probability in determining the cause of a failure swung toward the operator rather than the kit. However, whatever the cause the call for some steam locomotives to be used was again heard. On cross country Bristol Barrow Road's stock had been depleted, the condemnation policy of the Eastern Region for the Jubilees at Darnall was unhelpful, in

hindsight the transfer away of all of Saltley's Royal Scots and Patriots may have looked over hasty, but Derby's Black 5s and the Burton Jubilees would provide cover together with Holbeck's still reasonable stud and the North Eastern Region could continue to send V2s and pacifics.

On the London routes the planned run down of Kentish Town and Trafford Park depot fleets had been progressed. Any steam working out of St Pancras would be expected to be something returning home and in its final weeks it was not unusual to see up to ten passenger or mixed traffic type tender locomotives in the yard, predictably Derby, Burton and Holbeck examples plus strays from Carlisle and Manchester area depots appropriated as simply being locally available rather than on loan. Christmas Day/Boxing Day brought a flourish of steam activity both in London and, for other reasons, at Bristol. The former Midland depot at Barrow Road took on a more Great Western yard appearance with the allocation of multiple 2-6-2 and 0-6-0 tank locomotives from elsewhere in the area and secured its future at least whilst the transition to diesels was completely effected.

Closures of lines/services during the year:

- Beauchief station was closed with effect from 2 January 1962
- Bedford (Midland Road)–Northampton (Castle) 5 March 1962
- Coaley Junction–Dursley 10 September 1962
- Redditch–Evesham (due to condition of track) 29 September 1962.

Chapter Ten

1963: Hard Won Progress as the Elements and Politicians Take Charge

A late 1962/early 1963 review of traction types and facilities for maintaining fleets of diesel locomotives and multiple unit vehicles indicates how the transition from steam was being managed. In addition to Cricklewood (locomotives and multiple units), Toton (multiple units) and Derby (locomotives and multiple units) on the London Midland Region, an area of Holbeck depot at Leeds, North Eastern Region had been adapted to enable maintenance there of BR/Sulzer type 4 diesel locomotives in December 1962 and in the first week of that month received a block of consecutively numbered examples (D14-D32 inclusive). Meanwhile the modernisation plan for the Sheffield District of the Eastern Region had proceeded apace and the BR/Sulzer type 4s allocated to the Western Region were maintained at Bristol Bath Road. Work to establish a major locomotive maintenance depot for the Nottingham area was underway at Toton and work undertaken there on diesel multiple units was transferred to Etches Park depot, Derby.

Since the start in January 1960 of the St Pancras-Bedford diesel multiple unit service the resources at Cricklewood depot had been stretched continuously to manage the problems associated with that fleet of up to 120 vehicles (60 powered), the transitory needs of other units drafted in to maintain the service, the allocation of between 30 and 40 BR/Sulzer type 4 locomotives and a fleet of 37 BRCW type 2 locomotives (D5379-D5415 inclusive). Although with every month data upon which to base maintenance regime decisions was being amassed this was still new technology which had a capability to generate new technical challenges. An example related to the BR/Sulzer type 4s was the effect of the specified lubricating oil on piston rings. The expectation was of a need to change such rings every 12,000 to 15,000 hours of use; the emerging need was for a change every 2,000 hours. This was labour intensive work not envisaged and with a finite number of fitters/technicians it was inevitable that priorities would have to be assigned and decisions taken at a Regional level. A fire due to a seized engine on a diesel multiple unit conveying 650 passengers had been a worrying indicator and in

February a decision was taken to re-allocate to Derby for maintenance the entire Cricklewood set of BR/Sulzer type 4s and for periodic examinations of BRCW type 2s to be undertaken at Bedford, Wellingborough, Leicester and Saltley (the latter possibly being related to planned later use of BRCW type 3s into the Birmingham area). By March Derby had an allocation of 89 BR/Sulzer type 4s. However, actual availability of the type 4s on a daily basis was worryingly low and had been so throughout the winter (see later in this Chapter), reasons including the effect of the sub-zero temperatures, continuing problems with train heating boilers and the new one concerning lubricating oil. The consequence of the problems can be gauged from the number of the locomotives between D1 and D165 in and around Derby Locomotive Works and excluding newly built examples:

14 December 1962	16
21 January 1963	22
18 February 1963	24
10 March 1963	20
7 April 1963	22
15 May 1963	26
16 June 1963	29
12 July 1963	26
15 August 1963	36 (22% of fleet)
29 September 1963	28
16 October 1963	25
3 November 1963	22
16 January 1964	28

Interestingly the locomotives receiving Works attention very rarely included more than one from depots other than Derby and Toton; of the D1-D10 batch, mid-1963 consistently saw three or four examples under investigation/repair. Whilst all of this was not a good advertisement for new technology it still left a considerable fleet notionally available for traffic, even though confidence in cyclic diagrams being maintained over several days was realistically low. The intention of route management remained to progressively but quickly eliminate steam from the main line south of Leicester, but such intent had to be placed on hold.

Turning now to steam traction the position in summary at the start of the winter 1962/63 showed the following:

Holbeck	15 Black 5s 4-6-0
	11 Jubilees Class 6 4-6-0
	1 A3 4-6-2
	(Note: Royal Scots either
	condemned or re-allocated)
Derby	8 Black 5s
Barrow Road	3 Jubilees
	3 BR Std Class 5s
Trafford Park	3 Black 5s
Kentish Town	Closed
Cricklewood	2 Black 5s
Nottingham	6 Black 5s
Leicester	5 Black 5s
Saltley	35 Black 5s

(Note: Wellingborough had 23 9Fs and 21 at the end of the summer).

In addition Burton still had a large allocation of Jubilees in varying degrees of mechanical condition for use as required.

The response to the need for a larger pool of traction was met by Derby receiving from Burton eight Jubilees (45561/85/610/1/2/4/67/712). These were eased or pressed reluctantly into passenger traffic and, in some cases along the Midland line to St Pancras, directly substituted for BR/Sulzer type 4 diesels which were capable except in the critical area of the provision of steam to heat the carriages and, therefore, relegated to freight duties. The fleet of familiar Derby Jubilees was further strengthened by the addition of *Aden* and *Amethyst*, both new to the routes of interest during the period under review. That pair arrived in March and for the summer timetable three more (*Punjab*, *Hawkins* and (another newcomer) *Implacable*). During that period two Black 5s left to bolster the depleted fleet at Leicester Midland and three of the same Class went in the same month to Cricklewood. Three more arrived at Derby in May, being effectively swapped for three others which came from Blackpool depot.

A summary of re-allocations along the St Pancras routes during the first few months of 1963 shows a reversal of the trend towards a greater reliance upon diesels being replaced by a strengthening of steam resources. The depots particularly affected were Derby, Cricklewood, Leicester, Nottingham and, for cross

country, Saltley. Derby has already been detailed. Cricklewood – despite the demolition in part of its coaling facilities – received between early January and the end of March a total of ten Black 5s. Three were quickly re-allocated (for use on the former Great Central route) and three came from Derby's burgeoning fleet. Four BR Standard Class 5s followed, but were intended principally for inter-Regional workings to the Southern Region (which also operated the type and preferred the type to the Black 5s).

Nottingham depot had its allocation strengthened though not until the spring (four Black 5s).

Leicester received two Black 5s from Derby in March.

Trafford Park received four Black 5s and released one during the first four months of the year.

Holbeck was undisturbed and at Barrow Road one of the BR Standard Class 5s went (temporarily) to Shrewsbury.

Saltley received in March five Jubilees and all were newcomers to the cross country route, at least during the period under review (*Tanganyika*, *Sturdee*, *Barham*, *Duncan* and *Codrington*) followed in May by four Black 5s.

Out of chronological context here, but relevant in order to emphasise the point that the transition from steam to diesel traction was proving difficult and expensive is that Derby started the year with eight Black 5s and finished it with fifteen plus a dozen Jubilees … and seventy-five BR/Sulzer type 4 diesels. The diesel era timetables were difficult to maintain with steam and gross weights to be moved would in former days have justified requests for a pilot locomotive to be provided. It was for all concerned a very difficult time … and then there was the weather.

Winter 1962/63 was the most severe since 1947 and a combination of snow, ice, fog, fierce winds from the east and continuous sub-zero temperatures throughout the day-time as well as night made life for everyone difficult, including those involved with all forms of transport. The season had started in mid-November with a heavy fall of snow and this was followed by a cold snap with thick fog forming whenever day-time temperatures and a static area of high pressure combined. On the railways fog provided the usual barrier to progress and ice and snow quickly affected the gross tonnage of coal emerging from the Erewash Valley. Non-essential steam-hauled freight trains were either combined or cancelled and during the festive season fewer additional passenger services were run.

Diesel traction in both locomotive and multiple unit form did not take kindly to the sub-zero temperatures exacerbated by the effect of running at speed and consequently the common causes of failures were frost damage to exposed pipework and the seemingly constant winter problem of boilers to provide steam for heating carriages. Steam locomotives were not immune and their water tanks, water feed pipes to injectors and clacks being in need of protection whilst standing at depots awaiting duty. Yards at depots were characterised by lines of fire devils or braziers placed to protect the injectors themselves and to prevent the 4,000 gallons of water in most tanks becoming giant ice-lollies.

Passenger services were run with whatever was to hand and for those who ventured out to observe will have seen an array of traction which varied from day-to-day both on the Midland lines to London and cross country. Arrivals into St Pancras included the by then rare sight of Royal Scots plus more familiar at the time B1s, Jubilees, Black 5s and no doubt in some operational crisis the odd 9Fs which were not fitted with steam heating equipment.

January was a wretched month of arctic conditions affecting not only Scotland and Northern England, but nationally. The re-allocation of steam locomotives to various depots has already been noted earlier in this Chapter, but perhaps worth mentioning is the loss of the Holbeck Royal Scots in late 1962 which could have proven to be very useful over the next few months. The motive power depot arrangements for supplying traction for timetabled cross-country passenger trains were based upon the winter 1962/63 timetables and cyclic use of type 4 diesels from the Western (Bristol) and North Eastern (Holbeck and Gateshead) Regions, with the notionally large concentration of such types at Derby as a useful source of relief as and when needed. As the availability of the type 4 diesels fell away, frequently at little or no notice, it often fell to York (still with a good range of steam) to support the service with V2s, together with Jubilees and Class 5s from Holbeck, Derby and Saltley, plus Barrow Road's Jubilees and BR Standard Class 5s. At the Western Region locomotive exchange/provision point Barrow Road's now very limited quantity of steam locomotives suited to express passenger trains work, together with the Regional policy on the use of diesels having hydraulic transmissions (the Brush type 4s were yet to make an appearance), meant it was somewhat exposed and unable on occasions to maintain diagrams. This combination undoubtedly resulted in the first ever penetration of a V2 on a through working from the North East all the way to Bristol, a Grange (Western 4-6-0) and then the highly improbable pairing of a pannier tank (Western Region 0-6-0) plus B1 on the 6.46am Gloucester-Sheffield as far as Birmingham. As had been seen before with cross-country passenger services certain trains were the more likely to be steam worked, but during this particular January predicting anything was a fool's game; it was a case of wrapping up and setting off for a few hours and see whatever turned up. Two of the three signalmen at my vantage point – Breadsall Crossing – knew the small group of local diehards and were happy for us to light a fire in an old bucket and supplement the wood/lumps of coal we took with us. The third signalman was in a different category and did not welcome our attendance, our genuine interest and enquiries or the smoke from our warming fires; on one occasion calling the British Transport Police who came along, had a warm and went away. Observations were limited to reasonably bright days and day light hours only, but the following were enjoyed and cheered on their way:

8th	a pair of Black 5s (both Saltley) on the late running 8.25am Birmingham-Newcastle
10th	61337 (minus its pannier tank pilot!) on the very late 6.46am Gloucester-Sheffield
15th	45597 1.08pm Leeds-Cardiff

A fortuitous failure of the school heating system created extra viewing opportunities during the week commenced 21 January. Whilst it was perishing cold it was also bright and the unexpected holiday was enjoyed to the full. At a personal level I could hardly wait for the 27th to arrive. On that day (Sunday) the Derbyshire Railway Society was running a rail tour to Birmingham, Shrewsbury and Crewe with a Clan locomotive plus a pilot locomotive between Tyseley and Shrewsbury (presumably for use of automatic train protection equipment on the Western Region Hall Class locomotive). Although the 22nd produced a rare Jubilee (*Colossus* 45702) and a V2 (60837) the following day brought forth the same V2 and, on the 8.20 Newcastle-Swansea the barely believable sight of a Gateshead A3 (60042 *Singapore*). Unfortunately for me I was having my lunch at home and missed it! Well, you wait for years and then two come along together; the following day 60039 *Sandwich* of King's Cross depot was on the same train and unlike *Singapore* went beyond Derby, but failed before reaching Birmingham. The 24th brought a confirmation that the rail tour planned for the 27th had been deemed non-essential and was postponed until 24 March. The 25th was snowy, but the following day – Saturday – was bright and I wanted to know what had been through. To give one signalman a weekend off the other two worked twelve hour shifts (6 to 6) – thus allowing the lucky signalman to book off at 10pm on the Friday and then not book back on until 6am on the following Monday morning; the normal shift pattern being 6am to 2pm, 2pm to 10pm and 10pm to 6am. Breadsall Crossing signalbox was manned continuously. The reason for that was the need to close and open the gates for road traffic, for which duty an allowance was made in the weekly wages. At weekends the next signalbox open to the North was at Belper Goods, necessary to advise Ambergate South Junction box of routes required to be set. Little Eaton Junction and Duffield boxes would be closed at the weekend and distant signals placed into the 'on' position. The signalman at Breadsall Crossing would receive his first indication of an approaching train from the North when it was at or passing Ambergate and he would then time the closure of the gates dependent upon the classification of the train concerned as advised by bell codes; four bells, express passenger, three pause one bells local passenger trains for example. When previous Christmases had come around signalman Bill

Ayris would call on his way home early in the morning, taking with him one of our hens and it would then re-appear that night ready for the oven! Bill had retired and on 26 January I was unlucky in that the duty signalman was the one with no interest in sharing any information let alone vital information and Special Traffic Notices. I really wanted to find out whether the Clan locomotive for the (postponed) rail tour had been sent south, but irrespective of good intent my logic was badly flawed as I later found out that the tour was to originate in Leeds. However, I was well rewarded for my attendance at the lineside.

The first train to pass was Northbound and with a 2-6-4 tank (albeit a Saltley one) plus three carriages. I assumed (incorrectly) that it was the Derby-Manchester stopper running late. It was in fact a hastily arranged relief to the 7.35am Bristol-Bradford which had been very badly delayed between Bristol and Birmingham

Just after the start of a wonderful day out. The severe weather of early 1963 had caused the postponement of this railtour from 27 January to 24 March. The motive power for 'The Derbyshire Railway Society' tour to Tyseley (where Hall 7929 was added as pilot locomotive to Shrewsbury), Wolverhampton, Shrewsbury and Crewe (Works) was *Clan Macleod* (72008) and is seen here to glorious effect passing Branston. (*Phil Waterfield*)

and the relief ran as far as Sheffield. The Bradford train was run in the path of the Swansea/Cardiff-Newcastle and although the noise of its approach was lost on the Easterly breeze the sight was to remain a clear memory over half a century later. It was A3 60039 with German-style smoke deflectors, commendably clean and going well. As the locomotive passed, the Driver half turned in the bucket seat (that seemed so much better than the Stanier tip-up flat effort) and took in the initially stunned expression of one open-mouthed, young observer. Together with Britannia 70015 in 1959, Clan 72005 in July 1960 and a V2 to be introduced later in this Chapter it is in the pantheon of personal railway memories. Could anything follow that … and would anyone believe my sightings during the week? When the Swansea/Cardiff-Newcastle appeared it was double headed by a highly unusual combination of a BR/Sulzer type 4 diesel with a BR Standard Class 2 allocated to Worcester providing steam heat for the carriages. Cold days, short days, not days during which to linger and I suspect that many more unusual locomotive workings occurred which were never recorded, even with my pleas to friendly signalmen to record numbers in the Train Register. Another A3 (60084 *Trigo*) was seen on 12 February (8.20am Newcastle-Cardiff/Swansea), but I feel that more will have passed unobserved.

An interesting aspect of the first three months of the year was the regularity with which locomotives away from their normal operating area were seen. In steady state, good weather and with a few relief trains around it was perhaps only 3 per cent of sightings that were unusual. This winter period was different with every short session seeming to offer something new. As an example the Nottingham-Liverpool (via Derby and Manchester) morning passenger train had reverted to regular haulage by steam; seven Mark 1 carriages for which a Black 5 would be provided. Nothing unusual there so far, but locomotives from such depots as Fleetwood, Bangor and Carnforth were highly unusual.

The value of railways to communities nationwide was amply demonstrated throughout the winter, none more so than in January when thirty youngsters found themselves snowed in and marooned near Hartington on the Buxton-Ashbourne line and with others in that village in need of basic supplies. Three steam locomotives were coupled and then with a snow plough at each end of the trio were despatched to Ashbourne, followed by two more locomotives and a carriage to run as far as Hartington. Unfortunately this latter pair plus carriage became stuck in a newly forming snowdrift between Hindlow and Briggs Sidings and a further locomotive sent to assist could get no further

than Hindlow. Meanwhile the three locomotives with snowploughs could not achieve their original goal, but returned and collected the other locomotives (except one which was completely immobilised) and carriage, reaching Buxton late in the evening. Between 22 and 25 January passenger services were re-introduced between Buxton and Ashbourne, with two trains each day utilising the one carriage and two locomotives.

At last, in late March, the winter weather patterns were replaced with something more tolerable. However, a storm of a different nature – a political storm – was soon dominating the National news agenda.

The Transport Act 1962 had received Royal Assent on 1 August 1962 and became effective from 1 September of that year. The Act put into place the enabling legislation to assist the Conservative government to effect radical changes to the railways of the nation. The British Railways Board came into being on 1 January 1963 and its first Board meeting was held during the first week. The Board had in effect been operational since June 1962 when it was constituted as a Committee and most of its membership was unchanged in name and function. Sir Steuart Mitchell was now Vice-Chairman also with a responsibility for workshops and (six) full-time executive Members had responsibilities for manpower and planning, technical matters, finance and commercial matters. In addition there were five part-time Members representing Regional Boards.

In July 1962 maps illustrating the density of passenger and freight traffic had been made available.

In September proposals to re-organise the railway workshops had been announced and trade union reaction had included a strike. More positively, in October Dr Beeching addressed the Institute of Directors regarding how the railways could seek to win the £90 million worth of traffic currently moved by road, but well suited to rail.

Dr Beeching had made attempts to try to persuade civil servants and politicians of the benefits of productivity deals with the workforce and readers of previous Chapters will conclude that in areas of depots and locomotive workings alone there was vast potential waiting to be explored. The government was not keen to allow any such negotiations to start, fearing that their straight-jacket on public purse expenditure could be opened. Pay for railway personnel again started to slip behind contemporary sectors of industry.

What had not emerged publicly was the management information which arose from the extensive surveys of traffic and the additional areas which Dr Beeching had required to be studied and analysed. The conclusions from the analysis were included in a Report which was published on 27 March 1963 by Her Majesty's Stationery Office on behalf of the British Railways Board ('The Re-shaping of British Railways'). Throughout the legislative process the position and expressed view of the government was that a railway service would be operated if users were prepared to pay an economic price for it. Service to a community was no longer a pressing consideration. General subsidisation from the public purse was at an end and proposals affecting closures of services and lines would be taken locally by third party bodies. Where decisions based on grounds of national economy or of social needs needed to be taken the Minister of Transport would be responsible, having sought the approval of parliament.

The Report was brutal in its assessment of the problem and its proposed remedy to that problem. The case was made on a basis of national economics. In that regard it was useful for the government to be able to point out that in 1962 the British Transport Commission made a profit on all of its operations except inland waterways and railways and that in 1962 the working deficit of the railways was £104m (17m worse than 1961), gross traffic receipts down by £10m and working expenses up by £7m. The least used 50 per cent of 4,300 stations open to passengers in 1960 contributed only 2 per cent of total passenger revenues and one third of the route carried just 1 per cent of total passengers.

Recommendations in the Report included that 6,000 miles of route (out of a total of some 18,000) should be closed entirely and some of the remaining lines be for freight only, 2,363 stations should close (including 435 already listed and being considered) both on lines to be closed and along those to remain open.

There was seemingly no consideration of branch lines being necessary to support main lines, of seasonal traffic to the coasts, for the railways to be reorganised as part of a wider future, national transport policy or any far-reaching thinking to retain the one main line built to the continental loading gauge (the Great Central).

This book is not about the Beeching Report. It is though relevant to consider here the effects of the proposals upon our routes of specific interest.

The proposals made in 1962 for the workshops included:

Derby Locomotive Works:	To continue as a locomotive works with some increase in staff in 1963 and 1964.
Derby Carriage & Wagon Works:	To continue as a carriage and wagon works, but reduced in size to employ 3,200 (currently 4,000).
Bromsgrove:	To close in the third quarter of 1964 (219 staff).

Lines: Passenger services to be withdrawn:
Buxton–Miller's Dale
Derby Friargate–Nottingham Victoria
Derby–Burton-on-Trent–Tamworth–Birmingham
  (local services)
Derby–Sheffield (local)
Derby–Trent–Nottingham (local)
Kettering–Leicester
Kettering–Melton Mowbray–Nottingham
Leicester–Burton-on-Trent
Leicester–Melton Mowbray
Leicester–Nottingham (local)
Leicester–Peterborough North
Manchester–Chinley–Derby (local)
Northampton (Castle)–Peterborough
Northampton (Castle)–Wellingborough Midland Road
  (including Higham Ferrers)
Nottingham–Lincoln
Nottingham–Melton Mowbray
Nottingham–Sheffield (local)
Nottingham–Worksop
Rugby–Peterborough
Wolverhampton–Burton-on-Trent

Lines: Passenger services to be modified:
Birmingham–Barnt Green
Birmingham–Leicester–Nottingham
Birmingham–Redditch
Birmingham–Worcester
Crewe–Derby
Derby–Nottingham
Gloucester–Bristol
London–Nottingham
Worcester–Gloucester

Stations: To be closed
Alfreton and South Normanton
Ambergate
Ashby-de-la-Zouch
Ashwell
Awsworth
Bagworth and Ellistown
Bakewell
Barrow-upon-Soar and Quorn
Basford North
Bedford St John's
Belper

Berkeley Road	Kirkby-in-Ashfield
Blaby	Langley Mill and Eastwood
Bleasby	Lincoln St Marks
Borrowash	Long Eaton
Burton Joyce	Lowdham
Buxton	Lubenham
Chapel-en-le-Frith Central and South	Luffenham
Charfield	Mangotsfield
Cheadle Heath	Menton
Chorlton-cum-Hardy	Matlock Bath
Churchdown	Melton Mowbray Town
Clay Cross	Miller's Dale for Tideswell
Coalville Town	Millhouses and Eccleshall
Codnor Park and Ironville	Moira
Corby	New Basford
Cromford	Peak Forest for Peak Dale
Croft	Pear Tree and Normanton
Darley Dale	Pye Bridge
Derby Friargate	Radford
Derby Nottingham Road	Repton and Willington
Desborough and Rothwell	Rolleston Junction
Desford	St Albans Abbey
Disley	Sheepbridge
Dore and Totley	Sileby
Dove Holes	Spondon
Draycott and Breaston	Stanton Gate
Dronfield	Stapleford and Sandiacre
Duffield	Stockport Tiviot Dale
East Langton	Stoke Works
Fiskerton	Syston
Gresley	Trent
Gretton	Trowell
Harpenden East	Wellingborough London Road
Hazel Grove	West Hallam
Humberstone Road	Westhouses and Blackwell
Ilkeston Junction and Cossall	Whatstandwell
Ilkeston North	Wheathampstead
Irthlingborough	Wickwar
Kegworth	Wigston Magna
Kibworth	Willington
Kimberley East	Wingfield
Kirby Muxloe	Yate

The process for closure was quickly in evidence and during the course of 1963 the following closures were effected:

- Kimberley–Eastwood & Langley Mill (passenger 7 January 63
- (Nottingham Victoria) Eastwood & Langley Mill–Pinxton (South) 7 January 63 (Note: both of these sections had been managed under 'old' arrangements)
- Ripley–Marehay Crossing (goods 1 April 63; closed to passengers 1 June 30)

- Ripley Goods Depot 1 April 63
- Kettering–Loddington mineral branch 6 May 63
- Redditch–Ashchurch 17 June 63 (London Midland) 9 September 63 (Western)
- Harpenden (Central)–Hemel Hempstead 1 July 63
- Tewkesbury–Upton-on-Severn 1 July 63
- Middleton Incline (Cromford and High Peak) August 63

- Wraggs Siding (Swadlincote)–Woodville Goods Junction 9 September 63
- Ashbourne–Hartington (goods; closed to passengers 1 November 56)
- Heanor South branch (goods 7 October 63; closed to passengers 1 May 28).

Notices were posted regarding the proposed withdrawal of passenger services from the following:

- Northampton (Castle)–Peterborough (to include Motor/push pull service to Wellingborough) 9 September 63
- Derby (Friargate)–Nottingham (Victoria) 9 September 63.

The period between Notices being posted and any subsequent closure varied from the statutory minimum period (for example where there was satisfaction with the adequacy of replacement bus services and/or there were no formal objections to the proposals) to years (where there were substantial objections to be considered and potential/actual referral to the Minister for Transport). The Derby (Friargate)-Nottingham (Victoria) service was closed to passenger stopping services a year after the Notices were posted.

The reaction from the trade unions was to use the statutory closure procedure to make their concerns heard at a local level. At national level the concerns were centred upon arrangements for Members' terms of redundancy, seeking alternative employment within the industry, transfer, resettlement and lodging allowances. All of these concerns were legitimate, but it took the threat of a three-day national strike in May before the Railways Board conceded.

Returning now to our mainstream subject, the early months of the year had brought considerable observational interest to a yard near Derby Midland station. St Andrew's yard contained multiple examples of a type of diesel locomotive built at Hatton (near Derby) with Paxman power units developing 900hp. The initial production batch of fifty-one was destined for the Scottish Region and a small number entered service there before three successive failures of crankshafts prompted concerns over a possible epidemic and a decision to halt further acceptance. Consequently February, March and April saw examples held at Derby (both St Andrew's and at the motive power depot) whilst the problem was resolved; a test run on 30 April with empty coaching stock to/back from Chinley with D8530 seeming to satisfy all concerned. With their centrally placed cabs and attractive livery the locomotives were unusual. Also adding a splash of colour around Derby were powered

cars from *Midland Pullman* sets (60091/3/731) together with a Trailer Parlour Car (60741) in the Works for modifications. Elsewhere successful trials were held on the Lickey incline with the first of the Brush Traction type 4 diesels (D1500) in a two-tone green livery and the forerunner of an extremely useful class which would eventually total some 500. The era of production of small batches of new locomotives was coming to a close although the Railways Board gave trials to *Lion*, a one-off diesel electric type 4 power range produced by Birmingham Railway Carriage and Wagon Ltd which appeared in a very brave, if ill advised, white livery. It also had trials on the Lickey.

Quite apart from the various diesels either static or passing through, the cumulative effect of withdrawals of steam locomotives was becoming apparent even though the effects of the winter weather disguised the fact. The year 1962 had seen the withdrawal of 2,928 steam locomotives and 69 classes became extinct. Along our lines of route the ranks of the familiar 2F and 3F 0-6-0 tender locomotives (which totalled 935) had been reduced to just ten; three 2Fs at Coalville (58143/8/82) and seven 3Fs (four at Derby and three at Bedford). The 2F survivors were from a class built originally in 1875/6 with a driving wheel diameter of 4 feet 11 inches and later rebuilt with small Belpaire boilers. Twelve examples of the class worked out their days at Coalville and the last turn of all fell to 58148 (14 December 63). The 3F survivors were from a class built between 1888 and 1902 with 5 feet 3 inch driving wheel diameters and later rebuilt with the larger Belpaire boilers. Bedford having seen its three either condemned or re-allocated to Derby, the final three (43620/37/69) was in steam up to 27 January 64. Both of these classes were necessarily prolonged due to restricted clearances of tunnels (Glenfield and Shirland respectively), but with both lines having something of a future, alternative motive power in the form of BR Standard Class 2 (78XXX) were deployed, that at Coalville (78013) having its cab profile modified. More positively, there were still 820 Black 5s, 661 8Fs, 393 4Fs and 145 Jubilees. It was though a time to start to make an increased effort to see the diminishing variety of types on offer and a small group of us tried to see the evening Burton-on-Trent–York freight (known to us as the beer train) on the Derby Friargate line which on increasingly rare occasions produced a York B16. To do this we walked or cycled to Breadsall hilltop where although the station was long closed the signalbox remained open and a lady signal person operated the section including GN somersault signals. Feeling pleased with our efforts, we were at Derby Midland when one day in April two

B16s passed through with rakes of new hopper wagons bound for Gresley (61454/61) and we decided to concentrate on other classes. Possibly in an attempt to hasten the withdrawal of Stanier three cylinder 2-6-4 tank locomotives Nottingham's 42636 found its way on 24 April into the pit of the 60 feet diameter turntable at Derby motive power depot.

With freight traffic there were several developments of interest. The *Condor* service from Hendon to Gushetfaulds (Glasgow) had gained the confidence of transport managers and was moving loads to full capacity with BR/Sulzer and on occasions steam traction. In January the concept was extended to a new service each way between Birmingham and Glasgow via Crewe and the West Coast route, normally using a single BR/Sulzer type 2 though on occasions North British Locomotive Co Ltd built type 2 D6123 ventured south. (Note: from early 1964 both *Condor* services were routed via the West Coast line).

In March the Esso Fawley refinery-Bromford Bridge storage tank sidings and empty returns were placed (progressively as training allowed) into the care of BRCW type 3 diesels. Five of the class (D6505/21/46/9/85) were based at Saltley and until such time as training was complete the diesels brought the trains as far as Gloucester. These trains required considerable banking effort up the Lickey incline, as did similar trains from Avonmouth, later also from Milford Haven to Coleshill and the trains from Avonmouth bound for Cadbury's at Bournville with large tonnages of cocoa beans.

Planning for new flows or for long overdue improvements to existing flows resulted in priorities having to be assigned for utilisation of two track sections with few passing refuge loops, for example Stenson Junction to Water Orton (excluding the Burton area). During the summer a traffic flow new to the route was introduced between Scunthorpe/ Frodingham steelworks and Severn Tunnel Junction. The actual traffic was not new and had previously been routed via Barnetby, Annesley, the Great Central line to Woodford thence to Gloucester, a journey taking several days and the long train composed of bogie

The special movement in 1963 of two rakes of new 24 ton capacity mineral wagons from the North East of England to Gresley brought the highly unusual sight of two B16 4-6-0s. Here 61454 of York is at Wetmore, Burton and near the end of its journey. (*Phil Waterfield*)

bolster wagons. The new route was via Doncaster (avoiding line) Mexborough, Swinton, Rotherham, Chesterfield, Derby and Birmingham using a single Brush type 2 diesel. At Birmingham (Saltley/Landor Street) a Western Region type 4 hydraulic locomotive took over and enabled the journey to be completed in less than twelve hours. Whilst the weight of this train was not excessive its length was such that access to certain passing loops was essential whilst passenger trains took priority. The return working of the empty wagons was spread between the 4am from Cardiff and 12.55pm from Margam which conveyed various other traffic to Birmingham, Barrow Hill and Staveley.

In parallel plans to improve the flow of coal traffic and empty returns between Toton and Washwood Heath envisaged a time of 101 minutes in each direction, with a terminal allowance of 65 minutes. Theoretically at least it would be possible to cover the eight daily trips with just two BR/Sulzer type 4 diesels, but pathing difficulties rendered such a bold move forward impracticable,

though improvements did accrue. Planning also began for the dieselisation of Toton-Brent services with BR/Sulzer type 2 diesels and brake tenders; pairs of locomotives being based at Toton and Wellingborough and a single unit at Cricklewood. The planning soon became limited daily practice and enabled the release of some BR/Sulzer type 4s to other duties. Wellingborough though retained a fleet of 9F 2-10-0s (twenty-four at the end of June and twenty-one at the end of summer) and these continued working both south to Brent and north further into the Midlands.

In June Saltley's three 9Fs equipped with mechanical stokers were re-allocated; 92165/6 went to Bidston (6F) to work the John Summers iron ore traffic from the docks and 92167 went (temporarily) to Tyne Dock (52H) for banking duties between there and Consett steel works.

Later in the year a new car service similar to the well-established Chiltern Green–Bonnybridge run was introduced between Coventry (Gosford Green) and

The diesel era and a Western Region hydraulic type 4 is taking forward a Scunthorpe-South Wales train of bogie bolster wagons. This was a train re-routed away from the former Great Central route and with an Eastern Region Brush type 2 diesel electric as far as Landor Street (Saltley) and a change of locomotive/crew, completed the journey in around twelve hours. The classification 6 in the train description indicated that the train had a proportion of its vehicles with vacuum brakes operable. (*Kidderminster Railway Museum 134537, Courtesy P. Riley*)

Glasgow (Shields Road) for Rootes taking Hillman Imp cars. The significance of that was not the route (West Coast) but the fact that on occasions the pairs of English Electric type 1 diesels which worked such trains throughout would spend time at Saltley depot. Dependent upon the timings it was possible to see at the depot locomotives from five Regions (D65XX Southern, D10XX Western, D81XX Scottish, D55XX Eastern plus numerous London Midland examples).

For passenger services the consideration is in two parts. First, the timetabled and seasonal/ relief services and secondly the range of excursion traffic which was considerable and included football, cathedral and tours for enthusiasts seeking a final opportunity to travel a line threatened with closure, a type of locomotive soon to be extinct or both of those relative attractions.

In April newly built (at BR Swindon Works) four-car inter-city diesel multiple units took over the existing and popular South Wales-Birmingham-Derby diagrams. However, on Summer Saturdays the 7.05am Derby-Swansea was extended to Pembroke and was (steam) locomotive and carriages.

The end of the steam heat season brought the usual increase in utilisation of BR/Sulzer type 4s and steam found less regular use on timetabled trains. Religious, Bank holiday and seasonal trains, however, brought forth plenty of 4-6-0s, on the Thursday before Easter seven Jubilees worked to St Pancras. Pacifics were a rarer sight, though in April Britannias were used on the 24th (Birmingham-Bristol special) 25th (7.55am Swansea–Newcastle from Gloucester) one was at Nottingham on the 23rd and another was on Derby depot on 12 May. The unusual aspect of these sightings was that they were all former Great Eastern lines examples, 70007/6/40/1 in the order mentioned. I do not have the Works shopping dates for the Britannias, but it is possible that they had been or were to be overhauled at Crewe (rather than Doncaster) and briefly were captive to the London Midland Region.

For whatever reason – and I know not – the Midland Division seemed content to not impose a ban on steam workings south of say Leicester, Wellingborough or Bedford and throughout the year steam traction made appearances on passenger, parcels, milk (Appleby–

Jubilees were synonymous with the cross country route between York/Leeds and Bristol and here, a member of the class that was a newcomer to the route in 1963 – Saltley allocated *Duncan* (45674) – is in charge of the 2.15pm Bristol-York approaching Tramway Junction, Gloucester. The roots of the history of the railways around that area are evidenced by the 0-4-2 tank locomotive 1455 being held at signals with the 3.12pm Gloucester Central to Chalford auto train. 27 July 1963. (*Kidderminster Railway Museum 091663, Courtesy P. J. Lynch*)

Cricklewood) and freight (see also later section on excursion traffic); unusual workings including Jubilee 45560, 92086/180 on expresses from Nottingham and Clan 72006 on 15 December with the milk train. Pre-Christmas traffic actually included a resurgence in the use of steam on parcels and fitted freight work.

A problem with a bridge at Peterborough resulted in an interesting diversion of Saturday trains from Derby and Birmingham to Yarmouth; Class 5s taking the spur between Midland and St John's station at Bedford then via Cambridge.

Bedford as a steam depot suffered a lingering death through the year and even when in September it was decreed all diesel and the coal hoist was sold, steam continued to arrive from the North on an almost daily basis.

It was the cross country route which throughout the year continued to offer variety of steam traction types and some pleasant surprises. We enjoyed in particular the B1s which were plentiful on Summer Saturdays and on one such I went to Gloucester to enjoy the cross country trains together with trains from the West Midlands

coming from Stratford/Cheltenham. On the 27th July a procession along the Midland included 44666 with the 6.40am Leicester–Paignton, 45626 with the 7.05am Derby–Pembroke 45653 on the 7.05 am Newcastle–Paignton and 45667 with the 7.43am Nottingham/Derby–Bristol extended to Plymouth. In the afternoon 61090 had the 6.40am Paignton–Bradford and 61138 on the 9.15 Kingswear/Paignton–Bradford.

The highlight of the year for some was on 9 October when A4 streamlined pacific 60021 *Wild Swan* worked the 12.15pm Newcastle-Bristol to Derby. By that time, it was New England (Peterborough) based and its glory days well behind it, but an A4 at Derby was something remarkable. My father was travelling home from Nottingham and noticed it on Derby depot. In a matter of fact tone he said 'There's an A4 on the shed'. In no time at all I was at Breadsall Crossing signalbox where duty signalman David Stephenson noticed my high speed arrival on the bicycle he had sold to me, drew open the window and said 'I've been expecting you!' 'Is it going back on the 8.40pm York?' I asked, in hope of a positive response, 'No, 6.30am all stations

A little later after 45674 went north, BR Standard Class 5 73068 (with a regulator gland badly needing attention) crosses Tramway Junction with the afternoon Birmingham New Street-Fishguard Harbour service, by then a Monday to Friday inter-city diesel multiple unit duty, but not on Summer Saturdays. 27 July 1963. (*Kidderminster Railway Museum 091678, Courtesy P.J. Lynch*)

The Summer Saturday Nottingham-Plymouth service in 1963 was a regular Jubilee turn and on this day (27 July) *Jellicoe* (45667) worked it to Gloucester and is seen here after calling at Cheltenham. Although most of the carriages are BR Mark I design, note the two LNER designs second and fourth from the locomotive, the latter looks worthy of identification. (*Kidderminster Railway Museum 091666, Courtesy P. J. Lynch*)

A meeting of Jubilees at Burton on Trent with *Barfleur* (45685) arriving and *Trafalgar* (45682) accelerating hard under clear signals. (*Phil Waterfield*)

Widespread dieselisation resulted in previously front line express passenger steam locomotives being re-allocated and used to suit the varying needs of the operators. A4 60021 (*Wild Swan*) had been moved to Peterborough, but on 9 October 1963 found itself at the head of the 12.43 Newcastle-Bristol which it worked as far as Derby. Being too long for use of the turntable the locomotive was turned at Derby North Junction, placed in the shed yard and worked back to the Eastern Region with the 6.30am stopping passenger train on the following morning. (*Keith Platt*)

Sheffield in the morning.' An early 'rise and shine' followed. A York-Derby parcels train ran daily from mid-November up to Christmas and produced V2s and pacifics and we were surprised and delighted when A1s 60142/3 appeared; *Edward Fletcher* and *Sir Walter Scott* respectively. Number 60146 *Peregrine* (A1 60146) had started the trend on 15 October with the 4.05pm Newcastle -Bristol (to Derby).

Other notable occurrences during the year included:

• 46100 *Royal Scot* in LMS livery and as 6100 ex-works Crewe to Boston (then Butlins, Skegness) via Stenson Junction, Trent and Nottingham (hauled dead by 45038, replaced by 61177) 12 June 63.
• *Princess Elizabeth*, Light Engine Carlisle, Leeds, Derby, Saltley. 12-15 August. Towed dead to Ashchurch by 44045 on 22 August.

• 10001 diesel re-instated to traffic in July (to Willesden).
• D57 final production batch of BR/Sulzer type 4s in regular traffic having been de-rated from experimental 2750hp to 2,500hp.
• 75042. Final steam locomotive overhaul at Derby Locomotive Works. 20 September.
• Following a derailment on the Great Central line between Gotham and East Leake freight traffic diverted over Derby (Friargate)–Egginton Junction–Burton route. 3.30pm Hull–Plymouth and 4.30pm Grimsby–Whitland fish trains routed via Melton Mowbray, Market Harborough–Northampton–Bletchley–Oxford route to gain the Western Region. 3 October.
• A re-organisation of motive power arrangements included revised shed codes as follows:

Depot	Old Code	New Code	Depot	Old Code	New Code
Cricklewood (diesel)	14A	14A	Toton	18A	16A
Cricklewood (steam)	-	14B	Annesley	16D	16B
Bedford	14E	14C	Derby	17A	16C
Leicester Midland	15C	15A	Nottingham	16A	16D
Wellingborough	15A	15B	Kirkby	16B	16E
Kettering	15B	15C	Burton	17B	16F
Leicester Central	15E	15D	Westhouses	18B	16G
Coalville	15D	15E	Hasland	18C	16H
Saltley	21A	2E	Rowsley	17C	16J

- There were very few revisions to the public summer or winter (1963/64) timetables. There was an easing of timings for the Leicester-St Pancras section (up to five minutes) and with the 6.25pm from Manchester (retimed to 6.35pm calling additionally at Derby).
- To assist production of new type 4 diesels at Brush, Loughborough Works, final painting (and weighing) was undertaken at Derby Locomotive Works. D1696 was the first followed by D1698/1701/7/11 in November/December.
- Four Brush type 4 diesels allocated to Derby as part of route contingency plans. D1685/8/95/6 in December.

Passenger excursion traffic during the year brought much interest, not only in terms of locomotives, but also routings and rolling stock. Such traffic is now reviewed for certain sporting events, the new cathedral at Coventry, railway enthusiasts and finally BR commercial ventures.

Leicester City Football Club had another extended run of success in the FA Cup competition. Because of the prevailing weather and a lack of undersoil heating at most grounds, the third Round of matches (normally played at the end of the first week of the New Year) spanned from January to early March. Consequently the Cup Final was postponed from its usual early May date to the 25th. Leicester were fortunate to satisfactorily complete their third Round match away to Grimsby Town on Tuesday 8 January and then defeated Ipswich Town on Wednesday, 30 January; the difficulties of travel and uncertainty of matches being allowed to proceed restricting attendance to those living close by. However, for the match away at Leyton Orient on 16 March five locally based Black 5s took supporters to Leyton via the Midland line. The draw for the sixth Round paired Norwich City (with its fine recent form in the competition) and Leicester at Carrow Road, Norwich. At that time my father worked in Leicester and knowing how I had been thrilled by the exploits of Norwich in 1959 and of a developing interest in football arranged for us to travel on one of the six special trains run from Leicester and district, each with a Black 5. My hope was that at March our locomotive would be changed for steam, but in fact all the specials had Brush type 2 diesels forward. Leicester prevailed and the combination of a railway journey with steam and a football match made such a favourable impact on me that over the next five years I spent many a happy Saturday either in the North West, North East or along the South Coast (Southampton, Portsmouth and Bournemouth) of England.

We also attended the semi-final match at Hillsborough, Sheffield played on 27 April. The abiding memory apart from the vastness of the stadium compared with those I had previously visited was of the scene at Sheffield Midland station in the evening. The official Club party plus the players and manager were returning in style on a train double headed by a Black 5 and a Royal Scot. The dining train was routed via Beighton and the Old Road to Tapton Junction, then along the Erewash Valley to Trent and Leicester, a journey of perhaps one hour and a half which would enable the close victory to be celebrated. There was something a bit special about watching a long, heavy train eased out of Platform 1 at Sheffield Midland by two locomotives well prepared by their crews and on that particular evening it certainly was. Sadly for observers along the line from Leicester Midland on Cup Final day most specials were entrusted to BR/Sulzer type 4 diesels, though steam in the form of two Jubilees, a Black 5 and (on a relief from Derby) a BR Standard Class 5. Jubilees *Basutoland* and *Hyderabad* worked specials from Leicester Central. Again Leicester fell at the last hurdle ... 3-1 to Manchester United.

Two other matches played at Wembley that spring brought specials along the Midland lines to St Pancras. For the schoolboy international on 27 April two Jubilees and two Black 5s worked specials and for the Rugby League Cup Final on 11 May four Jubilees (45597/643/98/739) brought specials for supporters of Wakefield Trinity.

In May 1962 the Queen had consecrated the new (second) cathedral at Coventry, the original having been substantially rendered rubble during a campaign of bombing of industrial cities during the Second World War. The significance of such a development was not lost on the generation who had endured that war and captured in many a desire to visit. During late 1962 and throughout 1963 BR arranged special trains from far and wide. For such traffic the Divisions of the Railway Regions had available some excellently varied sets of carriages for which catering facilities could be added. The North Eastern Region could, and did, marshal fine dining sets of Gresley (teak) and Thompson designs and for the excursions to Coventry the commercial management teams seemed to attract every Women's Institute, British Legion Club, Rotary Club, Mothers'

Union and anyone else available for mid-week trips. From the North East came specials from Newcastle, Sunderland, Durham, Bishop Auckland, Sunderland and Bradford. From the Eastern Region came specials from Hull and Scunthorpe. Beyond Chesterfield the trains were routed via Ambergate, Derby, Burton-on-Trent, to Shackerstone Junction and Nuneaton to Coventry, the locomotive then being serviced at Nuneaton. It was arranged that the locomotive would work throughout in each direction and that V2 2-6-2s would be allowed. From a motive power perspective matters in 1963 started badly. On 25 March V2 60856 was failed upon arrival and on 1 April (when two specials ran; Newcastle and Durham) the V2 on one was failed at Derby (forward with 42768) though it was enabled to work north from Derby with the return. A list of sightings follows:

Date	Originating point	Locomotive Number	Class	Depot	Note
25 March	Newcastle	60856	V2	York	As in text
1 April	Newcastle	61049	B1	York	
1 April	Durham	?	V2	?	As in text
9 April	Newcastle	60969	V2	York	
16 April	Sunderland	61018	B1	York	
16 April	Newcastle	60828	B2	York	Failed on return 45653 forward from Burton
23 April	Newcastle	60810	V2	York	
29 April	Newcastle	D172	4	Gateshead	
6 May	Newcastle	D192	4	Gateshead	
27 May	Newcastle	D182	4	Gateshead	
10 June	Newcastle	60810	V2	York	
21 June	Bishop Auckland	61276	B1	York	
28 June	Hull	D6735	3	Hull	
12 July	Scunthorpe	70037	Brit	Immingham	
15 July	Bradford	45739	Jub	Holbeck	
9 Sept	Newcastle	D170	4	Gateshead	
9 Sept	Newcastle	D183	4	Gateshead	
16 Sept	Newcastle	D398	4	Thornaby	

Between its trips on 23 April and 10 June, 60810 could well have had an overhaul/repaint because on the latter it was in immaculate external condition. The long summer evening produced a reasonable sized gathering to watch its return and the gallery was not disappointed. An immaculate locomotive, twelve carriages including Gresley teak diners, a York crew not intending to be late home and really working their locomotive hard. Just wonderful.

In the era under review there was a continuing and in fact burgeoning national body of individuals of all ages

who were interested in railways. Magazines published monthly helped to keep individuals informed and to generate new interest. In addition were respected specialist Societies such as the Railway Correspondence & Travel (RCTS), the Stephenson Locomotive (SLS) and the Locomotive Club of Great Britain (LCGB) which published at varying periodicities their own highly informative journals and arranged visits and tours, usually by rail. Tours for enthusiasts had tended to be along particular routes or to major workshops, but as our era progressed the itineraries increasingly featured

One of the many excursions in 1962/63 to take visitors to Coventry to see the new cathedral, in this case having originated in the North East of England. The motive power – steam or diesel – worked throughout and during 1963 brought V2s to a route including the Burton upon Trent to Shackerstone Junction section. Here 60810 – which made two such forays – has taken the turn at Leicester Junction, Burton, with the yard of the motive power depot beyond the Derby-Birmingham line. These excursion trains are described in detail in the Chapter for 1963. (*Phil Waterfield*)

lines threatened with or known to be closing and classes of locomotives close to extinction. Other Societies, for example the Warwickshire Railway (WRS), Derbyshire Railway (DRS) and Halifax Railfans Club, developed their range of activities from tours by bus to multiple depots in a particular geographic area to include rail tours or the charter of a train to convey a large number. The WRS organised tours in 1963 (and 1964) by rail from Birmingham to Glasgow (overnight Friday into Saturday), a tour by bus to up to fourteen depots and a return overnight Saturday/Sunday back to Birmingham from Edinburgh.

The tours which attracted attention along our lines of route in 1963 were:

27 January (postponed to 24 March). DRS Leeds to Tyseley via Sheffield, Chesterfield, Codnor, Butterley, Crich Junction and Derby with Clan 72008. After a visit

to the depot, Hall 7929 piloted the Clan (presumably because the latter did not have Western Region compatible warning system equipment) to Shrewsbury (via a pause at Wolverhampton Stafford Road) and then with 72008 Crewe Works and back to Leeds via Stoke and Derby.

10 February. Home Counties Railway Society. On this snowy day Bulleid pacific 34094 in original form returned from Crewe to London Marylebone via Stoke, Egginton Junction Derby (Friargate) and Nottingham (Victoria) with B1 61409 as pilot between Crewe and Nottingham. By the time Aylesbury was approached 34094 was virtually out of coal and passengers alighted and went forward by service train.

17 and 18 April. Ian Allan Ltd. Bulleid pacific 34031 in re-built form worked (both days) from St Pancras to Derby for a visit to be made to the Locomotive Works.

11 May. RCTS/LCGB North Midlands tour. Bulleid pacific 34006 in original form worked St Pancras–Derby (B1 61004)–Trent–Codnor–Butterley–Ambergate–Miller's Dale–Buxton (48519 used locally)–Parsley Hay– Uttoxeter–Dove Junction–Burton (34006)–Ashby–Coalville– Knighton–St Pancras.

12 May. WRS. Bulleid pacific 34094 worked from Birmingham via Derby (depot visit)–Barrow Hill (depot visit) to Doncaster for a Works visit.

5 October. Midland & Great Northern Joint Railway Society. Wandering 1500 tour. Sole surviving B12 61572 worked London Broad Street–Hitchin–Bedford Midland–Northampton Castle–Rugby (and beyond).

13 October RCTS. East Midlander Number 6. Crab 42896 worked Nottingham–Chaddesden–Derby–Stenson Junction–Lichfield Trent Valley to Crewe and Horwich Works. Returned via Halifax–Cudworth–Chesterfield–Ambergate–Derby–Sawley Junction–Nottingham.

Of interest to me at least was the fact that when 34006 reached Derby on 11 May it was virtually out of coal. The run had been beset with problems and the locomotive possibly over fired by a Fireman unfamiliar with the type, but it does again raise the question of their suitability (considered in 1958) for the St Pancras-Manchester line.

BR commercial ventures included the concept of an autumn weekend package trip to the illuminations at Blackpool. Trains were run from Nottingham and Chesterfield on Friday evenings, returning on the Sunday usually with the locomotive which took the train on the Friday, Black 5s and B1s usually. Also marketed were rover tickets valid for travel over seven consecutive days within a railway geographical area. The Midlands rail rover had boundaries of Matlock, Malvern, Shrewsbury, Rugby, Leamington and Grantham and represented excellent value for money. Our small band set off each morning for Birmingham and if the Wolverhampton-Birmingham-London Euston train was awaiting departure time with a Princess Coronation we would go to Coventry with it, if not we would eschew the Britannia or Royal Scot and head for Snow Hill and the delights of the Shrewsbury-Leamington section. The Saturday coincided with August Bank Holiday and was particularly busy in railway terms though incessant rain reduced the number travelling. I went to Shrewsbury with a Castle and spent an hour there regretting that my ticket would not allow me to go to Crewe with Princess Coronation 46256 which was awaiting the Plymouth-Manchester/Liverpool, and so came back via Snow Hill with a Hall and from New Street to Tamworth with a Black 5. A pause there allowed a sight of Britannia 70030 on the Euston line before Jubilee 45674 arrived with the Newquay-Newcastle. I travelled back to Derby in a 68 foot, 12 wheel former dining carriage…and hoped things would never change.

The unusual sight and shape of a Bulleid pacific at Derby. *Mortehoe* of the West Country Class – paying its third visit of 1963 to the Midlands – paused whilst the participants on the tour made a visit to nearby railway facilities, before continuing to Doncaster. 12 May 1963. (*Kidderminster Railway Museum 033944, Courtesy R. H. W. Whitworth*)

Chapter Eleven

Performance Logs

One of the personal pleasures of train travel in the days of steam was to compare performances over a particular section of track. Included here is a selection of logs of parts of journeys made between 1957 and 1962. At that time my family was making regular trips along the Midland line to St Pancras, occasionally also to Bristol and my father took an interest in recording times and speeds. Southbound towards London our approach was to note how the locomotive and crew seemed to be going about their collective business during the climb from Market Harborough to Desborough North; if it appeared that they were showing intent then we would organise ourselves for the compilation of a log over the Bedford North to Luton section. In our experience only rarely were such sectional runs completed without a slowing for work on the permanent way, but we enjoyed better fortune when Northbound over the same section.

Southbound, apart from the prevailing weather, the ideal conditions were for a late start by a few minutes from Leicester (London Road) and with a Kentish Town crew heading for home or an evening at the local dog racing track! It has to be remembered that whilst these journeys were something of a novelty for us as a family, the Driver would have made the trip thousands of times, knew the passing times by heart and feel, probably had driven the same locomotive a few days previously and if the locomotive was steaming well then in all probability he and his Fireman would settle for 'right time'. Therefore, it was always expecting a lot for anything truly exceptional, but therein lay the rest of the interest.

The logs are not intended to be comparative between types of traction or classes of power; rather, they simply record how it was. Each log is of course unique and analysis can only extend as far as to suggest that with D5700/D5701 the Driver was learning how to keep to time with units limited to a maximum of 75mph, whilst with Britannia 70042 the Driver was intent on regaining time lost further north. The runs with the *Midland Pullman* were compiled by my father. With the advent of the type 4 diesels it was impressive to see how easily they could achieve times well within the then Working

Timetable allowances and as such was in stark contrast to the physical hardship of working steam.

The audibly evident effort and physical hardship involved with getting the double headed steam hauled train to St Pancras on time was just part of the job, but two aspects of such workings endure. First, anyone who thinks that life on the footplate was somehow glamorous or that the rails had something of romance about them never fired a 2P 4-4-0 at 80mph on any of fifty cold, wet and windy winter's nights and, secondly, anyone who feels that there was no role for trade union representation of the concerns of railwaymen did not fully understand or appreciate the railway environment.

On the Derby to Manchester route, the section that interested me was either side of Peak Forest where a combination of any of a poorly steaming locomotive, weather/rail head conditions and a permanent way speed restriction would make life difficult. After the hard climb came the exhilarating dash down the other side; it was a wonderful route to travel in any of the ten months of winter or two months of rain that prevailed annually. Many of my runs were in successive autumns and the walk rather than run with the Patriot Class locomotive was not untypical of wet, foggy mornings.

Although I became quite familiar with the London and Manchester routes from Derby, to Sheffield and towards Bristol never really excited much interest, at least until the Eastern Region men showed off with the B1s and V2s! I have though included a couple of runs along the Derby to Birmingham line, albeit they were Summer Saturday reliefs and I did not have Working Timetable or Special Traffic Notice information. The run with Jubilee 45658 was memorable in that having arrived at Derby quite satisfied with the performance, I was aghast to see running into the station a 9F plus ten carriages which had been hampered in its progress from Birmingham by the very train upon which I had chosen to travel. What, at New Street I had assumed was a Paignton-Leicester, was in fact a Paignton-Sheffield relief, also non-stop to Derby.

Alongside the track were placed posts spaced at one quarter of a mile, with every fourth one indicating the mileage to/from the end/start point. By use of a stopwatch the time in seconds taken by the train to cover one quarter of a mile could easily be converted to a speed; for example fifteen seconds indicated a speed of 60mph, or one mile in sixty seconds. Alternatively, the jointed track sections were 60 feet and as the carriage bogie wheel passed over the joint the number of clicks in the space of fifteen seconds would enable a speed to be calculated. For example, as eighty-eight sections of track formed one mile (5,280 feet), twenty-two formed one quarter of one mile (1,320 feet) and, therefore twenty-two clicks in fifteen seconds equated to 60mph. To assist logging we had a line graph of time in seconds for one quarter of a mile and simply read off the speeds shown on the other axis. On the logs we also recorded the total weight of the vehicles forming the train (usually the Guard would save the trouble of walking the length of the train and noting each individual weight) and then adding on a percentage (usually five, but less if the train was very lightly loaded) to give an estimated gross tonnage.

The planning for the introduction of the *Midland Pullman* included the application by British Railways of their own Elliott computer technology to train performance and scheduling. By calculating full utilisation of the power equipment of the diesel unit and programming the train weight, speed restrictions and gradients it was possible to compute sectional timings, which in physical practice were proven to be correct. In parallel, outputs from the Deuce and Pegasus computer systems of English Electric Co Ltd and Ferranti Ltd were being made available to British Railways for planning timetables for diesel and electric traction with trains of a uniform consist over particular sections of route. From that came standard, section timings such as E285 of E420, i.e. timings applicable to a 25kv ac electric locomotive with trains weighing 285 tons/420 tons respectively. Once standard timings became the norm the fascination for many of logging performance waned and disappeared.

A few notes about the characteristics may assist understanding.

After observance of the speed restriction at Market Harborough, Southbound, the crew and locomotive would face some 4½ miles of hard work until relief came with the sight of Desborough North signal box, followed by a rapid acceleration down the 6½ miles to Kettering. In the opposite direction the entertainment was similar.

Southbound from Elstow (milepost 47¼) to milepost 34 is – apart from a favourably graded section between Ampthill and Flitwick – a continuous, steady climb, much of which is at the Midland Railway's ruling gradient for goods trains of 1 in 200. in the reverse direction high speed running was the norm with a top speed often attained approaching Elstow.

The demanding nature of the Rowsley–Cheadle Heath section through the Peak District is described at page 75.

Derby to Birmingham has no significant gradient, but generally is more favourable Eastbound.

PERFORMANCE LOGS

Market Harborough–Kettering (pass to pass)

Dist Miles	Location	Sched. Mins.	Act m s	Speed m.p.h.	Sched. Mins.	Act m s	Speed m.p.h.
0.0	Market Harborough		–	55		–	59
4.5	Desborough North S.B.		6.02	45		5.37	54
7.4	Glendon		8.50	60		8.23	70
10.9	Kettering	12	11.44	70	12	11.08	71
	Locomotive(s)	45597			40537 + 45626		
	Load: carriages/tare/gross	8/300/315			11/372/390		
	Year of run	1957			1958		
	Weather	Dry			Dry		
0.0	Market Harborough		–	52		–	58
4.5	Desborough North S.B.		5.02	55		5.00	54
7.4	Glendon		7.40	71		7.38	68
10.9	Kettering	12	10.40	73	12	10.42	72
	Locomotive(s)	D5700/D5701			70014		
	Load: carriages/tare/gross	9/285/315			10/335/352		
	Year of run	1958			1960		
	Weather	Showers			Dry		
0.0	Market Harborough		–	53		–	57
4.5	Desborough North S.B.	6	4.37	61	4½	4.01	77
7.4	Glendon		6.58	80		6.30	90
10.9	Kettering	12	9.56	72	9½	8.43	76
	Locomotive(s)	D3			*Midland Pullman*		
	Load: carriages/tare/gross	10/335/355			6/298/302		
	Year of run	1960			1962		
	Weather	Showers			Dry		

Locomotives: 45597 and 45626 Jubilee Class 6: 40537 2P Class 2
70014 Britannia Class 7
D5700 and D5701 Metrovick type 2 1200 h.p.
D3 BR/Sulzer type 4 2300 h.p.

Notes: Speed restrictions through Market Harborough and Kettering
D5700 and D5701 maximum permitted speed 75 mph
Sched = Working Timetable schedule
Act = Actual time achieved. m.s. = minutes/seconds
S.B. = signal box
Tare = weight of train in unladen condition
Gross = weight of train in laden condition (estimate)
Pass to Pass = train did not stop at either station

Kettering–Market Harborough (pass to pass)

Dist Miles	Location	Sched. Mins.	Act m s	Speed m.p.h.	Sched. Mins.	Act m s	Speed m.p.h.
0.0	Kettering		–	54		-	70
3.6	Glendon		3.22	54		3.13	67
6.5	Desborough North S.B.		6.16	48		5.54	61
10.9	Market Harborough	12	12.34	58	12	9.32	58
	Locomotive(s)	44839			70017		
	Load: carriages/tare/gross	8/255/270			10/340/360		
	Year of run	1957			1960		
	Weather	Dry			Raining		
0.0	Kettering		–	65		-	68
3.6	Glendon		3 22	61		2.54	78
6.5	Desborough North S.B.		6.03	58		5.10	75
10.9	Market Harborough	? 11.0	9.42	57	8½	8.37	52
	Locomotive(s)	46103			*Midland Pullman*		
	Load: carriages/tare/gross	9/305/315			6/298/302		
	Year of run	1961			1962		
	Weather	Dry			Dry		

Locomotives: 44839 Black Class 5: 46103 Royal Scot Class 7
                           70017 Britannia Class 7

Note: Speed restrictions through Kettering and Market Harborough

This photograph was taken from the Fireman's side of the cab of Jubilee 45627 *Sierra Leone* and illustrates the gradient for passenger trains heading up to Sharnbrook. The train has just passed Irchester where the goods lines had diverged to take the Wymington deviation with less demanding gradients. (*G. Morris*)

Bedford North–Luton (pass to pass)

Dist Miles	Location	Sched. Mins.	Act m s	Speed m.p.h.	Sched. Mins.	Act m s	Speed m.p.h.
0.0	Bedford N Junc		–	74		–	73
8.1	Ampthill		7.17	55		7.16	58
9.7	Flitwick		8.12	62		8.15	62
12.6	Harlington		11.51	53		11.29	61
17.1	Leagrave		17.23	57		16.44	58
19.6	Luton	19	19.49	69	19	18.58	70

	Locomotive(s)	45564			40513 +		
	Load: carriages/tare/gross	8/270/285			45626		
	Year of run	1957			11/372/390		
	Weather	Dry			1958		
					Dry		

Dist Miles	Location	Sched. Mins.	Act m s	Speed m.p.h.	Sched. Mins.	Act m s	Speed m.p.h.
0.0	Bedford N Junc		–	74			76
8.1	Ampthill		7.02	74		7.03	63
9.7	Flitwick		8.24	71		8.36	70
12.6	Harlington		11.08	65		11.03	65
17.1	Leagrave		15.23	64		15.31	60
19.6	Luton	19	17.30	73	19	17.39	73

	Locomotive(s)	D5700/D5701			70042		
	Load: carriages/tare/gross	9/285/315			9/285/315		
	Year of run	1958			1959		
	Weather	Showers			Dry		

Dist Miles	Location	Sched. Mins.	Act m s	Speed m.p.h.	Sched. Mins.	Act m s	Speed m.p.h.
0.0	Bedford N Junc		–	65		–	79
8.1	Ampthill		7.31	61		6.22	77
9.7	Flitwick		8.43	67		7.40	78
12.6	Harlington		11.32	64		8.03	82
17.1	Leagrave		16.01	64		13.23	82
19.6	Luton	19	18.04	79	17½	15.18	83

	Locomotive(s)	46131			D77		
	Load: carriages/tare/gross	9/285/315			9/285/315		
	Year of run	1959			1961		
	Weather	Showers			Raining		

Dist Miles	Location	Sched. Mins.	Act m s	Speed m.p.h.	Sched. Mins.	Act m s	Speed m.p.h.
0.0	Bedford N Junc		–	86		–	83
8.1	Ampthill		5.43	84		6.03	74
9.7	Flitwick		6.47	89		7.17	77
12.6	Harlington		8.45	85		9.36	73
17.1	Leagrave		12.01	80		12.12	76
19.6	Luton	14	13.48	85	16	15.15	85

	Locomotive(s)	*Midland Pullman*			D154		
	Load: carriages/tare/gross	6/298/305			11/370/390		
	Year of run	1962			1962		
	Weather	Showers			Dry		

Locomotives: 45564 and 45626 Jubilee Class 6: 40513 2P Class 2
70042 Britannia Class 7: 46131 Royal Scot Class 7
D77 and D154 BR/Sulzer type 4 2500 h.p.
D5700/D5701 Metrovick type 2 1200 h.p.

Luton–Bedford North (pass to pass)

Dist Miles	Location	Sched. Mins.	Act m s	Speed m.p.h.	Sched. Mins.	Act m s	Speed m.p.h.
0.0	Luton		–	72		–	75
2.5	Leagrave		2.22	68		2.07	71
7.0	Harlington		6.02	83		5.42	83
9.9	Flitwick		8.09	86		8.44	88
11.5	Ampthill		9.20	80		9.13	81
19.6	Bedford N Junc	? 17	15.22	78	16	15.07	81

	Locomotive(s)	46157			45616		
	Load: carriages/tare/gross	12/410/435			9/315/330		
	Year of run	1958			1958		
	Weather	Showers			Dry		

Dist Miles	Location	Sched. Mins.	Act m s	Speed m.p.h.	Sched. Mins.	Act m s	Speed m.p.h.
0.0	Luton		–	75		–	90
2.5	Leagrave		2.13	68		1.45	85
7.0	Harlington		6.01	75		4.52	85
9.9	Flitwick		8.26	75		6.58	85
11.5	Ampthill		9.43	71		8.04	88
19.6	Bedford N Junc	17	16.38	71	13½	13.46	77

	Locomotive(s)	D5700/D5701			*Midland Pullman*		
	Load: carriages/tare/gross	11/368/390			6/298/302		
	Year of run	1958			1960		
	Weather	Raining			Dry		

Dist Miles	Location	Sched. Mins.	Act m s	Speed m.p.h.	Sched. Mins.	Act m s	Speed m.p.h.
0.0	Luton		–	80		–	78
2.5	Leagrave		2.22	77		2.20	78
7.0	Harlington		5.23	85		5.24	83
9.9	Flitwick		7.42	88		7.40	90
11.5	Ampthill		8.55	80		8.48	85
19.6	Bedford N Junc	?16	15.01	82	16	14.54	82

	Locomotive(s)	46103			D144		
	Load: carriages/tare/gross	9/305/315			11/370/398		
	Year of run	1961			1962		
	Weather	Dry			Showers		

Locomotives: 45616 Jubilee Class 6: 46103 and 46157 Royal Scot Class 7
D144 BR/Sulzer type 4 2500 h.p.
D5700/D5701 Metrovick type 2 1200 h.p.

Chinley–Miller's Dale (start to pass)

Dist Miles	Location	Sched. Mins.	Act m s	Speed m.p.h.	Sched. Mins.	Act m s	Speed m.p.h.
0.0	Chinley		–	–		–	–
2.0	Chapel-en-le-Frith		3.58	46		5.15	36
5.6	Peak Forest		9.24	43		11.38	34
8.4	Peak Forest Junc		12.01	42		15.14	40
10.2	Miller's Dale	17	14.19	–	17	17.34	–
	Locomotive(s)	70021			45622		
	Load: carriages/tare/gross	8/270/285			9/274/295		
	Year of run	1959			1959		
	Weather	Dry			Raining		
0.0	Chinley		–	–			
2.0	Chapel-en-le-Frith		4.09	47			
5.6	Peak Forest	11	9.17	39			
8.4	Peak Forest Junc		13.02	40			
10.2	Miller's Dale	17	15.16	–			
	Locomotive(s)	D78					
	Load: carriages/tare/gross	7/237/252					
	Year of run	1962					
	Weather	Raining					

Miller's Dale–Chinley (start to pass)

Dist Miles	Location	Sched. Mins.	Act m s	Speed m.p.h.	Sched. Mins.	Act m s	Speed m.p.h.
0.0	Miller's Dale		–	–		–	–
4.6	Peak Forest	8	8.41	36	8	7.24	53
8.2	Chapel-en-le-Frith		13.19	60		11.41	60
10.2	Chinley	14	14.58	71	14	13.29	68
	Locomotive(s)	44809			70015		
	Load: carriages/tare/gross	7/238/250			8/270/285		
	Year of run	1959			1959		
	Weather	Misty/fog			Dry		
0.0	Miller's Dale	–	–	–			
4.6	Peak Forest	8	10.22	26			
8.2	Chapel-en-le-Frith	–	15.37	56			
10.2	Chinley	14	17.30	62			
	Locomotive(s)	45520					
	Load: carriages/tare/gross	7/238/252					
	Year of run	1959					
	Weather	Fog/sleet					

Locomotives: 44809 Black Class 5: 45520 Patriot Class 6
45622 Jubilee Class 6
70015 and 70021 Britannia Class 7
D78 BR/Sulzer type 4 2500 h.p.

Derby–Birmingham (start to stop)

Dist Miles	Location	Sched. Mins.	Act m s	Speed m.p.h.	Sched. Mins.	Act m s	Speed m.p.h.
0.0	Derby Midland	–	–		–	–	
1.4	Pear Tree and Normanton		–	32		2.42	54
4.8	Stenson Junc	6.53		61	7	5.48	72
6.3	Repton and Willington		–	64		6.59	82
11.0	Burton-on-Trent	13.02		35	13	11.01	34
16.25	Wichnor Junc	18.34		62	19	15.58	78
23.75	Tamworth	24.45		75	26	21.36	89
29.4	Kingsbury	28.56		75	31	25.20	81
33.6	Water Orton	32.21		–	34½	28.15	–
33.85	Castle Bromwich	34.08		79		–	–
41.2	Birmingham New St	?	★			★	
	★ signal checks Saltley area		41.06	–	44	38.06	–
	Locomotive(s)	46123			D40		
	Load: carriages/tare/gross	9/304/320			10/340/360		
	Year of run	1961			1962		
	Weather	Dry			Dry		

Birmingham New St–Derby (start to pass)

Dist Miles	Location	Sched. Mins.	Act m s	Speed m.p.h.	Sched. Mins.	Act m s	Speed m.p.h.
0.0	Birmingham New St.	–	–		–	–	
5.35	Castle Bromwich		7.04	64		6.48	70
7.6	Water Orton		9.29	65		8.54	65
11.6	Kingsbury		12.59	76		12.12	81
17.5	Tamworth		16.42	80		16.18	82
30.2	Burton-on-Trent		27.04	45		26.37	45
34.9	Repton and Willington		33.04	63		31.35	69
36.4	Stenson Junc		34.28	60		33.01	64
39.8	Pear Tree and Normanton		37.58	56		36.22	64
41.2	Derby Midland	?	41.20	–	?	38.54	–
	Locomotive(s)	45658			D153		
	Load: carriages/tare/gross	8/264/280			12/410/435		
	Year of run	1960			1962		
	Weather	Dry			Raining		

Locomotives: 45658 Jubilee Class 6: 46123 Royal Scot Class 7
D40 and D153 BR/Sulzer type 4 2500 h.p.

Notes: Speed restrictions through Burton-on-Trent and Water Orton
D40 time/speed at Castle Bromwich not noted
46123 time not noted at either Pear Tree or Repton
All trains except that with D40 were relief trains. No WTT/Special Notice details to hand.

Chapter Twelve

The Human Element I: Geoffrey Morris – Locomotive Fireman

Whilst researching for this book I had several objectives; factually interesting information for railway historians and enthusiasts, something to acknowledge the social history of the time and, thirdly to try to find a human element. After all, railways were full of interest and served the needs of the nation only through the efforts of many hundreds of thousands of men and women who undertook the huge variety of tasks on all 365 days of the year around and against the clock.

Over the years I have worked with, contacted, spoken with and exchanged correspondence with many who had or have documents and credible recollections, many of which have been referred to in the various Chapters. However, apart from particular notes for 1960 the human element is not as strong as I would wish to be the case.

To address this whilst meeting my other objectives, and with his permission I have included in this Chapter an item about one particular locomotive footplateman. He was based at Derby between 1954 and 1966 mainly as one of some 750 Drivers, Firemen and Locomotive Cleaners at Derby 4 Shed, 17A which in the mid-1950s had an allocation of roundly 140 steam locomotives plus always a range of locomotives either new or freshly overhauled at the adjacent Locomotive Works.

Geoffrey (Geoff) Morris was a son of a professional soldier and was born in July 1939 at army accommodation at Tidworth, Hampshire. Father was a tank corps man and was soon on his way to Afghanistan, then Turkey, and throughout the ensuing world war was engaged in the Libyan and other North African theatres of war though never in Europe. The policy of the army was such that Mrs Morris and family would be better placed in civilian accommodation so a move was made to Staines, Middlesex. This proved less than ideal in that an aircraft production factory was nearby and therefore was an area targeted by the Luftwaffe. The local authorities let it be known that Geoffrey and his brother should be evacuated, but Mrs Morris would not agree to a separation and instead opted to move to relatives at Chadderton in Greater Manchester. The journey to Manchester in 1943 was from Marylebone and upon arrival at the Manchester terminus the two very young boys were placed upon a station seat and instructed to stay there until mother returned with information for the final short leg of the long journey. The Fireman of the locomotive that had hauled the train noticed the youngsters and lifted them onto the footplate of the locomotive (LNER B17 2848 *Arsenal*) where they could get warm very quickly. Young Geoffrey was entranced by this new-found environment and when an initially alarmed mother re-appeared thanks were exchanged and one excited little boy was hooked for life! The extended family accommodation at Chadderton was somewhat cramped and far from escaping the attention of the enemy the family was again in an area of high risk. At the time Germany had developed pilotless rockets known as Doodlebugs which would fly for a specific duration at which time the propelling engine would cut, forward momentum would be lost and the deadly rocket would fall and explode upon impact. One day Mrs Morris was out with the youngsters when a Doodlebug approached and to her horror the engine noise ceased. In panic she ushered the boys up against a wall only for a fortunately passing local bobby to shout 'Get away from that wall and lie down here in the road.' There, he covered them with his cape, bicycle and himself as the deadly rocket did its work and in the process brought down the very wall against which shelter had been sought. It was too dangerous to stay longer in the area and as soon as practicable, accommodation was found with relatives of father, at Abergele, North Wales. There, accommodation was in unconverted former London & North Western Railway sleeping carriages stabled adjacent to the Crewe-Chester-Holyhead main line. The passing railway traffic attracted Geoffrey and included at least one of the streamlined Princess Coronation pacifics no doubt then in wartime drab, but hugely impressive nevertheless.

The war having come to an end, the family found itself briefly united and for a while at an army establishment at Preston Park near Brighton which also served as a prisoner of war camp. Then, because father had never been involved in the European theatre of war, he was eligible for and selected to be an usher at the war crimes court of justice in Nuremberg and re-location to Germany followed. Back in the UK in 1952 the family was placed at a camp in Derby, then Corsham in Wiltshire where Geoffrey watched in awe the morning departure from the local station regularly entrusted to the gas turbine powered locomotive 18000 or its classmate. Another move in 1952/3 brought the family to Chilwell where they found some stability and at Bramcote Hills where Geoff continued his very fragmented schooling. He made friends with a group who enjoyed railways and regularly cycled together to nearby Trent where trains came in all directions and on a regular basis. Derby was attainable on Saturdays and a cycle ride of some 10 miles each way was nothing when an afternoon at mecca was in prospect. The popular viewing position was at the extreme south end of (the extension to) Platform 1 where part of the yard of the motive power depot could be reviewed, together with newly ex-works locomotives; arrivals, departures and shunting movements. By that time the Ian Allan locospotters' books were available and the assembly was keen to see whatever they could. One afternoon popular rumour had it that there was something extremely rare 'on the shed', but just out of sight. Geoff was intent on finding the rare locomotive and calculated that by using the staff footcrossing across the Birmingham lines and then the staff footcrossing across the London lines he could, if the sequence of trains allowed, complete the route whilst the vision of signalmen was in turn blocked by passing trains. The 'something rare' was not there, but lines of other locomotives were and a 'field day' was enjoyed uninterrupted. It had been so good that Geoff(rey) decided upon a return visit the following day.

On that Sunday afternoon he was soon spotted. 'Oy you what are you doing?' It was the Shed Foreman on an inspection. Geoff politely told him that he was collecting numbers. 'Show him out when you have a minute Joe' was the instruction. Joe was a Polish fellow who, like many of his countrymen had stayed on in the UK after the war and all of them were known simply as Joe the Pole. Joe was a firelighter and steamraiser and on a Sunday afternoon/evening would be responsible for cleaning, on twenty or more locomotives, their firegates, then laying and lighting warming fires so that when night shift came on steam pressure could be established in readiness for the increased number of locomotives required for service on Mondays. He was also a kindly soul and showed Geoff out via a slow, circuitous route which took in the outside turntable area, covered shed and part of the Locomotive Works. 'If you want to

come back on another Sunday be at the Hulland Street entrance at around 1.30pm, my shift starts at 1.45pm.'

An opportunity such as that was not to be spurned and was taken on a regular basis. By the time he was fourteen and a half Geoff knew how to lay fires, knew something of the arrangement of the different locomotives and, importantly was known around the depot, by its weekend staff and in its mess rooms. He loved it and had no difficulty in deciding where he wished to seek employment.

On his fifteenth birthday and having demonstrated an ability to read and write, be medically sound with good eyesight Geoffrey Morris was employed by British Railways as a Locomotive Cleaner. Sunday involvement had ensured that he had a 'head start' and was well prepared for the banter and the day-to-day reality of working in sometimes harsh environment of ashpits, coal dust, grime and overdoses of lubricating oil.

As one of four young Cleaners his gang was expected to clean two locomotives per shift (8am to 4.30pm) and by his own admission his first attempts with Black 5 44851 left that locomotive worse at the end than at the start of the shift. From time to time his duties were varied to work in the ash disposal pits and on general labouring duties; thirsty work that would be well slaked later in the bar at the Railway Institute opposite the station.

The first year passed and at the age of just sixteen Geoff was eligible to be assessed to become a Passed Cleaner and therefore eligible, subject to being passed by a Footplate Inspector, for firing duties on locomotives in service. The week-long assessment involved that Inspector with a group of a total of ten Cleaners, from Derby (four), Burton, Coalville and Rowsley two each. Each day two of the Cleaners would travel with the Inspector on the footplate of a locomotive on a service passenger train and each Cleaner in turn would take a turn in firing the locomotive to instructions given, whilst the booked Fireman travelled in the train. In that way each Cleaner had a trip away from his own depot; in Geoff's case to Rowsley. A group question and answer session then followed and having successfully negotiated both practice and theory, Geoff became a Passed Cleaner.

His first week as a Passed Cleaner involved five consecutive Carriage & Wagon Works shunt turns and as spare on the Saturday was allocated to work an 8F hauled train as far as Wichnor Junction; just 17 miles, but a mainline turn. The second week was a mirror image of the first, at least it was until the Saturday. He was summoned to the Foreman's Office, introduced to Derby Driver Claude Randall and told he would be doing some shovelling. Over to Derby Station, south end of the Platform 6 and it was becoming clear that this would be more than 8F to Wichnor. It certainly was. In rolled the noon Bradford to St Pancras express with Holbeck's Jubilee 45619 *Nigeria* at its head. Pleasantries having been briefly exchanged with the incoming crew they were off to London. Fireman/ Passed Cleaners were not required to have a detailed knowledge of each route; only Passed Firemen and Drivers had to meet such requirement and sign for it following an annual assessment. Driver Randall had not only full responsibility for his locomotive and timekeeping in accordance with the Working Timetable and Sectional Appendix, on this occasion he also needed to keep an eye on his young Fireman. Tending the fire was the main constant requirement, as long as some water could be seen in the gauge glasses that gave confidence and thankfully the exhaust steam injector was functioning reliably. Having successfully picked up some water from the troughs approaching Loughborough things generally were going well. They continued to do so and by the time the locomotive forged into Elstree Tunnel it was almost time to let the

fire look after itself. It was a summer afternoon with clear visibility and as Geoff looked along the boiler side of *Nigeria* he could clearly see the bright daylight beyond the profile of the tunnel portal. To his horror he could also see the outline of an adult human between the rails of the track. 'Claude, there's someone in the four foot!' 'I've seen him, we can't stop in time, get your head in.' The inevitable occurred without distress to either of the crew and Driver Randall continued to St Pancras. Bringing the train to a gentle stop in advance of the buffer stops Randall instructed Geoff to check the front of the locomotive in case there was a need for screening prior to alighting passengers making an exit. Nothing visible so a report was then made and interviews taken. Claude and Geoff were relieved as usual by Kentish Town depot men, had a couple of hours off and then made their way to the north end of the platform to receive their locomotive for the 6.33pm return express (to Manchester Saturdays Only) as far as Derby. No counselling, no relief crew, no nothing. The location of the suicide was a well-known high risk location, being as it was close to the grounds of an institution for patients having mental instability.

Jubilee 45619 *Nigeria* is at Sheffield Midland station with a train of empty stock heading south. (*Rail-online*)

For the 6.33pm Kentish Town had sent a Black 5 (44772) and it would have it all to do to maintain time. As soon as the train cleared West Hampstead Geoff started to build and maintain the fire for the initial thirty or so miles to near Leagrave at which point the gradient became favourable for the 17 miles or so to Bedford. Driver Randall's instruction was unequivocal; 'keep shovelling.' He wanted steam and a plentiful supply, the sharp climb over 5 miles to Sharnbrook was at the back of his mind and the last thing he would want would be a shortage of steam and consequential loss of time. The coal was very large lumps requiring the attention of the pick to be broken into pieces... 'no time for that... if it fits in the firehole get it in with your boot' instructed Claude. By the time Bedford was approached at the usual high speed Geoff knew that he had worked to instructions. In fact the firebox was as full as it could possibly be and burning extremely well. Just beyond Bedford there was water to be taken from Oakley troughs and having done so it was time for a brief rest on what Stanier laughingly called a seat.

Claude had of course been watching the signals and had not had the luxury of knowing the condition of the fire. He was not pleased to see young Geoff sitting down and shouted 'What's the matter, are you tired. I told you to keep firing.' 'It's full.' 'What do you mean; it can't be!" Claude checked the next signal then took a quick look at the fire...and sure enough the firebox was as full as possible. The climb to Sharnbrook was on in earnest, the locomotive going well and joy of joy to Claude's ears the safety valves lifted even against the demand for steam he had required. A thick-set man of average height, he crossed the cab, gave Geoff a fatherly hug and returned to his position smiling and muttering in some disbelief 'safety valves lifting on Sharnbrook!'

Geoff had earned some admiration and upon arrival at Derby and the train having exchanged locomotives Claude and Geoff booked off duty. Claude asked Geoff to accompany him to the Railway Institute. 'A pint of bitter for me, and a half of shandy for my Fireman please.' As the barman passed to Geoff the pathetic half he winked and said 'a bit of a comedown for you this isn't it?' Claude then became a little concerned about Geoff being under age for drinking and sought an assurance that Geoff's mother would not be made aware. As far as Geoff was concerned this was just great.

'Go on, I dare you', implored one of Geoff's contemporaries. 'Have a go, nothing to lose.' He was referring to an item on the weekly listing of vacancies, in this case for two Firemen to be based at Derby Slack

Manchester Central and the end of a routine passenger duty from Derby Midland for Derby crew of Driver Cecil Folwell (left) and Fireman Geoff Morris, plus Black 5 44920. Note the polished boots, white shirts and the ties worn as normal. (*Geoff Morris*)

Lane (former Great Northern Railway) depot as a sub-shed of Colwick. The 'depot' was closed later in 1955 due to the dangerous condition of the roof, but continued to provide a dozen sets of men for workings either side of Derby Friargate, to Tutbury and Burton in the West and via Nottingham Victoria to Grantham in the East. On Summer Saturdays Derby men and J6 0-6-0 tender engines would be exercised on holidaymakers' trains to Skegness, Mablethorpe and Cleethorpes, each being a traditional destination from the East Midlands industrial cities, towns and communities.

Promotion in the footplate grades was determined on seniority and having been told on joining the railway that he faced a long and hard road, any opportunity to sidestep the many more senior men should at least be considered. Many men did not want to move to a backwater shed with few opportunities for mileage bonuses on top of the basic pay for a 48 hour week and that may present an opportunity for a young aspirant. An application was promptly submitted and equally promptly rebutted with the advice that no young man ever wants to hear…wait a while.

Something must have registered somewhere because only a couple of weeks later, after another successful weekend spare job, the Driver said on return to the depot that he would have no objection if Geoff was to fire to him on a regular basis. 'I doubt you or he will have the chance, there's an envelope waiting for you Morris' said the Foreman. Sure enough there was an envelope and it contained news that he should report to Slack Lane, Derby for work as a Fireman. Geoff was at that time the youngest Fireman registered with British Railways. Life at Slack Lane was much quieter, traffic volumes were relatively light and locomotives rostered for work were essentially out based from Colwick and maintained in rudimentary conditions. The locomotives worked varied from A5 4-6-2 and L1 2-6-4 tank locomotives, Austerity and O4 2-8-0s, K2 2-6-0s plus the very occasional B1 4-6-0 (The Ivatt Class 4 2-6-0s displaced from the Midland and Great Northern Line did not arrive until later). Diesel multiple unit services were introduced in 1957 (Sundays Only) and when those initial, additional services were augmented at the expense of steam diagrams the draught of change was in the air. Colwick felt the draught and, it being the dominant shed, its men's representatives there sought to protect jobs, even at the expense of sub-shed work. Geoff could see the 'writing on the wall' and applied for a move back to 17A, which was accepted. After a break of some four years he was back. It was 1959 and in terms of motive power the Midland lines were stretched.

Working arrangements for footplate men from Derby were organised into a number of links and at that time the standard working week had reduced to forty-four hours. That was achieved by one week being forty-eight hours and the next forty, often by having a day off. A summary of the links is:

Top South link:	St Pancras and also Manchester with express passenger. (Always the premier link)
Second South link:	St Pancras/Nottingham/Lincoln/Leicester passenger/parcels and some Chaddesden to Nottingham freight turns
Top West link:	Birmingham/Gloucester parcels and fast fitted freight work (also included North Staffordshire line passenger work to Stoke and Crewe)
Top North link:	Sheffield/York/Leeds express passenger work (Second only to the premier link)
Second North link:	Mainly freight as above plus Stourton/Rowsley/Gowhole
Spare link:	20 sets of men work as required
Control link:	Two x 20 sets of men to work to Control instructions
Old Man's link:	Working Chaddesden/St Mary's/St Andrew's/Works shunts/Ripley branch/Wirksworth branch/Shirland Colliery trip/Trent trip. (Usually manned by men who had been ill, but passed to return to work, or for some other reason could not work in the other links)

Additional summer jobs included to Peterborough East and Llandudno, and prior to closure of the M&GN had included Yarmouth and South Lynn.

Rather than the bulk of the workings being with originating or terminating trains, much of the Derby's work was to relieve crews on trains passing through Derby, both passenger and freight. Derby had just one lodging turn and it was at the end of the long Sundays Only parcels train job from Derby (depart around 10.30am) which occupied staff at all principal stations over an elapsed journey time of some eight hours. This was one of the heaviest non-freight trains handled, often grossing at over 600 tons. Lodging accommodation was a dormitory style arrangement near Kentish Town where the locomotives on the former North London line would rattle the windows and disturb all but the deepest of sleepers.

The Chapter for 1960 introduced Geoff and his later regular Driver, Reg Beardsley and also a run with Bill Duff. It was on the return from that eventful run with the Crosti 9F/4F/Black 5 that Geoff had what he considers his finest run from St Pancras. The locomotive provided for the return express passenger run was an ex-works Jubilee (5X as Geoff would prefer) 45610 *Gold Coast* (later renamed *Ghana*). Everything about it was right and here was a machine to enjoy. The LMS type exhaust steam injectors could be very temperamental, but this one could be finely adjusted, left and trusted. By the approach to Bedford they were very well up to time and both enjoyed the evident response from increasing the cut off by two or three per cent … so much so that Houghton Conquest and Elstow were passed at some speed and a half causing Bill to have to sharply brake for the 80mph restriction at Bedford North. Many stories of steam have 'grown' somewhat over the years, but this was the only reference made by Geoff to very fast, controlled running and I have no doubt that a log of that run would have made for exceptional reading. (46143 was recorded at 100mph passing Elstow in 1961).

I asked Geoff for his recollections of items of particular interest that feature in the various Chapters. Here, in summary, are his thoughts:-

The Fell diesel mechanical:	A marvel in danger of shaking itself to pieces. Better when its continuously coupled cranks were replaced to make a 4-4-4-4 and when it was downgraded to local rather than express passenger work
2P 4-4-0 double heading	The 1912 built batch (40332-40557) was far more lively at speed than the 1928 batch (40563-40700) (As at 1959)
Double heading generally	Unpleasant, particularly if one is on the train (second) locomotive and particularly in tunnels and on adverse gradients. When on a pilot (leading) locomotive bringing forward coal from the rear of the tender with a 5X hammering away a few feet from you was just awesome
Sighting signals in fog, particularly at night	Very difficult and dangerous. If the Driver shouted for help, to leave the glare of the fire and hope the eyes would adjust to the darkness and cold air rushing past was difficult in the extreme. (Every sympathy extended to the Fireman involved in the Lewisham disaster)
Firing technique for different classes of steam locomotives	Tips on how to fire Britannias, Royal Scots/Patriots, Jubilees 5X, Black 5s, Standard 5s, V2s given and recorded! Note: on former LMS types never close the firehole door, just close as far as the combustion plate
Water level	When on the road… as long as you can see some water in the gauge glasses do not worry too much

When the BR/Sulzer type 4s took over former steam duties the role of the Fireman was much reduced, but between each October and the end of April the requirement for steam heating of carriages fully tested the idiosyncrasies of the boilers, causing countless failures. Characteristically, Geoff wrote to the various manufacturers and received from each sufficient technical information to enable a better working understanding of their products.

By 1966 the railway and 17A had changed out of all recognition. Again the 'writing on the wall' was clear and with some emotion Geoff handed in his notice and took a final walk over the bridge to Hulland Street … and to a new career with the Post Office. In an industry where to end employment is normally a total severance it was a measure of the standing Geoff had at 17A when the Superintendent advised him that, by exception, agreement had been reached with the trade union Branch that his job would be held in abeyance for six months just in case he changed his mind.

Railways and steam remained in his blood and when the heritage railway movement gained some momentum Geoff became a volunteer Driver at the North Yorkshire Moors Railway and the Great Central Railway.

Chapter Thirteen

The Human Element II:
Leslie Askin – Rolling Stock Inspector (1962)

Leslie Askin was born in 1928 and became a member of a family living in Derby. Mother was a companion/char lady at a nearby larger house which in addition to the family there also took in lodgers. One such lodger was David Mathieson who was in the early 1930s the Midland Division (of the LMS) Headquarters Passenger Inspector and was also a son of a long since retired and deceased former General Manager of the Midland Railway, John Mathieson. Through this connection young Leslie was introduced to the world of railways at Derby Station. A mischievous boy with an enquiring mind he combined the two characteristics by standing on the passenger overbridge and dropping an apple into the chimney of a locomotive, the intention being to see how high the apple would reach when the exhaust blast took effect upon departure. Admonishment was more along the lines of a waste of food rather than possible damage to the station roof!

In the mid-1930s David Mathieson was promoted to be Station Master at Bedford Midland Road and moved south from his Derby lodgings. In doing so some members of the family with whom he had lodged went with him and all were accommodated in a modern house close to the LMS station. The housekeeper did not enjoy good health and invited Leslie's mother (with Leslie) to temporarily fulfil the role. The invitation was accepted and for several months in 1935/36 Leslie was able to enjoy friendly access to the workings of Bedford Station and area. A little later in the 1930s (January 1938) a serious accident occurred at Oakley Junction. A train of empty carriages was being propelled off the main line and onto a siding at the start of the line to Northampton. The length of the train exceeded the available capacity of the siding and therefore a second shunt had to be arranged and carriages disconnected. Crucially the Driver of the locomotive (2893) eased forward a few yards and then stopped, awaiting the train's Guard. However, the movement had locked a set of points and correctly placed the main line signals at danger. Unfortunately the signalman had accepted the afternoon St Pancras-Bradford express (5569) and

although the Driver saw and reacted to a signal placed at caution he was unable to bring to a halt his train before an impact at 25mph which killed three persons and injured eight more.

In 1942 Leslie sought employment with the LMS at Derby and having the necessary two personal character testimonials (one from David Mathieson) plus that from his school, he was employed as a Messenger/Train Reporter and in 1946 – then as a young soldier – Leslie was proud to travel from Derby to Bradford Forster Square where David Mathieson was then Station Master. A return to civilian life followed and with it a resumption of railway service at Derby in the organisation of the Divisional Operating Superintendent (as referred to in the Chapter 'Setting the Scene').

One of the many recollections which Les told and amused me with concerned his time as a Rolling Stock Inspector. It relates to his involvement with arrangements for special trains to be run for supporters of Tottenham Hotspur Football Club in an FA Cup semi-final match at Hillsborough, Sheffield, on 31 March 1962.

In the normal course of events and to ensure that all was in order, engineering and operating staff were designated by the Regions. For the trains for Tottenham Hotspur, the Midland Divisional Operating Superintendent deputed two Passenger Rolling Stock Inspectors – Bill Mellady (running gear) and Les Askin (equipment) – to travel to Cricklewood (North London) carriage depot to arrange the formations to accommodate the maximum number of spectators (nine trains) and to cater for the needs of the official party of the football Club which would travel on the final departure from St Pancras. The VIP train would be required to offer silver service catering and with at least one first class dining only carriage. That final departure would be in the 'path' immediately following the 10.05 London-Scotland service, *The Thames-Clyde Express*, and follow it as far as Kettering where, to ensure a timely arrival at Sheffield, it may need to be regulated. Les Askin would travel with this train, and upon its return, would leave at an out of course stop at Loughborough (then home to Derby) whilst, with his task completed, the VIP party either enjoyed a dinner following a victory or not quite so enjoyable in defeat.

Coaching stock at Cricklewood was also required for two specials early on that same day to Liverpool for the Grand National. Bill would travel with the first, empty to Luton thence via Kettering, Harringworth and Oakham (where a stop would be made to enable the Duke of Rutland to join); the second train would start from St Pancras. In all, Bill and Les were looking for some 120–130 vehicles of the types required, including catering.

Bill and Les started work trying to identify and select vehicles with maximum seating and whilst such was generally common, it was necessary to request the Regional Operations Manager to bring in rakes of coaches stored serviceable along the Bedford (Oakley Junction) to Northampton line. Even with many coaches being potentially available the difficult train to source would be the 'first class diner'; functional kitchen car, restaurant car/first class dining car… it was a nagging concern and contemporaries elsewhere would also be looking to safeguard such vehicles and their utilisation.

Others were watching carefully as another sphere of the transport industry then facing huge change – shipping and docks – looked likely to need the provisions of adjusted special train services. During the two weeks since BRB determined the strategy for special traffic on 31 March, there had been a worsening of industrial relations between the unions representing 70,000 dockers plus affiliated trades, and their employers. This was particularly so at Liverpool/Birkenhead, but such was the fraternity amongst dock workers that any shipping expensively diverted to other UK ports would probably be 'blacked' upon arrival.

Unrest at the docks was strongest on Merseyside where, on 22 March, union labour had been withdrawn on both sides of the river. By the 28th, 10,500 workers were on strike there and 93 ships idle. More worryingly for the passenger shipping lines management was a supportive 24 hour stoppage at Southampton with resultant, consequential delays to stevedoring for the following days heavy tonnage movements also dictated by the tides. The general feeling of uncertainty and the sensitivity needed to deal with any diversions of inbound ships to alternative ports were further factors; the role of the railway was simply to respond as best possible.

Although London's Tilbury Docks were being worked normally, the tonnage/draught restrictions meant that only certain ships could be considered; for example Cunard's *Sylvania* inbound to Liverpool from New York. It was a volatile situation that, frankly, was of little concern to Bill and Les as they worked to have

marshalled their sets, label them either IT… or IX … as applicable and have them placed ready for movement on the Saturday morning for the few miles into St Pancras. By Thursday afternoon matters were well in order and both Les and Bill made their way back to Derby; the latter with a rabbit snared somewhere between Oakley Junction and Northampton! Upon arrival at the Derby office, they were advised that as a result of the likely strike action at some docks – particularly Southampton – ships were to be diverted to Tilbury and that some of the sets of rolling stock had been requisitioned by Regional HQ for use in services from there.

So … on the Friday a further, urgent 'draw down' of stock was made and sets quickly marshalled at Cricklewood. Les was particularly pleased with the VIP train, leaving the sole other catering vehicle at the end of a siding. That old vehicle had seen many better days as a first class dining car, but had been reported for poor riding and it probably had one journey only yet to be made. Job done, Les and Bill made their way for a well-earned rest; Les to the 'barracks' (the loco men's hostel) and Bill to the Fist Aid room at the carriage sidings. An early night for very early morning calls. In parallel the stocking of provisions and rostering of catering staff had been completed by others, as had provision for motive power and crews.

The railway never sleeps. Cunard were very concerned about the arrival of their *Sylvania*, off Ireland and awaiting instructions. No small vessel at 21,989 gross tons she had a crew of 450 and accommodation for 878 passengers. Built in 1956 for the Liverpool-Montreal service, she spent the winters on the New York service and it was from there that she was headed for her home, strike-torn port. Being of a size suitable for Tilbury, Cunard's management took the decision to divert the vessel and as part of the consequential actions, requested British Railways to arrange the transport of passengers, crew and luggage to Liverpool. The boat trains to/from Tilbury were operated from St Pancras and were dedicated sets suitable for short distance journeys and not for the 200 miles down the West Coast Main Line during which a meal service would be expected. So, night shift was looking for suitable stock and power. The availability of sets of rolling stock including a diner at Cricklewood must have been a godsend, so off they went into the night.

Imagine if you will the scene at Cricklewood as Les Askin arrived early on site to see empty sidings where some of the carefully marshalled sets should have been! In fact they were nowhere local at all and with the diner probably north west of Crewe. Other sets would have been used to convey immigrants newly arrived into the cold of England and heading for the Midlands and northern towns.

During the night alternative arrangements had been made to organise three trains at Hornsey for departures from Kings Cross. Les was able to pick up this information from the early shift control, but he was left with the not insignificant need to put together the VIP train, and in a hurry.

It being a Saturday with less suburban traffic to be dealt with, he managed to encourage the depot shunters to put together a mixed rake including a provisioned catering car capable of cooking the required number of meals, the rostered catering crew was available, but he still lacked a first class dining car. Only the 'down at heel' poor riding vehicle at the end of the siding seemed available. Even the shunting staff had reservations about its use and considered it may be a bad omen for their fellow North Londoners ... but there seemed no alternative. Unless, unless... given the nature of the occasion maybe the diner out of *The Thames–Clyde Express* could be swapped, the Scottish Region would probably not notice and by the time the set arrived back on the Sunday evening a reverse swap could be effected. A promise of an end of shift bonus of a crate of stout encouraged the participation of the shunting staff and at 10.05. *The Thames-Clyde Express* departed St Pancras 'right time' with the VIP special following its tail lamp north. Prior to joining the special Les sent a telegram to the Scottish Region advising a battery problem with 'their' dining car, but did not say it was not actually in the trainset.

For those on the VIP train there was no need to know of the drama that had unfolded and no doubt coffee and a pleasant lunch was enjoyed. Imagine though, lunch, afternoon tea or dinner on *The Thames-Clyde Express*, bad enough the mining subsidence of the Erewash Valley and South Yorkshire without a poor riding vehicle for the staff and passengers to endure. The Scottish Region would certainly notice, particularly when the train passed through tunnels with no lighting for the diners and the increasing gloom of an early dusk! It was a happy football club party that re-joined their train at Sheffield Midland for the journey home. Les was still with the train and was to travel with it as far as Loughborough where an out of course stop would be made to enable him to alight and make his way back to Derby. The stop was made, no one got off, an exhausted Les had 'nodded off' and actually left at the later, booked service stop, for water, at Kettering.

Monday brought with it the adverse reaction and Gaelic ire of the Scottish Region who were most upset and, later in the week, a letter of thanks to the Commercial Manager of the London Midland Region from Tottenham Hotspur Football Club was passed on to the Passenger Controller, Divisional Operating Superintendent, Derby.

The motto of Tottenham Hotspur Football Club is 'To dare is to do' and in dealing with the criticism from north of the border, Les's boss recognised the daring initiative that had been shown. The formal, verbal instruction to not repeat such action was given with a certain measure of acknowledgement of the initiative shown.

Tottenham Hotspur went on to win the FA Cup, the dockers returned to work on 2 April and in various guises and under various owners the *Sylvania* sailed on until 2004. Les Askin had an enjoyable career of fifty years with the railways, completing his time assisting Mr Dick Hardy as arrangements to sustain the legacy of engineering excellence via a formalised training and development structure were put into place.

Les recounted this story and several others to the author whilst travelling from Derby to London and many years 'on', it is worthy of record of how things were done and how problems could be solved without 'stopping the job'.

Chapter Fourteen

The Human Element III: John Heydon

One of the facts of working lives on and around the railway was (and is) a need for everyone to recognise that the work was continuous and had to be done strictly and consistently in accordance with the regulations; with a shift work arrangement it could be no other way. A second fact was that very little could happen without individuals working together for mutual benefit. Neither of these characteristics is unique to railways, but the level of both within the railways has been acknowledged time and time again in official records and, latterly, also by newcomers to the railway industry following privatisation.

It is the second of the characteristics – call it teamwork if you wish – which attracted me to the following piece. It provides an example amongst many of how individuals respected their employment I feel sure will be self-evident. The wording is as recorded by Mr John Heydon and made available by his son Patrick.

On one of my routine visits to the C&HP during the late 1950s when I was Freight Rolling Stock Inspector at Rowsley, I sat talking with Jack Smith, the late District Inspector for the line, in his office at Middleton Top.

Jack was very concerned with the difficulty of working the Middleton Top to Parsley Hay section, especially the Hopton Wood Quarry Branch, with the ageing North London (Class 2 freight) 0-6-0 locos. Tests had already been carried out with Liverpool Dock 0-6-0 tank No. 47164 – I believe on 17 February 1956 – but it was found to be unsatisfactory. The Divisional Motive Power people at Derby were unable to find a suitable, more powerful, short wheel base loco that would be suitable for Gotham Curve with a radius of only 55 yards and a super elevation of 10½ inches, and also be able to cope with the heavy limestone traffic the line was producing at that time.

Having spent four years in the Royal Engineers (Railway Operating Department), I knew much about the J94s, which had a similar tractive effort to a Class 4F. I knew of their capabilities and the very heavy trains they worked on the Longmoor Military Railway, which had several severe gradients. Jack Smith was very interested, so I set out to get as much information about the locomotives. My FRS duties also took me to

Ancoats, Ashton Road and Belle Vue shed. I knew that they had some J94s at the nearby Gorton shed, so on one of my visits I had a long chat with the Running Shed Foreman, telling him that I was from Derby and that we were interested in these locos. He very kindly took me to look round one. We measured the wheel base and diameters, and he gave me details about coal and water capacities. Armed with this information, and certain details from my lad's trainspotting book, Jack Smith submitted a suggestion to our Divisional Operating Superintendent that we should carry out tests with a J94 with a view to replacing the North London engines with locomotives from this class.

Comparisons between the J94s and the North London locos are as follows:-

	J94	Ex-N.L.
Wheel arrangement	0-6-0	0-6-0
Tractive effort	28,870 lbs	18,140 lbs
Weight	48 tons 5 cwt	45 tons 10 cwt
Wheelbase	11ft 0in	11ft 4in
Water capacity	1,500 gallons	850 gallons

I understand that the Divisional Motive Power people at Derby were initially reluctant due to the suggestion coming from the Operating Department, but they arranged for the temporary transfer of 68030 from Bidston to Rowsley for a trial period.

By this time I was the District Traffic Inspector at Rowsley, and the D.O.S. at Derby gave me permission to carry out tests on the C&HP line. I was to act as Guard, and with 68030 and a standard brakevan, one Monday morning (I think it was 10 April 1956) we set off from Rowsley via Buxton. We had two loco fitters, re-railing ramps, jacks and sprags, in case of a derailment. Rowsley Driver Len Fern, who had road knowledge for the whole of the route carried out all the tests; I am afraid that I have forgotten who the Fireman was.

At Buxton, we were joined by the Permanent Way Sub-Inspector for the C&HP line and a man from the Civil Engineer's Department in London. We also had a Motive Power Inspector from Derby for all of the tests – I think it was Lou Crane.

When we got to Friden we had to wait for the arrival of the 9.05am from Middleton Top and then followed the return working back to Middleton. Gotham Curve was the first obstacle, but the loco made easy work of the fifty-five chain curve. Number 68030 was then held at Middleton Top for the trials until the following Friday, when it returned with the brakevan to Rowsley.

In the meantime, trials were made with the engine and brake over every siding between Middleton Top and Friden, including the Hopton Wood Branch, where several loaded limestone wagons were worked up to Hopton Bottom. On another day, tests were made up Hopton Incline with two, three, four and finally five loaded wagons at a time. It was a very damp, foggy morning and at one stage with the five wagons and the regulator full open, the whole train slid backwards on the wet rail. The outcome was that three loaded wagons should be the maximum to be conveyed up Hopton Incline.

Number 68030 created great interest from all Departments – Operating, Motive Power and Permanent Way. I believe that the J94s were sometimes referred to as *Heydon's tanks* in the early days. The outcome is, of course, history and subsequently J94s 68006/13/30 were reallocated in August 1956 from Bidsten to Rowsley and Middleton Top to replace the North London tanks.

Chapter Fifteen

The Human Element IV: Alen Grice – Locomotive Maintainer

Alen Grice was born in 1932 at Kirkby-in-Ashfield, Nottinghamshire, and an early expedition alone to find and watch steam locomotives from a footbridge resulted in the 3-year-old being led back by the constabulary. Later, in boyhood and during the Second World War, Alen spent time at home, which was near Kirkby South Junction where he watched train after train loaded with artillery, tanks and American personnel heading South for the 'push' into Europe and beyond; a quick dash to the station was often rewarded by him being given something new in the form of chewing gum.

From a vantage point on top of a rock cutting, Kirkby South Junction was a fine location at which to watch a seemingly constant procession of trains. A more comprehensive description will provide an insight into the legacy left by the development of competing railway companies and the sheer volume of traffic being moved. The single-manned junction signal box controlled tracks diverging (ex-Great Northern Railway Leen Valley extension} North towards Langwith Junction. secondly (ex-Great Central Railway} North towards Mansfield and, thirdly (ex-Great Central Railway main line) North towards Heath/Sheffield Victoria and East towards Clipstone/Edwinstowe. Hereabouts, the Midland Railway line followed a North/South axis approximately half a mile to the East, and it was along that route towards Mansfield, Langwith Junction and the coalfield of North Derbyshire that the small town of Kirkby-in-Ashfield was situated.

In 1947 Alen's father paid a sum of £25 to the London Midland and Scottish Railway for his son to have the benefit of an Indentured Apprenticeship in mechanical engineering and maintenance of locomotives. For the purpose of the apprenticeship, Alen was to be based at Derby 4 Shed; 17A. Homeward bound at the end of the week, young Alen caught the 5.10pm Melton Mowbray train as far as Sawley Junction (now Long Eaton); a Derby locomotive (Compound) and crew turn. Although unauthorised riding on footplates was forbidden, the ample proportions of a macintosh hung up by a friendly driver would hide a 15-year-old until such time as the train was away from Derby. One evening, on 1006, Alen was allowed to accelerate the train away from Draycott, along the favourably graded 'golden mile'. Having rapidly attained quite some speed, and with Sawley Junction station in sight, Alen received instruction on how to bring a train to a gentle stop in a platform, and in having the awareness and confidence in the working of a locomotive.

The period of the apprenticeship coincided with the post-war Nationalisation of the railways and an end to the 'big four', private railway companies including the LMS. Alen's developing interest in locomotive engineering prompted him to request a 'letter of introduction' from his senior manager to enable access to depots in mainland Europe, then recovering from the war. Whilst in Germany he noted on locomotive tenders the slogan *räader mus rol fur den Reich* (wheels must roll) and – as a potential way of encouraging staff – this was of interest to his seniors. A later trip allowed Alen to sample the footplate of one of the eight 4-6-4 U Class, four cylinder compound locomotives of the French Railways.

Having mostly served his apprenticeship at Derby, the final stage was requested to be at a depot nearer to his home in Nottinghamshire. There were several depots within a few miles of each other; Mansfield, Kirkby-in-Ashfield and Toton. Kirkby-in-Ashfield was domestically ideal, though the Crewe-trained Chargehand Fitter had no time for Derby ways and told Alen in no uncertain terms. More on that later.

North Nottinghamshire was in the midst of a rich source of income for British Railways; king coal, by the many thousands of tons weekly and transported from collieries in rakes of 13-ton/16-ton wagons not having continuous vacuum braking (although some of the latter were so fitted later). Whilst the scale of production at the various collieries varied, their collective tonnage had been a sole domain of the Midland Railway until first the Great Northern Railway, and then the Great Central Railway, built lines in the late nineteenth century to access new loading points and increase competition.

The Midland Railway's route through the Nottinghamshire coalfields began in 1848 when the section from Nottingham to Kirkby-in-Ashfield was opened. The Midland Railway also purchased the (horse-drawn) tramway between Pinxton and Mansfield and rebuilt it to form a new section of railway north from Kirkby to Mansfield. The area's railway activity was dominated by the needs of the coal industry and, as a consequence, passenger services were – at least as far as the Midland Railway was concerned – a secondary consideration. Mansfield, the largest town in the vicinity, was not on any railway (as opposed to a tramway, horse-drawn) system until April 1871, when the line (Midland Railway) from Rolleston Junction to Southwell (opened in 1847) was extended via Farnsfield. After that section suffered from a withdrawal of passenger services (19 August 1929), facilities were retained to enable seasonal and sporting excursion traffic to be offered. Services for passengers from the area were enhanced, firstly, in 1876 when the Great Northern Railway reached Pinxton and introduced a service to Nottingham (ceased in January 1963) and secondly, from 1917 when the Great Central's Mansfield Railway linked Annesley through Mansfield Central (thus allowing an alternative service to Nottingham Victoria, via Sutton in Ashfield, which ceased in 1956). In February 1956 the London Midland Region of British Railways experimentally introduced a passenger train service between Nottingham, Hucknall, Kirkby South Junction and Sutton in Ashfield Town (which had last enjoyed any service in 1931). It proved a short-lived experiment; lasting less than one year. Ironically, the final passenger train service between Nottingham and Mansfield (at least in BR days) was along the former Midland Railway route, services being withdrawn on, and from, 12 October 1964. Having outlined a chronology of events to explain the complexity of the many railways within the area, we can now return to Alen's progress within the ever-busy railway operations of the time.

Alen started work as an apprentice fitter in 1949. Apart from a two-year spell of National Service between 1953 and 1955, Alen was employed at Kirkby until 1962 when he left on promotion to be Workshop Supervisor (Mechanical Foreman grade) at Annesley. During his time at Kirkby, Alen also spent much time on loan for similar duties at Mansfield until its closure in 1960.

Kirkby-in-Ashfield depot (16B) was established principally to serve the needs of the collieries nearby; twenty-seven in total: Annesley, Bestwood, Cresswell, Clipstone, Kirkby, Mansfield, Hucknall, Newstead, Thoresby, Sherwood, Rufford, Welbeck, Maltby, Dinnington, Firbeck, Manton Wood, Whitwell, Foxlow, Langwith, Blidworth, Ollerton, Warsop, Shirebrook, Bentinck, Langton, Brockhill and Linby.

The allocation of locomotives in 1948 totalled sisxty-six of power classes two (two), three (two), four (sixteen) and eight (forty-six), all of which were with tenders. The total allocation was dominated by the 8F

2-8-0s, built for the LMS between 1935 and 1945. The locomotives of that class allocated to Kirkby included several of the initial build of twelve, which had domeless boilers and, unlike the rest of the class did not have vacuum brake equipment and therefore relied solely upon a steam brake on the engine and a hand brake on the tender. Of this initial build, 48003 was later fitted with a more conventional boiler with dome and top feed separate, thus providing a spare spoiler for use by the remaining eleven. For a depot with a steady workload, Kirkby had a high turnover rate of 8Fs with the more conventional design of boiler. The reason for this was related to the quality of water. At Kirkby the supply to the depot was drawn from the town supply and was, therefore, treated and of good quality with beneficial results for boilers and washout periodicities. In fact the periodicity between washouts at Kirkby was extended to be beyond every twelve to sixteen days, as was the norm for locomotives with a boiler working pressure of 225lbs per square inch. Each day four samples of water were taken for analysis; town supply untreated, town supply treated, water taken hot from a locomotive and cold from a locomotive. 8Fs suffering the effects of poor water at other depots, but not due a shopping, were temporarily re-allocated to, and then away from, Kirkby after a period of several months (though those from the initial build largely remained within the motive power district). That will explain many a 'rare' sighting in notebooks!

Also of related interest to the fleet at Kirkby was that several locomotives benefitted from the BR programme of balancing 50 per cent of the reciprocating weights, which allowed running at up to 50mph with such locomotives denoted by a painted white star beneath the number on the side sheets of the cab. The programme was at least equally beneficial in terms of reducing the incidence of cracked frames, the rate of wear on the axleboxes within the horns and wear to the motion.

Passenger train workings for Kirkby locomotives were few and for the publicly timetabled excursions on Summer Sundays to Belle Vue (gardens) and Matlock, 4Fs and 8Fs were provided. Other irregular excursion traffic (for example horse racing at Doncaster/Southwell and football matches) would have motive power provided typically from Burton and Rowsley, both of which had examples of the Crab 2-6-0 mixed traffic type allocated.

At Mansfield the allocation of locomotives as at 1948 totalled thirty-six of power classes one (one), two (seven), three (seventeen), four (five) and eight (six), of which seven were side tank engines. For the passenger services the types were the ex-Midland Railway 2P 4-4-

0 with tenders and ex-LMS-built 4-4-2 tank. Of these the latter (three by the time Alen became involved, 41940/3/7) were the bane of many a working footplate and maintainer's daily shift life. They were far better suited to the flat of the London Tilbury & Southend route for which they were originally ordered and were deployed along than the switchback of the subsidence-affected Nottinghamshire coalfield routes they were locally unpopular. 41940 was the worst; having been one of the five built in 1925 by Nasmyth, Wilson & Company of Patricroft, Manchester, with a steam operated reverser which was ill tempered at best. These locomotives were known locally as 'crooners' (you had to sing to them by way of encouragement). All three left in 1956 (41943 and 41947 in February, both for scrapping, though the former was first assessed at Bow Works, and 41940 re-allocated in April to Toton). They were replaced by 2-6-2 tank locomotives built in 1935; 40096, 40146/84, known locally as flying fleas and also unsuitable for the traffic, though for reasons of being under powered. Matters improved belatedly when the flying fleas and were replaced by Fairburn modified (1945) versions of the original Stanier 2-6-4 tank design that were power class four and had a wheelbase more suited to tight curvature track. The closure of Mansfield depot in 1960 brought to Kirkby some of its men, its locomotives, workings (including passenger to Nottingham) and its brakedown vehicles, including a recently converted bogie carriage fitted out as a 'packing and staff van'.

Kirkby depot was (until modernisation in 1958 by installation of an additional covered area over two tracks to one side of the main building, a mechanical hopper coaling plant, a separate ash plant and electricity!) a three-road, dead-end covered shed with a Midland-style coaling stage, a turntable, reception, disposal and preparation pits – and little else. The main depot building lacked doors and as it was North facing was a very cold depot at which to work.

As with all motive power depots, the daily requirements for power were shown on the prominently displayed Train Board. A typical weekday would show locomotives off shed between 4.20am and 5.00pm.

- colliery work local (up to twenty 8F locomotives on weekdays/Saturdays as required)
- line work departures on weekdays and Saturdays to:
  Rowsley (5)
  Gowhole (1) (between Matlock and Chinley)
  Belle Vue (1) 1.17pm
  Garston (1) 11.20pm (export coal)
  Wichnor (1) 9.50pm (between Burton and Tamworth)

  Branston (1)
  Bromford Bridge/Washwood Heath (2) Birmingham
  Bristol Barrow Road loco (1, Mondays only)
  Bescot Loco (1, Thursdays only)
  Wellingborough (2) see later note
- power station train work on weekdays and Saturdays as required:
  Repton and Willington (1)
  Castle Donington (1)
  Drakelow (1)
  Staythorpe (6)

(Note: the longer hauls of coal south to London were mainly handled by Toton depot from the marshalling yard, which received and returned wagons from the many collieries). Kirkby also had two lodging turns; both were to Wellingborough and were worked on weekdays including Saturdays, the trains continuing South to Brent, North London.

The infrastructure, curvature and gradient profiles, plus the weight of trains from many of the collieries, demanded the greater steam brake power of the 8F 2-8-0s rather than the 4F 0-6-0s. These operational characteristics caused wheel tyres, particularly on tenders to work loose.

Unlike some depots with a similar level of allocation and demands for high availability and reliability, Kirkby did not have a Workshop Supervisory grade of Mechanical Foreman. The around-the-clock shift arrangements relied upon Leading Chargehand Fitters who's responsibilities fell within the general headings of examining and repairing. Working a three-shift system (6am-2pm, 2pm-10pm, 10pm-6am) for a standard forty-hour week, there was also a popular day shift (8am-5pm with one-hour lunchbreaks, which for many allowed a meal at home and a look at the garden/allotment). Teams were organised into ten fitters, plus mates, plus others solely deployed on boiler washouts. Additionally, there were two boilersmiths (days/nights), reduced later in the period under review to one, with provision for support from one more out based from Nottingham. Motive power depots such as Kirkby were essentially 'garages' to enable the fleet to be maintained on a day-to-day basis with an acknowledgement of a need for boiler washouts and submission for considerations of proposals for shopping into main works for overhaul based upon mileage accumulated/condition. In support of the depot staff the Regional Chief Mechanical and Electrical Engineer would provide advice via Boiler Inspectors and an experienced Outdoor Assistant.

The 'bread and butter' workload of the examining and fitting staff may be summarised as:

- daily examination of mechanical condition of locomotives prior to service
- responding to notes made by drivers at the end of their shifts
- changing brake blocks and replacement of 'consumable' components, for example, piston packings, drain taps
- washing out of boilers
- caulking of leaking stays (Boilersmith)
- fettling of injector cones/valves/lubricators and lubrication runs
- piston and valve examinations
- record keeping

Facilities at Kirkby were basic and did not extend to the inclusion of any machining or re-metalling of motion parts. One such task, the remetalling (white metal) and machining of the horizontal (sliding) faces of the crossheads, provides a good example of how the main depot (in this case Nottingham) provided support. The high incidence of particulates and colliery dust, plus the force exerted to provide motion, combined to require the crossheads to be removed, re-metalled, machined to size and re-fitted. The arrangement involved a locomotive coming out of traffic onto shed during depot night shift, the gudgeon pin retaining each connecting rod being knocked out, the retainer for each piston rod similarly treated, the crossheads removed from within the slide bars, placed onto a hand barrow and taken to the station for conveyance by early morning service to Nottingham, thence collected and taken to the shed. By 3.00pm the re-metalled/machined crossheads were ready for loading onto the 3.07pm train, met at the station, run on the handcart by four younger members of staff through the streets of Kirkby-in-Ashfield and the crossheads refitted to enable the locomotive (already in steam) to resume its diagram. Why the rush? The day shift could go home before 5pm if the job was completed before that time; the management having a locomotive not 'stopped' for repairs was ample, wider benefit.

During the period of Alen's time at Kirkby, a serious incident occurred with an 8F (48188), which lead to the death of the Driver John Axon at Chapel-en-le-Frith when he bravely stayed on the footplate despite scalding steam at pressure from a broken steam pipe joint. As a result of this, modifications were made at depots allocated with 8Fs to replace flat joints with a coned type for live steam to and from the driver's brake.

There were also unwanted demands placed upon fitting staff. On one occasion a Crab arrived on shed from Burton in readiness to work a passenger excursion. On the tender front was a chalked message 'Engine has two broken springs ... replacements are on top of tender.'

Thanks a lot! Another unwanted task regularly occurred on Sunday nights. During the weekends, juveniles of Mansfield took their pleasure by releasing on mineral wagons the internal drop doors, which would release whatever was in the wagon and then jam under the wagon in the four foot. The rakes of wagons were stabled on the long sidings (which had earlier formed part of the Pinxton tramway), pending movement on Monday mornings to local collieries. The 'gang' from Kirkby would be despatched in packing vans retained at the depot (and at Mansfield) for the purpose of derailments (Toton being the custodian of the brakedown crane/train).

Whilst minor derailments of wagons within collieries were not uncommon, significant incidents were, thankfully, rare. Reports of derailments and/or significant incidents would lead to a decision by Control as to whether the depot vans would be sent rather than the crane plus support staff from Toton. On one occasion there had been an incident at Portland Washery (Pinxton tramway route), with conflicting shunting movements of loaded and empty rakes of wagons conspiring to leave at least six wagons in a tangled heap. The Kirkby/Mansfield gang was despatched and were faced with the task of separating/righting the wagons with only hacksaws and hawsers. A very fine opportunity for some overtime!

Another reason for visiting certain collieries was considered something of a perk. These certain collieries had their own steam locomotive(s) for shunting of incoming/outgoing loaded wagons, which involved limited running rights over British Railways track. For insurance purposes it was necessary for all such private locomotives to be examined annually for mechanical and wheel tyre profiles suitability. Over a two-week period Alen would accompany a Leading Chargehand Fitter who, based upon the outcome of the examination, had the authority to remove the registration plate affixed to locomotive. Only on one occasion was such an action necessary; that being at Bilsthorpe where the warning of the previous year in regard to the wheel tyre profiles being badly worn had not been heeded. The colliery employee took the view that stopping the colliery was a greater threat to his continued employment than having a locomotive minus a registration plate. A pleasant drink was still taken at The Stanhope Arms!

Upon acceptance of a Proposal for Shopping (i.e. input into a main Workshop for an overhaul) of a (BR) locomotive, it would be assigned by the CM&EE Dept to (usually) either Derby or Crewe Works. Upon return of an overhauled locomotive, the fitters would (for the 8Fs) promptly remove a guard plate forward of the leading brake hanger, which, at depot level, effectively prevented ease of access to piston packings and glands, and replace all the tight 3/8″ cotter pins with 5/16″, again for faster maintenance work. Incidentally, the discarded guard irons made excellent dust pans!

It was probably those depot practices that had caused the Chargehand Fitter who was responsible for the final stages of Alen's apprenticeship, Harry Johnson (trained in the different ways of Crewe), to caution Alen as an apprentice in regard to Derby's ways being unwelcome. With such a surname he should have been a Midland man, but he wanted things done 'by his book' rather than what was best for production against the Train Board. Harry was one of life's contented souls; contented with his lot at work where he eschewed promotion opportunities, his quiet lifestyle as a bachelor and when the depot closed in 1962, soon found remunerative work elsewhere in the area.

As noted previously, electricity did not reach the depot until 1958, and this is an example of the rudimentary conditions under which the labour force worked, day in and out, season and out. Cutting gear was non-existent and removal of nuts, for example, was by hammer and cold chisel, whenever the usual heavy duty spanners proved inadequate. The management doubtless took a view that based upon the then only alternative work with the coal industry, life in the fresh air would always be preferred.

Even with sensible and appropriate arrangements, and the benefit of years of experience, railways carry for their operational staff a level of occupational danger. One such occasion involved Alen on the morning of 2 January 1962. One of the passenger train diagrams transferred upon the closure of Mansfield involved an early morning train from Mansfield to Nottingham; a diagram then entrusted to a Fairburn 2-6-4 tank locomotive (42222, as it happened). The locomotive required Fitter's attention to the lubrication feed to the underkeep of a trailing driving wheel axlebox. To undertake this task it was necessary for Alen to work in the pit directly under the locomotive, at a point where the rear hopper door of the ashpan was above him. The footplate crew were ready to take the locomotive off shed and, prior to going under the locomotive, Alen advised Driver Markiley as to his intention and that his fireman must not disturb the bed of the 27 square feet of fire by further addition of coal. The instruction was adhered to, but by cracking open the blower and opening the firehole doors (to check the state of his fire), the fireman did just enough to disturb the bed, which was reclining on the firebars, and much of which then cascaded into the ashpan and some embers straight out of a gap in the partially warped hopper door. Alen was caught, and sod's law applied in full as a large

ember found a way inside the top of his boot, which led to Nottingham General and Sheffield Burns Unit followed by a layoff of ten months.

By that time Alen was courting Patricia (herself a railway employee who transferred from Derby Locomotive Works to Mansfield (Central) Goods) and they were married in 1962. They settled locally with Alen moving on promotion to Annesley where he helped sustain steam motive power against a deteriorating agenda of change.

My own visits to Kirkby depot were on Sunday afternoons, usually as part of a tour of the area including Langwith Junction and Westhouses. Kirkby-in-Ashfield was always quiet on Sundays and a good example of a town where people respected and appreciated the day of rest. The only activity at the depot was seemingly the fire lighters and steam raisers with always over fifty locomotives to prepare for the following day and for night shift to examine for the start of the new working week.

Between 1953 and 1955, Alen undertook National Service. He was with the Royal Engineers, Corps of Transport, based at the Longmoor Military Railway between Liss and Bordon Camp in Hampshire. When the officers were made aware of Alen's training and employment in civilian life, he was quickly engaged with work on the small fleet of locomotives and was promoted to corporal. Whilst at Longmoor, a film starring Ava Gardner, Stewart Grainger and Lionel Jeffries, Bhowani Junction, was made and involved the creation of a train wreck. Once assembled, or disassembled as the case may be, the director decided that the scene was not quite right. It was made so by Alen going around smashing every window. Alen had, on occasions, a sense of humour that was tested by young and inexperienced officers; responding to a nonsense question as to the purpose of the hand-rail knobs along the side of the boiler, he advised that reins would be attached to enable the locomotive to be steered.

Towards the end of his career with British Railways, Alen was asked by the Divisional Manager, Nottingham, to 'keep an eye' on developments at the then fledgling base of the Main Line Steam Trust (now Great Central Railway) at Loughborough. Conditions there at the time made Kirkby of 1949 look palatial, but the allure of steam pervaded and long-term friendships were formed. Alen became the first paid employee of the Great Central Railway and, at the time of writing, remains a valuable member of staff, responding to end of turn notes by drivers of steam locomotives and passing on to the apprentices and volunteers alike the benefit of his years of experience. Alen also takes upon himself all things mechanical and operational concerning 8F 48624, one of only five restored members of that class.

Chapter Sixteen

You'll Never Believe What's Been Through!

This Chapter is for the enthusiasts; those who stood and admired, noted and memorised, cheered and booed, reflected, returned to the same locations time after time… and some of whom will probably recall numbers and names as though it was yesterday.

The Chapter is rich both in detail and depth. Listings are by date, by year, by route. Information includes the numbers of the locomotives, depot allocation at the time of the noting, class of train and where available details of the train worked. The railway culture was full of abbreviations and where detail shown is 'railway' rather than 'public' I have tried to guide readers and also have provided additional information for some obscure locations. Many, though, will not need help and will, I feel sure, quickly assimilate the information, absorb the detail, be surprised by some of the notings and find others to be scarcely credible. That, though, was the nature of the pass-time; perhaps 97 per cent of a session's notings would be as expected (locomotives allocated to depots locally or along the line of route and working in accordance with normal day to day arrangements). The interest and certainly the excitement was within the 3 per cent and whilst some days it would be 0 per cent others would produce more and it made attendance seem worthwhile.

An ability accurately to predict when the component parts of the 3 per cent would pass was beyond us all; certainly we had over the years noted trains that were the more likely of contenders, but we never really knew until the moment the locomotive(s) passed. Whenever something unusual or, to use popular parlance, 'rare' passed, the next souls who appeared on the platform, on the bridge or popular viewing position would be greeted with the refrain – usually accompanied by a grin – of 'you'll never guess what's just been through!' It was the 'just' that hurt most! This will bring back memories for many of arriving 'just' too late to see such and such locomotive making its only known venture in twenty years (a lifetime to us then) from its usual haunts. For East Midlanders arriving at Tamworth (with 45509 struggling as usual) to be told with unlimited glee that *Duchess of Buccleuch* was on the 9 o'clock stopper which had 'just' left was not a good start to the day. To all those who know what I mean, my commiserations, we have each been there!

Although the listings are extensive, they cannot be comprehensive, let alone fully comprehensive. The railway was operated twenty-four hours a day every day of the year and at the start of the period under review there were some 16,000 locomotives based at roundly 500 depots and sub-depots. Simply because I was Derby based there is a high incidence of sightings thereabouts. I have culled information from other credible sources, but feel that I have been somewhat short of sightings along the Erewash Valley (between Clay Cross and Trent) and therefore have been unable to identify the extent to which Holbeck 'Royal Scots' worked south to St Pancras prior to mid-1960. In addition there were trains of interest which produced unusual locomotive workings but which have eluded my research. I have in mind in particular a Friday's only train from the north-east of England (possibly Catterick Camp) to Birmingham for national servicemen going on leave. That train was heavy and produced pairs of Bls and an occasional V2 way before those classes became more frequent visitors. My message is that if anyone has real information about these two areas of interest or can add to the fund of knowledge, let's be having it!

For some readers only a fully comprehensive daily listing for the entire seven year period would suffice, but there is a limit to what could reasonably be incorporated. For example a weekly listing of the locomotives entering or leaving Derby Locomotive Works would make a separate volume. Also, there are inevitable omissions; for example it was far more exciting to note something new rather than when something ceased.

The benefit of research, reflection, deduction, probability, access to credible records and discussions with some of those directly involved at the time should provide a basis of confidence in what is stated. Where significant doubt exists no reference has been included. Nearly sixty years may not for some have diminished the memories, but as I progressed the research I was surprised by the pace of developments along and affecting the railway routes of interest, how one timetable period merged with the next and how subtle changes could conspire to cloud what I thought was a fact. Therein lies the importance of the record and I hope you will enjoy the listings.

An end to end, self-contained route such as Bristol to Sheffield (Regional boundaries)/ Leeds/York/Newcastle should have been able – and generally was very able – to maintain a strong control on the locomotives deployed. Nothing from the Western Region (former Great Western classes) could venture more than a very few miles east of Birmingham and the locomotive exchange point at Sheffield (for most passenger trains to/from the North thereof at least up to 1961) provided an effective barrier for anything bigger than a Bl. Manchester Central/Sheffield Midland to St Pancras passenger trains usually had locomotives from depots at either end of the routes (Trafford Park/Millhouses and Kentish Town) and interest between 1957 and 1961 for steam lay in the turnover of front line locomotive classes and individual locomotives allocated rather than in the encroachment of 'foreign' locomotives. It was, therefore, the passenger train services from Leeds that potentially provided much of the (3 per cent) unusual sightings, due in part from a failure by the 'gatekeepers' to prevent Carlisle and Scottish based locomotives from straying south and, occasionally, west. Leeds, Holbeck depot and its workings were interesting because in meeting general, day to day running requirements the authorities maintained a strong control over what locomotives were turned out for the work over the Carlisle, London and Bristol routes. For example, their Royal Scots rarely seemed to stray from the section north of Leeds (at least until diesels and some A3 pacifics arrived) and for London trains in need of Class 7 power, an available Britannia would generally be favoured over deployment of a Scot. Similarly it seemed at times of stress on resources that Carlisle or Scottish locomotives of Class 6 would be sent south rather than a Holbeck based example, of which there seemed to be a generous allocation.

From time to time events and traffic flows would disturb arrangements; for example the Glasgow Fairs holiday traffic would produce a welter of Southbound trains requiring a change of locomotive at Leeds and with no immediate, balancing return working that could create a disturbance. As an insight, take a preview look at mid-June 1957 for the Midland lines – a week when the 3 per cent was exceeded. Wakes Week traffic was similarly demanding on locomotives, rolling stock and crews, but had the relative advantage of 'out and home' workings. Any backlog of maintenance, washouts, an unfortunate run of mechanical failures, locomotives being called to Works, a need to provide power to help

out elsewhere … each an uncontrollable variable which conspired to maintain interest for lineside observers. Another arrangement that could generate the unusual was the use of cyclic diagrams whereby a locomotive could be away from its home depot for two or three days. One such involved the locomotive off the Northbound *Pines Express* from Bath to Birmingham then being used on a following train from Birmingham to Sheffield. If arrangements were followed that sometimes brought a BR Standard Class 5 from a Southern Region depot to Sheffield, and could on occasions also be used to get such a locomotive to Derby for Works attention (and if luck was unusually favouring the Operators) plus enabling another to be sent back. Finally, there were many practices involving locomotive workings that could be traced back to the days of pre-grouping whereby, for example, Longsight examples found their way to Leicester and Derby.

Dieselisation (and withdrawal of facilities for servicing steam locomotives) created huge disturbances to long established arrangements and when the new technology ran up against teething problems and the British weather, there was an opportunity for an extended flourish with steam which was savoured by many, though not including the management.

The year by year listings will probably best be appreciated when read in conjunction with the main Chapter for each year. The chapters include additional information and in some cases will answer questions that arise from a study of the listings. Many of the questions will start with WHY.....? For example, WHY did Nuneaton based locomotives start appearing on an afternoon freight train through Derby in 1961 (answer, a diversion of many trains due to electrification work around Crewe) and WHY was there an influx of V2s and pacifics from North Eastern Region depots in 1962/63 (answer, a combination of diesel problems, weather and a management decision to not change locomotives at Sheffield).

During the seven year period the balance of the extent of the unusual swung from the Midland lines to London to the cross country route. It was that which largely drove the decision to combine the two routes into one book. Anyone living between Ambergate and Derby or was able to spend time at Derby had a particularly interesting and rewarding time. It is difficult to think of other routes which over the same period witnessed such a variety of both change and traction. Banbury to Oxford and Reading maybe, the Great Central perhaps.

You'll Never Believe What's Been Through: 1957 – Midland Lines to/from St Pancras

Date	Loco No.	Loco Class	Loco Shed	Train Class	Detail
January	10201	SR3	17A	1	Regularly allocated to work 12/5 Dby–St P and
	10202	SR3	17A		4/15 return 1
	10203	SR3	17A		
1 Jan	45544	Pat6	8A	1	9.15 Nottm–Lpl (to Man)
26 Jan				1	Footex traffic. Refer to Chapter text
19/20 Mar	10800	BTH1	17A	2	Dby–Man and return
27/28 Mar				Grove	Royal Train movements. Refer to Chapter text
April	61318	B1	40B	1	At Buxton off Scunthorpe excursion
6 April	70032	Brit	9E	1	5/55 Man–St P (double-headed)
	45641	Jub	14B		
May	61198	B1	36A	1	At Buxton off Scunthorpe excursion
12 May	62571	D16	40A	1	Enthusiast excursion. Nottm–Yk via Erewash
16 May	90763	WD10	68A	-	At Westhouses
June	45696	Jub	68A	1	Various Lds–St P and return workings
18 May	45511	Pat6	9A	2	Pilot on Dby to Lcln (to Nottm for Nottm–Lpl 1 19 May)
12-17	45704	Jub	68A	1	Various Lds–St P and return workings
June	45715	Jub	68A		
	45724	Jub	68A		
	45728	Jub	68A		
	45731	Jub	68A		
14 June	73154	Std5			Final new steam locomotive built at Dby Loco Works (2,941st)
15 June	72009	Clan	68A	1	10.30 Brdfd–St P (ex Lds) returned with 11/00 St P–Shfld 3 (parcels)
16 June	46117	Scot	55A	1	Glgw–St P (ex Lds) returned with 9/15 St P–Edin to Lds 1
17 June	45665	Jub	67A	1	10/45 Glgw–St P.
18 June	30308	700	70C		At Cricklewood
22 June	31622	U	70C		At Cricklewood
23 June	45599	Jub	68A	1	11.30 St P–Brdfd
24 June	45519	Pat6	9A	1	7.20 Brdfd–St P (ex Lds)
26 June	45510	Pat6	1A	1	10.25 St P–Man (ex Dby)
July	45550	Pat6	9A	1	Various Man/Shfld–St P workings
July	45550	Pat6	9A	-	Loaned to Toton
3 July	45671	Jub	26A	1	10.5 Edin–St P (ex Lds) returned with 9/15 St P–Edin 1

You'll Never Believe What's Been Through: 1957 – Midland Lines to/from St Pancras

Date	Loco No.	Loco Class	Loco Shed	Train Class	Detail
9 July	45507	Pat6	5A	2	Bletchley–Bedford workings
10 July	45503	Pat6	5A	2	Bletchley–Bedford workings
13 July	45677	Jub	67A	1	4/55 St P–Shfld
13 July	44964	Bl5	21C	1	9.20 Glgw–St P (44964 ex Lds, 40585
	40585	2P	15C		pilot from Shfld)
15 July	45687	Jub	67A	1	Noon Brdfd–St P (ex Lds)
21 July	45720	Jub	67A	1	10.40 Brdfd–St P (ex Lds)
22 July	45101	Bl5	26A	1	9.20 Glgw–St P (45101 ex Lds, 44805 pilot
	44805	Bl5	21A		from Shfld)
22 July	45156	Bl5	26A	1	10.5 Edin–St P (45156 ex Lds, 73000 pilot
	73000	Std5	16A		from Shfld)
1/4 Aug	70045	Brit	6J	1	Scout Jamboree excursions. St P–Sutton Park
3 Aug	61306	Bl	53B	1	Glgw–St P relief ex Lds
Sept	D8000	EE1			Trial workings from Toton
October	46110	Scot	14B		Allocated to work on St P–Man
	46116	Scot	14B		class 1
	46127	Scot	14B		
	46131	Scot	14B		
	46152	Scot	14B		
	46157	Scot	14B		
14 Dec	44491	4F	2E	1	Dudley–Luton (Footex)
	44524	4F	2E		
21 Dec	41078	Com	21A	1	2/25 Man–St P (ex Dby) (double headed)
	41143	Com	17A		
16-31 Dec	44725	B15	68A	1	Various Glgw/Edin/Lds
	44790	B15	68A		St P and return workings
	44792	B15	68A		
	44795	B15	68A		
	45481	B15	68A		
	45696	Jub	68A		
	45704	Jub	68A		
	45732	Jub	68A		

You'll Never Believe What's Been Through: 1957 – Cross Country

Date	Loco No.	Loco Class	Loco Shed	Train Class	Detail
5 Jan	61306	Bl	53B	1	Footex Nottingham Forest v Goole Town
26 Jan	45741	Jub	3B	1	Footex West Bromwich Albion v Sunderland
26 Jan	61083	Bl	35C	1	Footex traffic Huddersfield Town v Pboro United
	61168	Bl	40B		
	61211	Bl	36E		
31 Jan	62586	D16	32E	2	3/5 Lcln–Dby (D16/3 replacing D11/1 at that time)
2 Mar	61056	Bl	38A	1	Footex traffic. Nottm (Vic) 5/ Shirebrook 1 to Bham via Egginton Jn Birmingham City v Nottingham Forest
	61046	Bl	38A		
	61141	Bl	38A		
	61208	Bl	36E		
	61272	Bl	38B		
	61367	Bl	34A		
18 Mar	62571	D16	40A	2	6.57 Lncln–Dby returned with 12/12
29 April	65584	J17	31B	7	Colwick–Egginton Jn
14 May	45614	Jub	14B	3	Stoke–Basford via Egginton Jn
10 June	45687	Jub	67A	1	Lds–Btl relief
11 June	61738	K2	38A	4-6	6/55 Burton–Yk via Egginton Jn
24 June	46126	Scot	68A	1	8.20 Ncl–Cdff (ex Shfd)
26 June	61205	Bl	35C	1	At Worcester off excursion from Eastern Region
29 June	60132	A1	52A	0	Turned on Dore triangle
13 July	60082	A3	52B	0	Turned on Dore triangle
20 July	60018	A4	52A	0	Turned on Dore triangle
20 July	45720	Jub	68A	1	10.15 Brdfd–Pgntn (ex Lds to Btl)
29 July	46145	Scot	55A	1	3/57 Ncl–Btl (ex Shfld)
August	46111	Scot	9A		At Burton (ex Sutton Park Scout Jamboree excursions)
	46168	Scot	1B		
	70045	Brit	6J		
3 Aug	42815	Crab	5B	1	Kidsgrove–Skegness via Egginton Jn
10 Aug	45441	Bl5	71G	1	1/18 Dton–Bham (ex Shfld)
13 Aug	46135	Scot	5A	1	Sutton Park–Ncl via Dby
14 Aug	45625	Jub	5A	1	Sutton Park–Pboro via Egginton Jn (to Colwick)
17 Aug	45441	Bl5	71G	1	1/18 Dton–Bham (ex Shfld)
24 Aug	60154	A1	52A	0	Turned on Dore triangle
8 Sept	61010	Bl	53B	1	Hull–Bournville trade excursion
8 Sept	45501	Pat6	9A	1	10.15 Brdfd–Pgntn (ex Lds to Btl) (double headed)
	73068	Std5	22A		

You'll Never Believe What's Been Through: 1957 – Cross Country

Date	Loco No.	Loco Class	Loco Shed	Train Class	Detail
11 Sept	61248	Bl	40B	2	2/55 Lcln–Dby
29 Oct	63686	04	39A		At Glos
26 Nov	61416	Bl6	50A		At Dby
29 Nov	61416	Bl6	50A	7	Wwd Hth–Ncl via Trent/Erewash

You'll Never Believe What's Been Through: 1958 – Midland Lines to/from St Pancras

Date	Loco No.	Loco Class	Loco Shed	Train Class	Detail
January		2P			Several examples on loan from Western Division of LM Region for piloting work
3/4 Feb					Derailment on Western Division resulted in diversions along part of Midland route
3 Feb	45528	PatR	5A	1	*The Caledonian* London Euston–Glgw C via Northampton, Market Harborough, Trent, Erewash
4 Feb	45601	Jub	1B	1	9/17 Euston–Glgw C
	45512	PatR	12B	1	10/20 Euston–Glgw C (double headed)
	45244	Bl5	12B		
14 Feb	47994	Gar		0	Hasland–Crewe for dismantling
26 Feb	45666	Jub	12A	1	Glgw C–Euston diverted via Erewash (double headed)
	45412	Bl5	17A		
March		Std4/5			Bedford allocated 3 Cl5 and 1 Cl4
March		8F			Various examples noted with white star on cabsides (denoted re-balanced)
March	10800	BTH1	17A		At Dby carriage shunting
10 Mar	45547	Pat6	1A	4-6	Willesden–Clsle diverted as 3 Feb
13 Mar	D8203	BTH1x		0	Trial workings from Toton
16 Mar	60855	V2	14D	0	Clearance trials St Pancras area. Refer to Chapter text
23 Mar	60855	V2	14D		Clearance trials St Pancras–Wigston Jns
30 Mar	40682	2P	17A	1	Due to late running of 8.55 Man–St P, worked a relief, but failed at Bedford (forward with 75042 BR4)
8 April	44883	B15	12A	1	Various workings into St. P
	44885	B15	12A		Ex Glgw/Edin/Lds
	44903	B15	12A		
	45715	Jub	12A		
9 April	45546	Pat6	5A	2	4/6 Shfld–Dby
10 April	45516	Pat6	8A	1	7.50 Buxton–Man
14 April		dmu		2	17 x 3 car sets introduced on some Lcln–Nottm–Dby, Lstr–Nuneaton–Bham and Bham–Dby (B8/B9) workings
5 May	46145	Scot	55A	1	Noon Brdfd–St P (ex Lds)
10 May	44690	B15	27A	1	Cup Final relief trains
	45717	Jub	27A		Ex Manchester, to St. P.
13 May	45677	Jub	12A	4-6	Clsle–Lstr
22 May	61390	Bl	40B	1	At Buxton off Scunthorpe excursion
29 May	61158	Bl	36A	1	At Buxton off Scunthorpe excursion

You'll Never Believe What's Been Through: 1958 – Midland Lines to/from St Pancras

Date	Loco No.	Loco Class	Loco Shed	Train Class	Detail
30 May	44682	B15	5A	1	Pilot on Folkeston Hbr–Leeds also conveyed 3 Pullman Cars
May/June		Scots			Progressively replaced by Britannias Refer to Chapter text
	70004	Brit	14B/9E		
	70014	Brit	14B/9E		
	70015	Brit	9E		
	70017	Brit	9E		
	70021	Brit	9E		
	70042	Brit	14B/9E		
		9F		1/3	Resumed seasonal workings.
			Scottish		At Millhouses (T Th SuO) off 6/38 Glgw–Marylebone. Returned North with balancing working (ex Beighton)
20 June	30909	Sch	73A	1	At St Albans on returning excursion to Southern Region (Whipsnade Zoo)
24 June	30939	Sch	73A	1	Maidstone (East)–St Albans excursion
1 July	D6501	BCW3	73C	1	Fawkham–St Albans excursion
25 July	61136	Bl	14D	1	7.33 Brdfd–St P (ex Lds) (double headed)
	45627	Jub	17A		
28 July	D5700	Metro	17A	3	Driver training Dby–Hope Valley (also Churnet Valley) Locomotives in multiple
	D5701	Metro	17A		
1 Aug	92122	9F	15A	1	Relief to 12/25 Man–St P (ex Lstr)
2 Aug	92128	9F	15C	1	12/15 Nottm–St P
1–4 Aug		Com/2P		1	Total of 16 noted in use over Bank Holiday weekend (also includes cross country route)
6 Aug	46109	Scot	55A	1	2/15 St P–Brdfd
Sept	D5700	Metro	17A	1	Commenced revenue working with 9.0 Nottm–Lpl and 2/30 return 1
	D5700	Metro	17A		To Cricklewood for trials with vacuum braked, roller bearing, freight set
	D5701	Metro	17A		
	10201	SR3	17A	1/2	Regularly allocated to work St P–Man and
	10202	SR3	17A	1/2	return workings; also Dby–Man and return
	10203	SR3	17A	1/2	Trial workings from Toton (ecs)
	D8000	EE1		3	
9 Sept	D5700	Metro	17A	1/2	Dby–Man and return workings
	D5701	Metro	17A	1/2	Singly or in pairs
	D5702	Metro	17A	1/2	
	D5703	Metro	17A	1/2	
October		Brit	9E		Availability generally poor

You'll Never Believe What's Been Through: 1958 – Midland Lines to/from St Pancras

Date	Loco No.	Loco Class	Loco Shed	Train Class	Detail
	D57XX		17A		St P–Man workings in pairs. Worked Britannia diagrams
	46103	Scot	14B		Allocated to Kentish Town (Ex Holbeck)
	46133	Scot	14B		Refer to Chapter text
1 October	60831	V2	38C		At Derby
16 Oct	10100	Fell	17A		Caught fire at Man
20 Oct	92022	9F	15A		Noon Brdfd–St P at Luton
December	51232	0F	27A		Temporary re-allocation to Dby for Works shunting
12 Dec	45610	Jub	17A		Named *Ghana* (previously *Gold Coast*)
28 Dec	70051	Brit	66A	1	5/15 Man London Road–St P
30 Dec	46169	Scot	9A	1	10.37 Brdfd–St P (ex Lds)

You'll Never Believe What's Been Through: 1958 – Cross Country

Date	Loco No.	Loco Class	Loco Shed	Train Class	Detail
4 Feb	45670	Jub	8A	1	Lpl–Btl military
11 Feb	61151	Bl	41A	3	1/32 Dby–Btl
15 Feb				1	20 Footex excursions through Dby (11 for Sheffield United v WB Albion and 9 for Wolverhampton W v Darlington)
26 Feb	61200	Bl	34A	1	Cleethorpes–Bournville trade excursion
3 April	45234	Bl5	26B	1	Relief Hull–Pgntn (to Btl)
8 April	45546	Pat6	5A	1	9.26 Lds–Btl
9 April	45546	Pat6	5A	1	8.35 Btl–Yk (to Shfld)
19 April	60076	A3	51A		At Shfld off footex
April/May	7235	GWT	85A		Trials on Lickey incline
	5226	GWT	85C		
3 May	41123	Com	17A	3	Bham area–Mangotsfield (pigeon (double headed)
	42787	Crab	5B		
9 May	45538	Pat6	24K	3	Bath–Crewe (pigeon)
10 May	45703	Jub	5A	3	Crewe–Bath (pigeon)
May/June		9F		1/3	Resumed seasonal workings
28 June	73116	Std5	71A	1	2/45 Bham–Shfld (locomotive off *Pines Express* Bath–Bham)
2 July	61374	Bl	40B		At Btl on Royal Show excursion
4 July	45730	Jub	12A	4-6	9/15 Edin Lothian Road–Stk Gifford (via Lds, Dby)
22 July	45154	Bl5	26A		7.43 Nottm–Ply (to Btl). Returned with 2/40 Btl–Nottm 1
9 August	45533	Pat6	8A	3	At Worcester. Up pigeon (double headed)
	44520	4F	21A		
12 August	46109	Scot	55A	3	At Bournville
24 August	61925	K3	36A		At Glos
25 August	61925	K3	36A41C	1	8 30 Cdf–Ncl (ex Glos)
	45725	Jub			
30 August	60524	A2	50A	1	8 45 Btl–Ncl (ex Shfld)
Sept	45509	Pat6			The route's then sole Pat6 re-allocated from 17A to 26A
8 Sept	45623	Jub	5A	1	Hull–Bournville, trade excursion
10 Sept	92152	9F	21A	1	8 30 Ncl–Cdff (ex Shfld)
11 Sept	92128	9F	15C	1	8 30 Ncl–Cdff (ex Shfld)
Sept/Oct		Std4	85E	1	Withdrawal of Compounds brought this type to Shfld as pilot locomotive (ex Glos)

You'll Never Believe What's Been Through: 1958 – Cross Country

Date	Loco No.	Loco Class	Loco Shed	Train Class	Detail
October	D5300	BC2		0	Delivery run ex Bham to Doncaster
November	45504	Pat6			Allocated to 82E. Grown men wept
	45506	Pat6			
	45519	Pat6			
13 Nov	45519	Pat6	82E	1	2/15 1 Yk–Glos
13 Nov	69820	A5	40A	1/2	Lcln–Dby workings (with 69805/12)
24 Dec	72006	Clan	12A	1	3/17 Shfld–Bham (relief). Returned with 7/5 Bham–Shfld (relief)

You'll Never Believe What's Been Through: 1959 – Midland Lines to/from St Pancras

Date	Loco No.	Loco Class	Loco Shed	Train Class	Detail
January				2	Bedford–Northampton/Hitchin Push/pull services reverted to steam
		Brit		1	Regularly allocated to Buxton–Man and return residential services
2 Feb	65437	J15	31A	2	10/15 Nottm–Lstr
8 Feb	46131	Scot	9A	1	5/15 Man–St P
11 Feb	46148	Scot	9A	1	2/25 Man–St P
14 Feb	46148	Scot	9A	1	12/15 St P–Brdfd
15 Feb	92163	9F	15B	1	6/00 Dby–St P
28 Feb				1	Footex traffic Nottm Forest v Bolton Wanderers (44845/91 45104/5). Sheffield Utd v Norwich City. Refer to Chapter text
March				1	8.15 Nottm–St P and 5/25 return named *The Robin Hood*
	D57XX	Metro	17A	1/2	Working in pairs on St P–Man and Dby–Man services
	9202X	9F	15A	-	Five in store at Wboro mpd
15 Mar	D57XX	Metro	17A	4	*Condor* service commenced between Hendon and Gushetfaulds. Refer to Chapter text
18 April	45081	Bl5	12A	4	*Condor* forward from Dent to Hendon (double headed). Refer to Chapter text
	45100	Bl5	12A		
20 April	45665	Jub	12A	1	Noon Brdfrd–St P (ex Lds)
21 April	40504	2P	16A	1	6/33 St P–Dby (double headed)
	73010	Std5	55A		73010 failed en route. 92125 9F piloted 2P forward
24 April	73157	Std5	17A	1	Luton–Portsmouth–Southampton schools excursion
May	62597	D16	31F	1/2	Pboro–Northampton workings. Locomotives previously deployed on (closed) Midland and Great Northern route
	62612	D16	31F		
	62613	D16	31F		
2 May				1	Footex traffic. Nottingham Forest v Luton Town. Refer to Chapter text
14 May		dmu	14A	3	First 4 car unit (of 30) at Cricklewood for driver training on St P–Bedford services
Spring		Scot			At Kentish Town/Nottingham. Refer to Chapter text
		PatR			
	50XXX	LY			Several dismantled at A Looms Ltd., Spondon. Refer to Chapter text

You'll Never Believe What's Been Through: 1959 – Midland Lines to/from St Pancras

Date	Loco No.	Loco Class	Loco Shed	Train Class	Detail
June	D1	BR4	17A	0	Dby–Cricklewood and return
	1000	Com	1		Restored in Midland Railway livery
	69805	A5	40E	2	Nottm–Chilwell Ordnance Depot trains
11 June	61329	Bl	32B	1	At St Albans on excursion from Eastern Region (Whipsnade Zoo)
29 June	45507	Pat6	12B	1	10 25 Man–St P
14 July	D1	BR4			Named *Scafell Pike* at Clsle
15 July	61002	Bl	50A	1	2/25 Man–St P to Dby. Forward with 44697 Bl 5 26A
27 July	61250	Bl	36A	1	At Buxton off Doncaster area excursion
1 Aug	D5018/9	BR2		1	St P–Man as a pair. Returned with 4/25 Man–St P
1 Aug		dmu	14A	1	New 4 car units in multiple used on Nottm–St P working and Dby–St P (second class only)
4 Aug	61268	Bl	56A	1	4/13 Dton–Bham relief. Returned 5 Aug with 8/50 Bham Lawley St–Yk 3
8 Aug	41101	Com	24J	0	Newton Heath–Dby Loco Works for dismantling. Refer to Chapter text
13 Aug	1000	Com	1	0/3	Test runs
25 Aug	45585	Jub	14B	3	High speed night test run St P–Man Returned 26 Aug. Refer to Chapter text
Sept	46127	Scot	14B		Allocated to augment class 7 power for routes
	46130	Scot	14B		
	46132	Scot	14B		
	46140	Scot	14B		
	46142	Scot	14B		
	46160	Scot	14B		St P–Man and return workings
	D1-D4	BR4	17A	1	
5 Sept	48101	8F	21A	1	8 5 Newquay–Ncl (ex Btl to Bham)
14 T/T change				1	Certain Manchester London Road–Euston trains (and corresponding returns) diverted via Stoke–Stenson Jn–Sheet Stores Jn–Lstr to St P. Refer to Chapter text
13 Oct	61269	Bl	26B	4–6	8 50 Stourton–St P Goods. Returned next day
November		dmu		2	Some Nottm–Shfld services via Erewash diselised
		MP		3	*Midland Pullman* on trials Lstr–Luton

You'll Never Believe What's Been Through: 1959 – Midland Lines to/from St Pancras

Date	Loco No.	Loco Class	Loco Shed	Train Class	Detail
2 Nov		dmu		2	Dby ltwt twin units commenced working Bletchley (ex Oxford)–Bedford St John's–Cambridge services
4 Nov	62612	D16	31F		At Cricklewood
6 Nov	61152	Bl	41C	1	1/57 Shfld–St P
8 Nov	61360	Bl	30E	1	Cambridge–Nottm excursion
30 Nov	61136	Bl	14D	1	8.15 Nottm–St P (double headed)
	45532	PatR	16A		
30 Nov	62012	K1	65J		At Toton
December		MP		3	*Midland Pullman* on trials Dby–Luton
15 Dec	45017	Bl5	8F	4	*Condor* in each direction

You'll Never Believe What's Been Through: 1959 – Cross Country

Date	Loco No.	Loco Class	Loco Shed	Train Class	Detail
10 Jan	45580	Jub	24E	1	Footex Derby County v Preston N End
	45721	Jub	5A	1	Footex Derby County v Preston N End
20 Jan	90732	WD8	36A		At Saltley mpd
26 Jan	61084	Bl	50A	1	12/48 Yk–Btl
30 Jan	45717	Jub	27A	1	12/48 Yk–Btl
February	45640	Jub	12A	1	Various Lds/Shfld–Btl workings as replacement for unavailable Pat6 at 82E
	D3586	08	17A		At Burton for crew training
	D3587	08	17A		
1 Feb	61002	Bl	50A	1	Following failure at Yk of 45627 Jub 17A on excursion ex Ncl, worked to destination of Dby
2 Feb	61002	Bl	50A	1	8.5 Bham–Ncl (ex Dby to Shfld) 12/43 1 Ncl–Btl (ex Shfld to Dby) 10/15 3 Dby–Shfld
7 Feb	61257	Bl	56B	1	12/48 Yk–Btl
9 Feb	62056	K1	50A	1	7.35 Nottm–Btl
9 Feb	61439	Bl6	50A	7	At Dby
12-14 Feb	41123	Com	85E	1	8 30 Cdff–Ncl (pilot ex Glos to Bham) Returned as pilot to Glos on 8 20 Ncl–Cdff
14 Feb	61141	Bl	40E	1	Footex traffic. Birmingham City v Nottingham Forest. Trains shown routed via Egginton Jn from Nottm Vic
	61177	Bl	40E	1	
	61381	Bl	15E	1	
14 Mar	61071	Bl	50A	1	12/48 Yk–Btl
22 Mar	45504	Pat6	82E		Re-entered revenue earning service
	45506	Pat6	82E		
	45519	Pat6	82E		
22 Mar	61002	Bl	50A	1	12/48 Yk–Btl
April	5226	GWT	85C		In use as bankers on Lickey incline
	92085	9F	15A		
	92135	9F	21A		
	92231	9F	86C		
4 May	61182	Bl	31A	1	At Bournville off Eastern Region excursion
5 May	45537	Pat6	12B	3	Stlg–Worcester (pigeon)
6 May	46114	Scot	8A	1	Coventry–Weston super Mare excursion
9 May				1	Excursion to Ashbourne–Buxton line
10 May				1	Refer to Chapter text
11 May	61233	Bl	30A	1	At Bournville off Eastern Region excursion

You'll Never Believe What's Been Through: 1959 – Cross Country

Date	Loco No.	Loco Class	Loco Shed	Train Class	Detail
9-13 June	D50XX	BR2		1	8.5 Bham–Ncl (ex Dby–Yk) in pairs Returned with 12/48 Yk–Btl 1 to Dby
10 June	61056	Bl	41A	1	Hull–Bournville trade excursion
19 June	45732	Jub	12A	1	9/30 Sutton Coldfld–Stlg
19 June	45528	PatR	5A	1	Kenilworth–Weston super Mare excursion. Failed at Glos on return
26 June	61164	Bl	41C	1	3/30 Ncl–Bham (pilot ex Shfld)
27 June	61164	Bl	41C	1	11.40 Bnmth–Cleethorpes (ex Bath to Bham) 61318 Bl 40B forward
27 June	61157	Bl	26A	1	12/15 Sboro–Kings Norton
28 June	61164	Bl	41C	1	Bham–Btl additional
10 July	61288	Bl	50A	1	12/48 Yk–Btl
12 July	45596	Jub	12B	3	Stlg–Mangotsfield (pigeon)
13 July	45515	Pat6	8A	1	7.36 Sunderland–Btl
16 July	45691	Jub	12A	1	8/55 Stlg–Sutton Coldfld
19 July	45531	PatR	8A	3	Stlg–Worcester (pigeon)
7 Aug	45141	Bl5	11A	1	11 8 Shfld–Btl relief
23 Aug	64930	J39	9G		At Btl and Glos mpd's
29 Aug	46137	Scot	9A	Grove	At Glos on Royal Train
31 Aug	1000	Com	1		At Burton (hot axlebox from previous day excursion)
October		D16		1	Still in regular use on Bham–Norwich service
10 Oct	64789	J39	31F		At Btl Barrow Road. Returned with 2/40 Westerleigh–Wwd Hth 7
November	51218	0F	82E		Replaced 51221 at Btl Barrow Road
16 Nov	60954	V2	50A	1	12/48 Yk–Btl
21 Nov	61961	K3	36A		At Cheltenham
21 Nov		Pan		2	Ashchurch–Upton on Severn services now with Western Region traction
29 Nov	61468	Bl6	50A		At Saltley mpd
9 Dec	46100	Scot	16A	1	8 40 Btl–Shfld
11 Dec	60839	V2	50A		At Bristol Barrow Road mpd

You'll Never Believe What's Been Through: 1960 – Midland Lines to/from St Pancras

Date	Loco No.	Loco Class	Loco Shed	Train Class	Detail
6-16 Jan	61312	Bl	41D	4-6	Rotherham–Brent/Somers Town and return
	61334	Bl	41D	4-6	Rotherham–Brent/Somers Town and return
8 Jan	34010	WCR	70A		At Cricklewood
11 Jan		dmu	14A	2	Inauguration of unit services on St Pancras–Bedford. Refer to Chapter text
30 Jan	D57XX	Metro	17A		Final example delivered
February	41157	Com	17A		Placed into store, serviceable at Dby
		Scot	41C	1	Rostered for Shfld–St P services rather than
		PatR	41C	1	Jubilees
March	61044	Bl	41A	4-6	Rotherham–Brent/Somers Town and return
	61285	Bl	36A	4-6	Rotherham–Brent/Somers Town and return
	61312	Bl	41D	4-6	Rotherham–Brent/Somers Town and return
	61660	Bl7	31B	1	7.5 Pboro–Rugby
	61664	Bl7	31B	1	7.5 Pboro–Rugby
19 May	65541	J17	31A	7	Rugby–Pboro
2 April	D5	BR4	17A	1	1/55 St P–Man Vic (D5 to Dby)
	46106	Scot	9A		(double headed)
4 April	45569	Jub	55A	1	12/25 Man–Dby extended to St P (1000 ex
	1000	Com	1		Dby) (double headed)
5 April	46123	Scot	14B	4-6	10/20 Somers Town–Crewe
6 April	46133	Scot	14B	4-6	10/40 Somers Town–Crewe
12 April	61660	Bl7	31B	1	7 5 Pboro–Rugby
14 April	61657	Bl7	31B	1	7 5 Pboro–Rugby
27 April	1000	Com	1	1	1/55 St P–Man Vic (1000 to Dby)
	46106	Scot	9A		(double headed)
30 April	61660	Bl7	31B		At Wellingborough mpd
Apr-May	D1-D10	BR4			Transferred to Western Division. Refer to Chapter text
4 May	45504	Pat6	82E	4-6	2 28 Rotherham–Brent/Somers Town and return
6 May	D230	EE4	5A	1	11 42 Man Vic–St P
9 May	46121	Scot	66A	1	11 42 Man Vic–St P
10 May	70043	Brit	9A	4-6	9/35 Somers Town–Ardwick
12 May	72001	Clan	66A	1	11 42 Man Vic–St P
12 May	61903	K3	50B	4-6	At Mkt Hboro on diverted fish train ex Grimsby to Western Region
16 May	45518	Pat6	8B	1	1/57 Shfld–St P
18 May	44297	4F	14A	1	3/25 St P–Lstr
18 May	92156	9F	18A	1	Shorncliffe Camp–Shfld military (ex Brent)
19 May	46137	Scot	26A	4-6	9/35 Somers Town–Ardwick

You'll Never Believe What's Been Through: 1960 – Midland Lines to/from St Pancras

Date	Loco No.	Loco Class	Loco Shed	Train Class	Detail
Summer		6-7			Refer to Chapter text
June		Metro			Up to 17 of Class (of 20) out of service at Cricklewood and Dby
2 June	92082	9F	15A	1	7.5 Shfld–St P
2 June	92124	9F	15A	1	8.15 Nottm–St P
3 June	92052	9F	15A	1	3/25 St P–Lstr
3 June	92077	9F	18A	1	7/5 St P–Lstr
9 June	45663	Jub	26F	4	Up *Condor*
13 June	64679	J20	30F		At Brent
14-17 June	92133	9F	15A	4	Down *Condor*
	92055	9F	15A	4	Down *Condor*
	92081	9F	15A	4	Down *Condor*
14 June	45542	Pat6	24K	1	9 25 St P–Lstr
15 June	73011	Std5	6J	1	Horsebox special Holyhead–Harpenden
20 June		Metro		4	Re-instated to *Condor* workings with enhanced loadings
4 July		MP		1	Introduced into revenue service. One 6 car unit Man–St P and return M–F
22 July	60038	A3	55A		At Nottingham mpd
23 & 30 July		dmu	14A	1	7.42 and 7.50 Lstr–St P
23 July	45505	Pat6	82E	1	3/15 St P–Brdfd
23 July	61216	B1	55H	1	10/50 Edin–St P (ex Lds)
	44985	B15	14B		(double headed)
27 July	D211	EE4	1B	1	7.25 Man–St P Returned with 2/25
30 July	61861	K3	31B	1	Morecambe–Dby excursion
30 July		dmu		1	4 x 2 car units 8 45 Dby–St P Returned 12/55 St P–Nottm
31 July	45673	Jub	63A	1	1/55 St P–Man Lon Rd
Summer					Saturday traffic. Refer to Chapter text
1 Aug	45673	Jub	63A	1	11 48 Man Vic–St P (92080 as pilot from some point) (double headed)
	92080	9F	15A		
2 Aug	45511	Pat6	8B	1	10 25 Man–St P Returned with 5/55
6 Aug		dmu	14A		7.42 and 7.50 Lstr–St P
6 Aug		Pat6		1	Refer to Chapter text
10 Aug	45506	Pat6	82E	1	10 5 St P–Edin (D5090 pilot ex Bedford) (double headed). To Nottm only
	D5090	BR2			
13 Aug	45478	B15	60A	1	Relief to Brdfd–St P
18 Aug	45478	B15	60A	1	7 50 Dby–St P (double headed)
	45628	Jub	17A		

You'll Never Believe What's Been Through: 1960 – Midland Lines to/from St Pancras

Date	Loco No.	Loco Class	Loco Shed	Train Class	Detail
18 Aug	64778	J39	31B		At Lstr ex Coalville
27 Aug					Dby Loco Works Open Day. Refer to Chapter text
29 Aug	61010	Bl	50B		At Lstr
12 Sept	70031	Brit	9A	1	2/25 Man–St P (double headed)
	70032	Brit	9A		(with track condition recording vehicle)
15 Sept	D11	BR4			First of production batch on initial tests
15 Sept		Metro			7 of Class in store at Dby (D5703/7/8/9/12/13/19)
October	D11	BR4			First of production batch completed at Dby
	D68	BR4			First of production batch completed at Crewe
5 Oct	61031	Bl	51L		At Dby
11 Oct	61021	Bl	51A		At Dby
13 Oct	67769	L1	40E	3	Dby–Nottm
14 Oct	61319	Bl	50A		At Dby
24 Oct	61388	Bl	50A		At Dby
November		Brit			6 re-allocated away from Midland Division after 18 month stay (70004/14/15/17/21/42)

You'll Never Believe What's Been Through: 1960 – Cross Country

Date	Loco No.	Loco Class	Loco Shed	Train Class	Detail
9 Jan	45694	Jub	55A	1	Footex traffic. Birmingham City v Leeds United
	45728	Jub	12A		
16 Jan	60915	V2	51L	2	4/8 Shfld–Dby. Returned with 5/15 Btl–Yk ex Dby
18 Mar	92220	9F			Last steam locomotive for British Railways out shopped (Swindon)
23 Mar	D5503	Br2	30A	1	At Bournville off Southend excursion
10 April	61202	B1	40A	1	Hull–Dudley excursion
11 May	D258	EE4	52A	1	At Shfld off 7/10 Ncl–Btl
12 May	70054	Brit	55A	4-6	9/18 Carlisle–Water Orton forward from Hellifield following failure of 92167 9F 21A. Returned with 5/5 Water Orton–Stourton 4-6
14 May	45662	Jub	82E	1	12/48 Yk–Btl (61853 ex Shfld as pilot) (double headed)
	61853	K3	56B		
18 May	61152	B1	41C	1	10 5 Man Vic–Bnmth (ex Bham to Bath)
26 May	5319	GW4		0	Not in steam. Oxley–Killarmarsh via Erewash for dismantling
	2840	GW2			
	2878	GW2			
	2880	GW2			
28 May	46119	Scot	26A	3	At Worcester (pigeon)
31 May	61027	B1	41A	1	As for 18 May
June					Sutton Coldfld–Stlg. Refer to Chapter text
Summer			6-7		Refer to Chapter text
2 June	61312	B1	41D	1	Appleby–Btl excursion
3 June	61249	B1	41A	1	10.44 Shfld–Btl. Returned 4 June as pilot locomotive ex Glos on 8.15 Cdff–Ncl to Bham
11 June				2	Final day of Burton–Tutbury passenger services
12 June	63610	04	16D		At Bromsgrove
15 June	61041	B1	41A	1	7 40 Btl–Shfld (72007 ex Dby) (double headed)
	72007	Clan	12A		
16 June	73XXX	Std5		1	7 40 Btl–Shfld (72007 ex Dby) (double headed)
	72007	Clan	12A		
16 June	45665	Jub	67A	1	10 44 Shfld–Btl. Returned 17 June 8 40 Btl–Shfld 1
25 June	45687	Jub	67A	1	9 50 Brdfd–Pgnton (ex Lds to Btl)
25 June	61334	B1	41D		7 30 Ncl–Btl (ex Shfld)

You'll Never Believe What's Been Through: 1960 – Cross Country

Date	Loco No.	Loco Class	Loco Shed	Train Class	Detail
29 June	45687	Jub	67A	1	As for 18 May. Returned 30 June With 9.45 Bnmth–Man Ldn Rd 1
July		Ivatt 4	4OE	2	43108/48/52/55 sharing duties with L1 tanks on Dby Friargate–Nottm Vic–Grantham services
2 July	45687	Jub	67A	1	9 50 Brdfd–Pgntn (ex Lds to Btl)
8 July	72005	Clan	12A	1	8/45 Brdfd–Pgntn (ex Lds to Btl)
9 July	72005	Clan	12A	1	7.45 Pgntn–Ncl (ex Btl St Phlps Marsh)
9 July	61195	B1	40B	1	7 36 Sunderland–Btl (ex Shfld)
	61223	B1	40A	1	8 15 Ncl–Cdff (ex Shfld to Glos) (double
	45566	Jub	55A		headed)
16 July	60077	A3	55A	1	Ncl–Btl (ex Shfld to Burton, where it was replaced)
19 July	73068	Std5	82E	1	7 40 Btl–Brdfd (72006 ex Dby) (double
	72006	Clan	12A		headed)
21 July	?	B15		1	7 40 Btl–Brdfd (72006 ex Dby) (double
	72006	Clan	12A		headed)
23 July	46164	Scot	5A	1	9 50 Brdfd–Pgntn (ex Lds to Btl)
25 July	46137	Scot	26A	1	10 25 Blackpool–Lstr (to Burton)
	73068	Std5	82E	1	9.15 Pgntn–Brdfd (46137 ex Burton) (double
	46137	Scot	26A		headed)
Summer		9F		1/3	Refer to Chapter text
8 Sept	46102	Scot	66A		At Burton
28 Sept	61338	B1	51A	3	Clsle–Dby (parcels)
29 Oct	61808	K3	41e	4-6	Wwd Hth–Stoke Gifford
18 Nov	63675	O4	40E	7	Civil engineering matls Colwick–Stoke Gifford via Egginton Jn
23 Nov	70015	Brit	9E		7/5 Ncl–Btl (ex Shfld)
26 Nov	70015	Brit	9E		12/48 Ncl–Btl (ex Shfld)
December		Jub	82E		Working through to Yk on Ncl trains
	D53XX	BC2		0	Being returned to builder for modification (ex Eastern Region)
5 Dec	34102	WCO	71B	1	9.45 Bnmth–Man Ldn Rd diverted (to Bham). Returned 6 Dec with 10 5 Man Ldn Rd–Bnmth 1
6 Dec	4942	Hall	82B	1	As for 5 Dec. (Returned 7 Dec)
7 Dec	34053	BBR	71B	1	As for 5 Dec, but did not work back on 8 Dec

You'll Never Believe What's Been Through: 1961 – Midland Lines to/from St Pancras

Date	Loco No.	Loco Class	Loco Shed	Train Class	Detail
January	D50XX	BR2		4	Regularly in pairs on *Condor*
5 Jan	61334	Bl	41D	1	2/25 St P–Lstr
7 Jan	45533	Pat6	2B	1	Footex. Luton Town v Northampton
7 Jan	61048	Bl	31A	1	Footex via Melton Mowbray Portsmouth v
	61052	Bl	31B	1	Peterborough United
February	D6504	BC3			At Dby for electric train heating trials
5 Feb	10800	BTH1			At Dby Loco Works for stripping prior to sale to Brush Traction Ltd
8 Feb	45548	Pat6	2B	1	11.25 St P–Lstr
March	D21	BR4			700th new diesel locomotive built at Derby Loco Works outshopped
9 Mar	D5680	Br2	41A	1	Footex Leicester City v Barnsley
	D5683	Br2	41A	1	
18 Mar	D210	EE4			All at Dby Loco Works
	D230	EE4			
	D232	EE4			
	D290	EE4			
25 Mar	D55XX	Br2	41A	3-6	Commenced regular through return workings between Rotherham–Somers Town/St Pancras Goods
26 Mar	92054	9F	15A	1	Replaced failed D320 EE4 at Wboro on up *Royal Highlander* diverted
May		9F		1	Regularly working seasonal 8.0 Shfld–Blackpool
6 May				1	Footex traffic. Leicester City v Tottenham Hotspur. Refer to Chapter text
8 June	61162	Bl	41A	1	10.5 St P–Glgw to Lds (double headed)
	45656	Jub	416		
9 June	34055	BB0	75A		At Bedford mpd off Portsmouth–Luton excursion
18 June	61011	Bl	9G		At Rowsley
22 June	45692	Jub	67A	4-6	Clsle–Lstr. (Returned with 4/30 Lstr–Normanton)
24 June	D5031	BR2	1A	1	8 45 Dby–St P
	D5022	BR2	1B		
24 June	45562	Jub	55A	1	Noon St P–Shfld relief
	45575	Jub	14B	1	2/0 St P–Shfld relief
	45602	Jub	55A	1	3/0 St P–Shfld relief
26 June	D34	BR4			1,000th member of BR mainline diesel fleet completed at Dby Loco Works

You'll Never Believe What's Been Through: 1961 – Midland Lines to/from St Pancras

Date	Loco No.	Loco Class	Loco Shed	Train Class	Detail
27 June	60038	A3	55A		At Derby. Refer to Chapter text
July		4F		1	Seasonal workings. Refer to Chapter text
11 July	D5693	Br2	41A	1	8.0 Shfld–St P
13 July	D5804	Br2	41A		At Buxton off Eastern Region Excursion
August	61820	K3	41C	1/2	All in regular use in Shfld/Nottm/Dby areas
	61821	K3	41C		
	61989	K3	41C		
	41168	Com			Final Compound withdrawn
5 Aug	D7005	Hy		3	Gorton Works–Dby trial run (repeated for subsequently newly built Hymek Class)
25 Aug	61989	K3	41C	1	9.0 Nottm–Lpl (to Man)
Sept	D77	BR4	82B		Trials from Toton with brake tender
23 Sept	D100	BR4	17A		Named *Sherwood Forester* at Dby station
2 Oct		MP			Commenced middle of day St P–Nottm and return workings
5 Oct	70010	Brit	32A	1	At Market Hboro on Norwich–Bournville trade excursion
29 Oct	70028	Brit	21D		In Leicester/Nottingham area
30 Oct		MP			Failed. Replaced by BR4 plus 5 carriages and kitchen car
November					Winter weather. Refer to Chapter text
13 Nov	46107	Scot	66A	1	1/55 St P–Man Picc
17 Nov	70025	Brit	21D		At Lstr
18 Nov	70029	Brit	21D		At Lstr
19 Nov	70001	Brit	31B		At Lstr ex Pboro
19 Nov	45518	Pat6	8A	4-6	Garston-Beeston spl
21 Nov	70011	Brit	31B		At Lstr ex Pboro
21 Nov	70048	Brit	21D	2	5/50 Dby-Darley Dale
23 Nov	70009	Brit	31B		At Lstr ex Pboro
23 Nov	70034	Brit	31B		At Lstr ex Pboro
3 Dec	D144	BR4			First BR4s to receive small yellow warning panels on nose end
	D145	BR4			

You'll Never Believe What's Been Through: 1961 – Cross Country

Date	Loco No.	Loco Class	Loco Shed	Train Class	Detail
February	45540	PatR	9E	1	Temporary lack of availability of suitable traction
	46106	Scot	9E		at Dby resulted in Trafford Park locomotives
	46122	Scot	9E		being allocated to 12/43 Ncl–Btl ex Dby on
	46141	Scot	9E		various dates
20 Feb	45540	PatR	9E	1	7.35 Nottm–Btl. Returned with 5/0 Btl–Yk to Dby
March	47190	Sent			At Saltley mpd
					Test runs (diesels) on Lickey incline. Refer to Chapter text.
1 Mar	45516	Pat6	8B	1	2/55 Btl–Yk
3 Mar	46126	Scot	1A	1	12/43 Ncl–Btl ex Dby
8 Mar	44913	Bl5	6H	1	10 15 Man Picc–Bnmth (Bham–Bath)
12 Mar	60812	V2	52B	1	5/0 Btl–Yk (to Dby) (double headed)
	45576	Jub	41D		
13 Mar	45345	Bl5	6H	1	As 8 March
17 Mar	45730	Jub	12A	4	9/20 Edin Lothian Rd–Stoke Gifford
					Returned 18 Mar with 5/0 Btl–Yk 1
17 Mar	46113	Scot	55A	1	12/43 Ncl–Btl (ex Shfld). Returned 18 Mar with 1.10 Btl–Shfld
18 Mar	70014	Brit	26A	4	9/20 Edin Lothian Rd–Stoke Gifford (ex Saltley)
18 Mar	46162	Scot	14B	1	8 15 Ncl–Cdff (ex Shfld to Glos).
					Returned 20 Mar with 2/55 Btl–Yk
21 Mar	70014	Brit	26A	1	As 8 Mar
22 Mar	D5622	Br2	41A		At Bournville off excursion from Eastern Region
24 Mar	92175	9F	36A	3	7 37 Yk–Btl
30 Mar	45548	Pat6	2B	1	Stoke Golding–Blackpool excursion
	1000	Com	1		(1000 pilot ex Dby)
12 April	70020	Brit	88A	1	At Cheltenham on Western Region–Bournville excursion
12 May	45558	Jub	26F	1	10 45 Shfld–Btl
13 May	42782	Crab	5D	1	Ashbourne–Belle Vue excursion
13 May	42587	St4	17A	1	Sutton in Ashfield–Tissington excursion via GN/Egginton Jn
20 May	45560	Jub	8A	1	10 15 Brdfd–Pgnton (ex Lds to Btl)
20 May	45512	PatR	12B	3	Preston–Mangotsfield/Bath (pigeon)
15 June	45541	Pat6	2B	4	9/20 Edin Lothian Rd–Stoke Gifford
					Returned 17 June 1.10 Btl–Shfld
17 June	46130	Scot	55A	1	10 15 Brdfd–Pgntn (ex Lds to Btl)
22 June	46137	Scot	9E	1	10 15 Brdfd–Pgntn (ex Lds to Btl)

You'll Never Believe What's Been Through: 1961 – Cross Country

Date	Loco No.	Loco Class	Loco Shed	Train Class	Detail
23 June	46161	Scot	24K	1	Walsall–Weston super Mare excursion
24 June	46123	Scot	21A	1	Walsall–Weston super Mare excursion
25 June	46150	Scot	6J	3	9 25 Dby–Btl (parcels)
June-July	46145	Scot	55A	1	Sutton Coldfld–Stlg/Inv. Refer to Chapter text
	46125	Scot	5A		
	46135	Scot	5A		
	46166	Scot	5A		
	60088	A3	55A		
29 July	46101	Scot	1A	1	10 15 Teignmouth–Shfld (ex Btl)
30 July	46145	Scot	55A	1	8 30 Cdff–Ncl (ex Glos to Shfld)
	46162	Scot	21A		(double headed)
5 Aug	D5680	BR2	41A	1	9 4 Bham–Ncl relief (ex Dby to Yk)
5 Aug	70044	Brit	55A	1	2/15 Btl–Yk
11 Aug	73087	Std5	71A	1	Btl–Shfld relief
28 Aug	45646	Jub	55C	1	12/43 Ncl–Btl (ex Shfld)
3 Sept	D29	BR4	82A	1	9 35 Brdfd–Btl diverted from Bham to Cheltenham via Honeybourne
12 Sept	45574	Jub	24E	1	12/43 Ncl–Btl (ex Shfld)
17 Sept	70025	Brit	21D	1	135 Sutton Coldfld–Stlg/Inv
24 Sept	70047	Brit	12A	1	9/35 Sutton Coldfld–Stlg/Inv
25 Sept	60835	V2	52B	1	7/5 Ncl–Btl (to Dby) Returned 26 Sept 8 5 Bham–Ncl (ex Dby)
16 Oct	GT3	BBo		0	At Dby Friargate to Crewe following trials on Great Central route
28 Oct	72009	Clan	12A	4-6	2/25 Water Orton–Normanton
November					Block oil trains. Refer to Chapter text
December		Jub	82E		Bristol Barrow Road allocation decimated. Refer to Chapter text
	30931	Sch			Not in steam. At Chesterfield en route to Swinton for dismantling
	32534	C2X			
	31177	H			
	31261	H			
	31579	C			
23 Dec	60076	A3	55H	1	12/43 Ncl–Btl (to Dby)
29 Dec	60065	A3	55H	1	12/43 Ncl–Btl (to Dby)

You'll Never Believe What's Been Through: 1962 – Midland Lines to/from St Pancras

Date	Loco No.	Loco Class	Loco Shed	Train Class	Detail
23 Jan	4/6/8 10/11 13	Met			At Kettering for dismantling
March	92022	9F	15A		Sole remaining example with Crosti equipment
18 Mar	46127	Scot	5A	1	9 20 Glgw–St P (ex Lds). Returned 19 March 8.15 St P–Nottm 1
20 Mar	46127	Scot	5A		Stanton Gate–Glgw Special goods
25 Mar	D5379	BC2	14A		At Cricklewood. First of batch of 37
25 Mar	61871 61986	K3 K3	50B 50B		At Toton
13 April	70028	Brit	9B	1	2/55 Man Picc–St P
14 April	D163	BR4	17A		Named *The Leicestershire and Derbyshire Yeomanry* at Dby station
21 April	61109 61315 61327	Bl Bl Bl	41A 41A 41A	1	Shfld–Blackpool excursions
5 May	D5381 D5383	BC2 BC2	14A 14A	1	8 15 St P–Nottm. Noon return 1 Regular diagram. In pairs
August	D43 D154	BR4 BR4	17A 17A	4-6	Trials with brake tender
2 Aug	D5403 D88	BC2 BR4	14A 17A	1	2/25 Man–St P (double headed)
10 Aug	34023	WCO	72A		At Cricklewood
13 Aug	60954	V2	50A	1	Relief to 10 15 St P–Glgw
18 Aug	60871	V2	34A	1	Relief to 2/0 St P–Shfld
19 Aug	92153 92158	9F 9F	18A 18A	4-6	Trials with vacuum braked mineral wagons
31 Aug					10,000th car conveyed on Chiltern Green– Bonnybridge Service
1 Sept	70039	Brit	40B	1	8 17 Chesterfield–Blackpool excursion
7 Sept					Diversions following incident on GN main line. Refer to Chapter text
8 Sept				1	12/10 Man Picc–St P (diversion) ceased running from timetable change
29 Sept		dmu		1	Lines to Wirksworth and Denby
October	10201 10203	SR3 SR3			In store at Dby (later joined by 10202 SR3 and 10001 BR3)
14 Oct	45543	Pat6	24L	1	Enthusiasts tour Dby–St P
5 Nov		dmu		2	7 44 Shfld–Nottm. Fire at Unstone

You'll Never Believe What's Been Through: 1962 – Midland Lines to/from St Pancras

Date	Loco No.	Loco Class	Loco Shed	Train Class	Detail
15 Nov	10800	BTH1			Transferred to Brush Electrical Engineering, Loughborough
December		2F	17C		Final example withdrawn

You'll Never Believe What's Been Through: 1962 – Cross Country

Date	Loco No.	Loco Class	Loco Shed	Train Class	Detail
January		A2 A3 V2 Brit		1	Refer to Chapter text
3 Jan	46128	Scot	8A	1	10 26 Shfld–Btl. Returned with 11/45 Btl–Dby 3
6 Jan	70044	Brit	55A	1	10 15 Brdfd–Pgntn (ex Lds to Br1)
17 Jan	D38	BR4	82A	1	9 15 Pgntn–Brdfd. Failed at Ashchurch. 92248 9F 82E forward to Bham with assistance from Bromsgrove by 9493 Pan 85A as pilot
February		A3 V2		1	Refer to Chapter text
1 Feb	45661	Jub	26A	1	8 40 Btl–Shfld
5 Feb	70034	Brit	31B	1	7 35 Nottm–Btl
10 Feb	45600	Jub	12B	1	8 40 Btl–Shfld
17 Feb	*Falcon*	BrX		3	Trials on Lickey incline
12 Mar	61986	K3	50B	4-6	Yk–Kings Norton car vans
12 Mar				1	Lickey incline. Banking of BR4 hauled trains up to 12 carriages ceased
April		Pat6	82E		Withdrawn
1 April	70054	Brit	55A	1	12/15 Yk–Btl
13 April		4F		2	Btl–Bham working
21 April	61281	B1	40E	1	12/48 Yk–Btl
22 April	45545	PatR	12B	1	9/35 Sutton Coldfld–Stlg/Inv
24 April	45526	PatR	12B	1	9/35 Sutton Coldfield–Stlg/Inv
24 April	60516 46121	A2 Scot	50A 66A	1	Refer to Chapter text
May		Jub	17B		Allocation at Burton reached 24
7 May		4F		2	Btl–Bham working
16 May	72005	Clan	12A	1	8/35 Stlg–Sutton Coldfield
June	46169 70017 70043 70045 70046 46115	Scot Brit Brit Brit Brit Scot	1A 21D 21D 21D 21D 9A	1 1	9/35 Sutton Coldfld–Stlg/Inv on various dates Various Dby–Btl and return workings
1 June	46143	Scot	9E	1	12/52 Yk–Btl
10 June	45529	PatR	1A	1	Coventry–Weston super Mare excursion
23 June	92134	9F	21A	3	Dorchester–Stlg via Dby and Manchester area. 22 bogie vans (pigeon)

You'll Never Believe What's Been Through: 1962 – Cross Country

Date	Loco No.	Loco Class	Loco Shed	Train Class	Detail
July		BR4	52A	1	Weekly delivery run Dby–Ncl as pilot to 8.5 Bham–Ncl
16 July	70039	Brit	40B	0	At Dby Friargate en route to Crewe Works for overhaul
28 July	61152	Bl	36A	1	Rotherham–Btl
	61360	Bl	36A	1	Rotherham–Btl
10 Aug	70025	Brit	21D	4-6	9/20 Edin Lothian Rd–Stoke Gifford Returned 11 August Pgntn–Shfld 1
17 Aug	D5814	Br2	41A	1	Rotherham–Dudley and return
18 Aug	42922	Crab	6A	1	9 5 Penzance–Brdfd ex Bt1
25 Aug	92118	9F	21A	1	12/45 Btl–Shfld
8 Sept	42756	Crab	16A	1	Enthusiasts tour in Leicestershire area
	58148	2F	15D		
	44109	4F	15D		
15 Sept	D34	BR4	82A	1	9 15 Pgntn–Brdfd failed near Blackwell. 43958 4F forward to Bham, then 45608 Jub 55A forward
14 October	64354	J11	36E	1	Enthusiasts tour Nottm Vic–Burton on Trent via Egginton, then reverse 43658 forward to Dby. Refer to Midland lines listing
	43658	3F	17A		
24 Oct	77004	Std3	50E		At Dby (ex Crewe Works)
3 Nov	61853	K3	56B		At Glos
7 Nov	60837	V2	50A	1	11 53 Yk–Btl to Bham
16 Nov	60855	V2	50A	1	8 20 Ncl–Cdff to Bham
December		dmu		2	Units from North Eastern Region allocated to support services in Midlands
18 Dec	61033	Bl	41D	3	Yk–Btl (parcels)
20 Dec	61026	Bl	40A	3	Yk–Btl (parcels)
22 Dec	61094	Bl	41A	3	Yk–Btl (parcels)
22 Dec	70051	Brit	6J	1	Catterick–Btl military. Returned 24 Dec 4/18 Btl–Lds 1

You'll Never Believe What's Been Through: 1963 – Midland Lines to/from St Pancras

Date	Loco No.	Loco Class	Loco Shed	Train Class	Detail
January		BR4 Steam			Response to severe winter weather and poor availability/reliability of BR4. Refer to Chapter text
7 Feb	D5384	BC2	14A	1	10.25 St P–Man to Derby
March–May					Footex traffic. Leicester City. Refer to chapter text
15 April	D1008	Wes4	81A	1	Footex. Peterborough United v Swindon Town via Northampton and Market Harborough
17/18 April	34031	WCR	70A	1	Enthusiast excursion St P–Dby
11 May		Jub		1	Footex traffic. Refer to Chapter text
11 May	34006 61004	WC0 Bl	70A 50A	1	Enthusiast tour. Refer to Chapter text
June	D4132	08			At Bedford mpd
July	10001	BR3	1A		Re-instated to traffic (Western Division)
20 Sept	75042	Std4	16C		Final steam locomotive overhaul at Dby Loco Works
3 Oct				4-6	Diversions following incident on GC route. Refer to Chapter text
5 Oct	61572	Bl2		1	Enthusiasts tour. Refer to Chapter text
December		BR4			Various examples to Dby Loco Works ex Brush Loughborough for painting

You'll Never Believe What's Been Through: 1963 – Cross Country

Date	Loco No.	Loco Class	Loco Shed	Train Class	Detail
January		A3			Response to severe winter weather and poor availability/reliability of BR4. Refer to Chapter text.
		V2			
		Jub			
		4F			Deputising for dmu's in Midlands
10 Jan		Bl		1	7 35 Btl–Brdfd at Bham (double headed)
	9453	Pan	85B		
16 Jan	46126	Scot	16D	1	6 46 Glos–Shfld
16 Jan	70029	Brit	21D	1	Footex. Bristol City v Aston Villa
17 Jan	6868	Grge	81E	1	6 46 Glos–Shfld to Bham
22 Jan	61033	Bl	50A	1	6 46 Glos–Shfld
28 Jan	60945	V2	50A	1	Yk–Btl throughout
23 Jan	46417	Ivatt2	26D		At Barrow Hill mpd
23 Jan	D8024	EE1	41A	1	Shfld–Penzance at Dby (double headed)
	D61	BR4	82A		
26 Jan	D6546	BC3	73C		At Saltley for crew training
February	D85XX	Clay	ScR		Stored at locations around Dby Refer to Chapter text
10 Feb	61409	B1	40A		Enthusiast tour (double headed)
	34094	WCO	70A		Refer to Chapter text
20 Feb	D1500	Br4		3	Lickey incline tests with empty stock
March		Bl		1	Excursion traffic to Coventry
- Sept		V2			Refer to Chapter text
		Jub			
		Brit			
		EE3			
		BR4			
		EE4			
March	D65XX	BC3		4	In use on block oil trains. Refer to Chapter text
12 March	61337	Bl	50A	4	3 25 Clsle Kingmoor–Stoke Gifford
24 March	72008	Clan	12A	1	Enthusiast tour. Refer to Chapter text
April		dmu		1	New ex Swindon 4 car units on South Wales–Midlands services. Refer to Chapter text
			85D	4	Equivalent to 6 banking locomotives on Lickey incline for block oil trains
22 April	61454	Bl6	50A	4-6	New ex works rakes of 24 ton hopper wagons to Gresley
	61461	Bl6	56D	4-6	
24 April	70006	Brit	31B	1	Relief to 12/20 Ncl–Btl ex Bham Refer to Chapter text for other Brits

You'll Never Believe What's Been Through: 1963 – Cross Country

Date	Loco No.	Loco Class	Loco Shed	Train Class	Detail
11 May	34006	WC0	70A	1	Enthusiast tour refer to Chapter text
	61004	Bl	50A		
12 May	34094	WC0	70A	1	Enthusiast tour. Refer to Chapter text
12 May	70001	Brit	1A		At Dby
18 May	60106	A3	34F		At Dby
3 June	70051	Brit	5A	1	5/25 Bham–Btl
4 June	6100	Scot		0	Not in steam Crewe–Boston. Refer to Chapter text
4 June	60876	V2	50A	1	Jarrow–Chesterfield excursion
8 June	61050	Bl	41A	1	Shfld–Penzance to Btl
8 June	73139	Std5	17C	1	10 45 Newquay–Dby ex Btl
	44757	B15	55A		(double headed)
15 July	D55XX	Br2		7	Scunthorpe–Severn Tunnel Junction to Bham. Forward with Western Region type 3 or 4. Daily M–F service
28 July	90393	WD8	40E	1	Dby Friargate–Skegness
27 July		Jub		1	Refer to Chapter text
		BL5			
		Bl			
August	45695	Jub	55C	4-6	WO/Wichnor Jn–Normanton. Ex Works Crewe
12-16 Aug	46201	Prin		0	Clsle–Ashchurch. In steam to Saltley via Lds, Dby
16 Aug		Lion		3	Trials on Lickey incline with empty coaching stock
3 Oct				4-6	Diversions following incident on GC route. Refer to Chapter text
9 Oct	60021	A4	34E	1	12/15 Ncl–Btl to Dby. Returned 10 Oct with 6 30 Dby–Shfld 2
13 Oct	42896	Crab	16D	1	Enthusiast tour. Refer to Chapter text
16 Oct	60146	A1	50A		At Dby
21 Oct	70002	Brit	31B	2	5/2 Nottm-Dby
December	60142	A1	52D	3	At Dby. Refer to Chapter text
	60143	A1	50A	3	

Abbreviations for locomotive classes (steam/diesel/electric)

Abbrev.	Denotes	Arrgmnt	Note
A1	Ex LNE	4-6-2	3
A2	Ex LNE	4-6-2	1
A3	Ex LNE	4-6-2	1
A4	Ex LNE streamlined	4-6-2	1
A5	Ex LNE tank	4-6-2	
Bl	Ex LNE	4-6-0	1
Bl2	Ex LNE/GE	4-6-0	1
Bl6	Ex LNE/NE	4-6-0	
Bl7	Ex LNE/GE	4-6-0	2
BB0	Ex SR Battle of Britain in original form	4-6-2	1
BBR	Ex SR Battle of Britain in rebuilt form	4-6-2	1
Bl5	Ex LM Black 5	4-6-0	1
Brit	BR Britannia	4-6-2	1
C	EX SR/SEC	0-6-0	1
C2X	Ex SR/LBSC	0-6-0	
Clan	BR Clan	4-6-2	2
Com	Ex LM/MR Compound	4-4-0	1
Crab	Ex LMS	2-6-0	1
D16	Ex LNE/GE	4-4-0	
Gar	Ex LM Garratt	2-6-0 x2	
Grge	Ex GW Grange	4-6-0	2
GW2	Ex GW 2800	2-8-0	1
GW4	Ex GW 4300	2-6-0	1
GWT	Ex GW tanks	2-8-0/2	1
H	Ex SR/SEC tank	0-4-4	1
U	Ex SR	2-6-0	1
700	Ex SR/LSW	0-6-0	
Hall	Ex GW Hall	4-6-0	1
Ivatt2	Ex LM	2-6-0	1
Ivatt4	Ex LM	2-6-0	1
J11	Ex LNE/GC	0-6-0	
J15	Ex LNE/GE	0-6-0	1
J17	Ex LNE/GE	0-6-0	
J20	Ex LNE/GE	0-6-0	
J39	Ex LNE	0-6-0	
Jub	Ex LM Jubilee	4-6-0	1
K1	Ex LNE	2-6-0	1
K2	Ex LNE/GN	2-6-0	
K3	Ex LNE/GN	2-6-0	
L1	Ex LNE	2-6-4	
LY	Ex LM/L&Y	2-4-2	1
04	Ex LNE/GC/ROD	2-8-0	1
Pan	Ex GW pannier tank	0-6-0	1

Abbreviations for locomotive classes (steam/diesel/electric)

Abbrev.	Denotes	Assgmnt	Note
Pat6	Ex LMS Patriot in original form	4-6-0	2
PatR	Ex LMS Patriot in rebuilt form	4-6-0	
Prin	Ex LM Princess Royal	4-6-2	1
Sch	Ex SR Schools	4-4-0	1
Scot	Ex LM Royal Scot in rebuilt form	4-6-0	1
Sent	Ex LM sentinel tank	0-4-0	
St4	Ex LMS tank	2-6-4	
Std2	BR	2-6-0	1
Std3	BR	2-6-0	
Std4	BR	4-6-0	1
Std5	BR	4-6-0	1
V2	Ex LNE	2-6-2	1
WCO	Ex SR West Country in original form	4-6-2	1
WCR	Ex SR West Country in rebuilt form	4-6-2	1
WD8	Ex MoS	2-8-0	4
WD10	Ex MoS	2-10-0	
OF	Ex LM/L&Y saddle tank	0-4-0	
2F	Ex LM/MR	0-6-0	
2P	Ex LM/MR	4-4-0	
3F	Ex LM/MR	0-6-0	
4F	Ex LM/MR	0-6-0	1
8F	Ex LMS	2-8-0	1
9F	BR	2-10-0	1

Key to origination of steam classes

BR	British Railways	L&Y	Lancashire & Yorkshire Railway
GC	Great Central Railway	MoS	Ministry of Supply
GE	Great Eastern Railway	MR	Midland Railway
GW	Great Western Railway	NE	North Eastern Railway
LBSC	London, Brighton and South Coast Railway	ROD	Railway Operating Division
LM	London Midland Scottish Railway	SEC	South Eastern and Chatham Railway
LNE	London & North Eastern Railway	SR	Southern Railway

Notes for steam classes

1. Example(s) preserved
2. Initiative to build a replica under development
3. Replica build Tornado
4. Look-a-like example in preservation

Abbreviations for locomotive classes continued (diesel/electric)

Abbrev.	Denotes	Bhp	Arrgmnt	Note
BB0	English Electric Gas turbine mech	2,750	4-6-0	1
BC2	BRCW Diesel electric	1,160	Bo-Bo	2,a
BC3	BRCW Diesel electric	1,550	Bo-Bo	3, a
BC4	BRCW Diesel electric	2,800	Bo-Bo	4
Br2	Brush Traction Diesel electric	1,250	A1A-A1A	5, a
Br4	Brush Traction Diesel electric	2,750	Co-Co	24, a
BrX	Brush Traction Diesel electric	2,800	Co-Co	6
BR2	BR Diesel electric	1,160	Bo-Bo	7, a
BR3	English Electric/LMS Diesel electric	1,600	Co-Co	8, b
BR4	BR Diesel electric	2,500	1Co-Co1	9,a
BTH1	North British Loco Co Diesel electric	827	Bo-Bo	10
BTH1X	North British Loco Co Diesel electric	800	Bo-Bo	11, a
Clay	Clayton Equipment Diesel electric	900	Bo-Bo	12, a
Dmu	Various builders	Various	-	13, a
EE1	English Electric Diesel electric	1,000	Bo-Bo	14, a
EE3	English Electric Diesel electric	1,750	Co-Co	15, a
EE4	English Electric Diesel electric	2,000	1Co-Co1	16, a
Fell	English Electric/LMS Mechanical	2,000	4-4-4-4	17
Hy	Beyer Peacock Diesel hydraulic	1,700	B-B	18, a
Met	Metropolitan Vickers 660V d.c.	1,200	Bo-Bo	-
Metro	Metropolitan Vickers Diesel electric	1,200	Co-Bo	19, a
MP	Metropolitan Cammell Diesel electric	2,000	-	20
SR3	BR Diesel electric	1,600	1Co-Co1	21
Wes4	BR Diesel hydraulic	2,700	C-C	22, a
08	BR Diesel electric	350	0-6-0	23, a

Key to Arrangement

A1A   3 wheelset bogie with centre set unpowered
Bo   Two powered axles on each bogie
B   Cardan shaft to two wheelset bogie with coupled wheelsets
Co   Three powered axles on each bogie
C   Cardan shaft to three wheelset bogie with coupled wheelsets
1   Unpowered wheelset at nose end of each bogie

Notes for diesel/electric classes

1	GT3 experimental	14	D80XX early examples
2	D53XX early examples (Bo indicates independent wheelsets)	15	D67XX early examples
3	D65XX examples	16	D2XX examples
4	*Lion* pre (hoped for) production run	17	10100 modified from 4-8-4
5	D55XX examples	18	D70XX early examples (B indicates coupled wheelsets)
6	D0280 *Falcon* pre (hoped for) production run	19	D57XX
7	D50XX early examples	20	*Midland Pullman* 6 car units (2)
8	10001	21	10201 10202 (10203 was 2,000 bhp)
9	D1-D193 (D1-D10 2,300 bhp)	22	D10XX early examples
10	10800 pre-production	23	Shunting locomotives
11	D82XX small scale production build	24	D15XX examples
12	D85XX early examples. Centre cab	a	Example(s) preserved
13	dmu in 2, 3 and 4 vehicle units, some powered	b	Initiative to build a replica under development

Motive Power Depot codes for locomotive sightings as listed

Code	Location	1957	1958	1959	1960	1961	1962	1963	Note
1	Derby			X	X	X			1
1A	Willesden	X	X			X	X	X	
1B	Camden	X	X		X	X		X	
2B	Nuneaton					X			
3B	Bushbury	X							
5A	Crewe North	X	X	X	X	X	X	X	
5B	Crewe South	X	X						
5D	Stoke					X			
6A	Chester M						X		
6H	Bangor					X			
6J	Holyhead				X	X			
8A	Edge Hill	X	X	X		X	X		

Motive Power Depot codes for locomotive sightings as listed

Code	Location	1957	1958	1959	1960	1961	1962	1963	Note
8B	Warrington				X	X			
8F	Springs Br			X					
9A	Longsight	X	X	X	X		X		
9E	Trafford Pk	X	X		X	X			2
9G	Gorton			X		X			3
11A	Barrow			X					
12A	Clsle Kingmoor		X	X	X	X	X	X	3
12B	Clsle Upperby		X	X		X	X		
14A	Cricklewood			X	X	X			
14B	Kentish Town	X	X	X	X	X			2,4
14D	Neasden		X						
15A	Wellingborough			X	X	X	X		
15B	Kettering			X					
15C	Leicester M	X	X						
15D	Coalville						X		
16A	Nottingham M	X		X			X		
16C	Derby							X	3
16D	Annesley				X				3
16D	Nottingham M							X	3
17A	Derby	X	X	X	X	X	X		2,3
17B	Burton						X		
17C	Rowsley						X	X	
18A	Toton				X		X		2,3
21A	Saltley	X	X	X		X	X		
21D	Aston					X	X	X	
22A	Btl Barrow Rd	X							2,3
24E	Blackpool			X		X			
24J	Lancaster GA			X					
24K	Preston		X		X	X			
24L	Carnforth					X			
26A	Newton Heath	X	X		X		X		
26B	Agecroft		X	X		X			
26D	Bury						X		
26F	Patricroft				X	X			
27A	Bank Hall		X	X					
30A	Stratford			X	X				
30E	Colchester			X					
30F	Parkstone				X				
31A	Cambridge			X	X				
31B	March	X			X	X	X	X	
31F	Pboro Sptl Br			X					3
32A	Norwich	X				X			
32B	Ipswich			X					

Motive Power Depot codes for locomotive sightings as listed

Code	Location	1957	1958	1959	1960	1961	1962	1963	Note
32E	Yarmouth V	X							
34A	King's Cross	X	X				X		
34E	New England							X	
34F	Grantham							X	
35C	Pboro Sptl Br	X						X	3
36A	Doncaster	X	X	X	X		X		
36E	Retford GN	X					X		
38A	Colwick	X							3
38B	Annesley	X							
38C	Leicester GC	X							3
39A	Gorton	X							3
40A	Lincoln	X	X		X		X		
46B	Immingham	X	X		X		X	X	
40E	Colwick			X	X			X	3
41A	Shfld Darnall		X	X	X	X	X	X	
41C	Millhouses		X	X	X	X			2,4
41D	Canklow				X	X	X		
41E	Staveley BH				X				
50A	York	X	X	X	X		X	X	
50B	Hull Dyctes				X				
50E	Scarborough						X		
51A	Darlington		X		X				
51L	Thornaby				X				
52A	Ncl Gateshead	X			X		X		
52B	Heaton					X			
52D	Tweedmouth						X		
53B	Hull Bt Gdns	X							
55A	Lds Holbeck	X	X	X	X	X	X	X	2
55C	Farnley Jn					X		X	
55H	Lds Nvl Hll				X	X			
56A	Wakefield			X					
56B	Ardsley			X	X		X		
56D	Mirfield								
60A	Inverness				X				
63A	Perth				X				
65J	Fort William			X					
66A	Glgw Polmadie		X		X		X		
67A	Corkerhill	X							
68A	Clsle Kingmoor	X							3
70A	Nine Elms				X				
70C	Guildford	X							
71A	Eastleigh		X				X		

Motive Power Depot codes for locomotive sightings as listed

Code	Location	1957	1958	1959	1960	1961	1962	1963	Note
71B	Bnmth C				X				
71G	Weymouth	X							
72A	Exmouth Jn						X		
73A	Stewarts Lane		X						
73C	Hither Green							X	
75A	Brighton					X			
81A	Old Oak Common Didcot							X	
81E	Btl Bath Road							X	
82A	St Philip's Marsh					X	X	X	
82B	Barrow Road Worcester				X	X			2,3
82E	Glos Horton Rd		X	X	X	X			
85A	Hereford		X						
85B	Bromsgrove							X	
85C	Glos Barnwood		X	X					
85D	Cdff Canton							X	
85E	Cdff Canton		X	X					
86C				X					3
88A						X			3

Note generally applicable

The summary is to assist an understanding of a sighting on a specific date. In many cases the Chapter text for the year will offer more information about specific workings (for example Nuneaton based locomotives in 1961) and provide additional information (for examples, winter 1962/63 and excursion train traffic in 1963 to Coventry).

Particular Notes

1. Plate affixed to preserved locomotive
2. Depot featured strongly in text
3. Depot had a change of code (Regional boundary change or Regional re-organisation). Certain other depots also had a change of code (eg Bushbury), but because no other sighting was recorded the replacement code (or preceeding code) is not listed
4. Depot closed

Abbreviations used for station names

Abbreviation	Denotes	Note
Bath	Green Park	
Bedford	Midland Road	
Bham	Birmingham New Street	
Blackpool	North	
Bnmth	Bournemouth West	
Brdfd	Bradford Forster Square	
Btl	Bristol Temple Meads	
Burton	Burton on Trent	
Catterick	Camp	
Cdff	Cardiff General	
Cheltenham	Lansdown	
Chesterfield	Midland	
Clsle	Carlisle	
Dby	Derby Midland	
Dby Friargate	Derby Friargate	
Dton	Darlington Bank Top	
Edin	Edinburgh Waverley	
Euston	London Euston	
Glgw	Glasgow St Enoch	
Glgw C	Glasgow Central	
Glos	Gloucester Eastgate	
Inv	Inverness	
Lcln	Lincoln St Marks	
Lds	Leeds City	
Lpl	Liverpool Central	
Man	Manchester Central	
Man Ldn Road	Manchester London Road	1
Man Picc	Manchester Piccadilly	2
Man Vic	Manchester Victoria	3
Marylebone	London Marylebone	
Mkt Hboro	Market Harborough	
Ncl	Newcastle	
Nottm	Nottingham Midland	
Nottm Vic	Nottingham Victoria	
Norwich	Thorpe	
Pboro	Peterborough East	
Pgntn	Paignton	
Ply	Plymouth North Road	
Sboro	Scarborough	
Shfld	Sheffield Midland	
Stlg	Stirling	
St P	London St Pancras	
Sutton Cldfld	Sutton Coldfield	
Wboro	Wellingborough	
Yk	York	

Notes for station names
1. Station re-named in September 1960
2. Station named in September 1960
3. Station used for certain trains that would normally have used Manchester London Road

Notes for Railway locations

BR   site developed by British Railways for new traffic
CLC   Cheshire Lines Committee
GC   Great Central Railway
GN   Great Northern Railway
LNW   London & North Western Railway
MR   Midland Railway
SR   Southern Railway
GW   Great Western Railway

Other abbreviations and expressions

	Meaning
Midland Pullman	name of train
mpd	motive power depot
multiple or pairs	locomotives coupled to provide power/braking
pigeon	train for consignment of racing pigeons
pilot	locomotive attached to front of another for part or all of journey (forms a double header)
production batch	build of locos following initial build being proven
push/pull	method of operation from each end of train
relief train	run in addition at busy times on busy routes
roller bearings Southern	modern axlebox technology
Region	organisational area of BR
T Th SuO	runs on Tuesdays Thursdays Sundays only
triangle (of tracks)	method of turning locomotives/trains
up	towards London or from Bristol towards Derby
vacuum	method of braking
Western Division	operating area within LM Region
Western Region	organisational area of BR
12 15	departure after midnight and up to noon
12/15	departure after noon and up to midnight
2 January	date of sighting as noted

Railway locations to which reference is made

Reference	Location	Note
Ardwick	goods depot Manchester area	L&Y
Barrow Road	mpd for Bristol	MR
Blackwell	station at NE end of Lickey incline	MR
Bournville	station, mpd and Cadbury's plant Bham area	MR
Brent	marshalling yard N London	MR
Chiltern Green	loading point S of Luton	BR
Chilwell	Ordnance depot between Nottm and Trent	HR
Churnet Valley	Leek–Uttoxeter	LNW
Cricklewood	yard and mpds N London	MR
Dore	Dore and Totley S of Sheffield	MR
Edin Lothian Rd	goods yard Edinburgh area	BR
Egginton Jn	between Derby Friargate–Burton	GN
Erewash	Trent–Clay Cross via Alfreton	MR
Gorton	loco works Manchester area	GC
Gushetfaulds	goods yard Glasgow area	BR
Hasland	mpd Chesterfield area	MR
Holbeck	mpd for Leeds	MR
Hope Valley	Dore–Chinley	MR
Kentish Town	mpd for St Pancras	MR
Killamarsh	between Chesterfield and Sheffield	MR/GC
Kings Norton	junction station S of Birmingham	MR
Lawley Street	goods/parcels depot Birmingham	MR
Lickey incline	between Bromsgrove and Blackwell	MR
Mangotsfield	junction station for Bath NE of Bristol	MR
Millhouses	mpd for Sheffield	MR
Newton Heath	mpd for Manchester	L&Y
Oxley	mpd for Wolverhampton	GW
Saltley	mpd for Birmingham	MR
Severn Tunnel Jn	between Bristol and Newport	GW
Sheet Stores Jn	between Derby and Nottingham	MR
Sharncliffe Camp	near Folkestone	SR
Somers Town	goods depot N London	MR
Stenson Jn	between Derby and Burton	MR
Stoke Gifford	yard NE of Bristol	GW
Stoke Golding	near Nuneaton	MR/LNW
St P Goods	St Pancras goods depot	MR
Stourton	goods yards Leeds area	MR
Sutton Park	station near Walsall	MR
Swinton	S Yorkshire	MR
Toton	marshalling yard and mpd near Trent	MR
Trafford Park	mpd for Manchester	MR/GC/CLC
Trent	extensive junctions between Nottm and Derby	MR
Wboro	yard and mpd for Wellingborough	MR
Westerleigh	yard N of Bristol	MR
Westhouses	mpd Chesterfield/Staveley area	MR
Willesden	yard and mpd N London	LNW
Water Orton/WO	yard Birmingham area	MR
Wwd Hth	yard Birmingham area	MR

Classification of trains (summary only)

Class	Denotes
1	Express passenger train, newspapers. Snow plough or breakdown train, light engine or fire brigade train going to attend an incident
2	Ordinary passenger train
3	Parcels, fish, fruit, horses, livestock, meat, milk, pigeon, perishables in vehicles conforming to coaching stock requirements. Empty coaching stock (ECS)
4-6	Express freight, ballast train with varying proportion of total vehicles with automatic brake in operative condition
7	Express freight, ballast train not fitted with continuous brake
0	Light engine or light engines coupled
Grove	Royal Train

Derby Locomotive Works Open Days

The final Saturday in each August was for many years the Annual Flower and Horticultural Show for staff at Derby Locomotive Works, but for many of the thousands who attended it was the locomotives on display in cold condition and not the fauna that had attracted them. Each year there would be assembled opposite Platform 6 of the station and in the yard in front of the Manager's office an array of up to half a dozen locomotives with access via steps to the cabs. Usually on the Thursday or Friday preceding the Open Day something big and (up to 1963) ex-works would arrive, normally from Crewe which for four consecutive years provided a Princess Coronation in the maroon livery applied in 1958 to some members of the Class.

To say that control arrangements were relaxed in the extreme does not understate the situations which quickly arose with youths climbing and walking along boiler tops, cab tops, in the coal space of the tenders, on top of the tender, peering down the chimneys and generally having a good time. The year 1960 was exceptional in that the invasion was huge and soon penetrated the admittedly flimsy defences of the motive power depot which were over-run with the same level of exploration ... except that many locomotives were in steam and un-manned. What does this do, what happens if I pull/push/open/close/turn this, where is the whistle? It was akin to New Year's Eve when at midnight locomotive whistles were blown, only in this case it was a Saturday afternoon and multiple Midland, Stanier and (one of two) LNER whistles were audible for miles. It was a wonderful experience that could not be allowed to be repeated.

From time to time I am asked whether or not I know what locomotives were on display in particular years. The following is a list of main exhibits for the years 1956-69 inclusive.

Year	Exhibits on display						
1956	46112	73128	92029	Two car dmu	350 hp diesel shunter		
1957	75057	92139	D3377	Two car dmu			
1958	70017	92166	D3542	D5001	D5700		
1959	70004	92165	D2	D3782	D5021		
1960	1000	71000	Std Class 5	BR/Sulzer type 2	350 hp diesel shunter		
1961	46254	92220					
1962	46256	70048	BR/Sulzer type 4				
1963	44094	46251	47581	D57	D2381	D3021	D5222
1964	45585	46245	92053	D94	D1756	D3016	D5293
1965	70012	92094	BR/Sulzer type 2		BR/Sulzer type 4		
1966	70028?						
1967	70013	D7643					
1968	44888	D55	D3292	D5187	HS4000 (Kestrel)		
1969	D100						

The annual Horticultural Show and Open Day at Derby Locomotive Works was held on the last Saturday in August. The principal locomotives on display were Royal Scot (*Sherwood Forester*) a Crosti 9F, newly built steam and diesel examples (the lightweight diesel multiple unit vehicles being from the Carriage and Wagon Works), plus ex-Mersey Railway 0-6-4 tank (*Cecil Raikes*) which had been working at Shipley Colliery and was the subject of possible preservation. 25 August 1956. (*Kidderminster Railway Museum 093497, Courtesy P. J. Lynch*)

Three years later and the same event drew a far larger attendance and with limited supervision the opportunity to explore the fine detail of a Britannia (70004) was not to be missed. No such possibility of anyone getting too close to preserved Compound 1000. A full listing of locomotives in the main displays over the years is included in the text of the book. (*Kidderminster Railway Museum 094244, Courtesy P. J. Lynch*)

Names

D2	*Helvellyn*	70004	*William Shakespeare*
D55	*Royal Signals*	70012	*John of Gaunt*
D100	*Sherwood Forester*	70013	*Oliver Cromwell*
		70017	*Arrow*
45585	*Hyderabad*	70028	*Royal Star*
46112	*Sherwood Forester*	70048	*The Territorial Army 1908-1958*
46245	*City of London*	71000	*Duke of Gloucester*
46251	*City of Nottingham*	92220	*Evening Star*
46254	*City of Stoke-on-Trent*		
46256	*Sir William A Stanier F.R.S.*		

The final Shop within the overhaul process for many locomotives at Derby Locomotive Works was the extensive Paint Shop. Here, in summer 1960 a line-up of engines includes, from the left a BR Standard Class 5, a 7F, 3F, 4F and 4MT whilst on the track adjacent new diesel shunting locomotives await completion of painting/numbering. (*Kidderminster Railway Museum 006610*)

After the 1960 show 71000 was placed on Spike Island pending a decision on its future use or otherwise. (*G. Morris*)

202

Concluding Remarks

The opening words of this book stated that it was about railways and change. I feel confident in that the content has reflected both of those topics.

In drawing together some concluding remarks my approach will touch upon the strategic decision-making, some of the decisions taken and the role of railway personnel through a period of great upheaval.

Until the terms of reference for the management of the corporate railway were changed by the government of the day, who could blame the British Transport Commission for the huge accumulated loss on revenue account over the period 1957-60? The Commission was attempting to 'meet the needs of the nation'. The government deserves some credit for recognising that the needs of the nation were changing and would continue to change and also for putting into place the necessary legislation to effect change. There were, though, poor decisions taken on the basis of the short-term economic need and the exclusion of the leaders in diesel locomotive technology from the process of traction developments was pure politics to protect UK industry.

Along the Midland lines to/from St Pancras the chronic need to have steam motive power that could reduce the very high incidence of double-heading was eventually met, but in the interim there is little doubt that those lines contributed handsomely to the operating losses of the time. The *Midland Pullman* was an expensive folly demanded by the business community which would surely have never countenanced such expenditure for their own businesses where a pay back on capital investment was required. Similarly, the experiments, with the 9F 2-10-0s were ill conceived and driven by private contractors with low probability of significant benefit. The campaign change to vacuum braking of mineral wagons of low capacity and lower

utilisation as immobile stockpiles was never a realistic investment opportunity. However, the move to bulk movement over distances exceeding 250 miles using containers was a success and provided a template for future development.

Had it not been for Dr Beeching and the arrivals of diesels the cross-country route would probably have run undisturbed and largely unchanged for another decade; seasonal and mail/parcels traffic continuing to influence patterns of services.

At the time, those responsible for maintaining a service faced huge, constant change and new challenges as, I hope, adequately described in the book. On a daily basis at an operational level there is no doubt in my mind that no matter what 'cards' were dealt to the individuals they did their best to play the best possible 'hand'. Since the late eighteenth century railway personnel had just tried to 'get on with it' and that continued at least through to the period covered by the book; they deserved support and some consideration as their industry was taken over by the politicians.

At an observational level this was surely one of the greatest railway shows of all time!

Finally, a few random thoughts. The first relates to what I assume was a headquarters Operations team of individuals who had – as far as I am concerned – the best job in the world as being close to operational requirements and being responsible for the allocation and re-allocation of motive power to meet changing needs and requirements. Surely there is a book yet to be written about their work. Secondly, and related to the first, is how did the Eastern Region manage to retain its twenty or so Britannias for so long? Finally, I would never have thought prior to setting out to write this book that I would learn so much about the needs of the Federation of Racing Pigeon Clubs and their dedicated train services!

Bibliography

Working Timetables of LMS and British Railways
Search Engine at the National Railway Museum
Sectional Appendices to Working Timetables
Special Traffic Notices
Public Timetables of British Railways
Records at Public Records Office, Kew
British Newspaper Library
The Reshaping of British Railways, HM Stationery Office
British Railways Atlas and Gazetteer, W. Philip Conolly Railway Publications Ltd
Various issues of *Trains Illustrated*, *Modern Railways* and *Railway Magazine*
Various issues of railway enthusiast society journals
British Railway – Main Line Gradient Profiles, Ian Allan Ltd
The Midland Railway, C. Hamilton Ellis Malaga Books
The Midland Railway London Extension, T. E. Rounthwaite
The North Midland – Part One, Bob Pixton
The Friargate Line, Mark Higginson
Rail Centres: Derby, Brian Radford
Websites on the Internet
Personal Records
Notes provided in relation to railway operations at specific locations/times

Index